Selected Letters of
RAINER MARIA RILKE

RAINER MARIA RILKE was born in Prague (then part of the Austro-Hungarian Empire) in 1875. As a young man he became a friend of Rodin and in 1901 married Clara Westoff, one of the sculptor's students. They had one child, a daughter, but because of Rilke's devotion to solitude the family never remained together for long. After he had written several volumes of poetry and prose, he published his "novel," *The Notebooks of Malte Laurids Brigge,* which appeared in 1910. In the years just before World War I, he began to write his *Duino Elegies,* but for many reasons could not finish them until 1922, when a burst of creative energy enabled him, in one month, to complete the ten *Elegies* and compose the fifty-five *Sonnets to Orpheus.* Rilke died of blood poisoning in a Swiss sanitorium in 1926.

HARRY T. MOORE, the editor, is professor of English at Southern Illinois University, in Carbondale, Illinois, and a Fellow of the (British) Royal Society of Literature. In 1958 and 1960 he held Guggenheim Fellowships. Among his books are *The Novels of John Steinbeck* (1939), *Life and Works of D. H. Lawrence* (1951), and *The Intelligent Heart* (1955), a critical biography of Lawrence. He helped Karl W. Deutsch to translate Karl Jaspers' *Tragedy Is Not Enough,* and his book reviews and critical articles have appeared in the New York *Times Book Review,* the *Saturday Review, The New Republic* and in other leading periodicals. At present he is at work on an edition of Lawrence's Letters.

Selected Letters of

RAINER MARIA RILKE

Edited by Harry T. Moore

Anchor Books
Doubleday & Company, Inc.
Garden City, New York
1960

TYPOGRAPHY BY SUSAN SIEN

COVER DESIGN BY HARRY FORD

Library of Congress Catalog Card Number 60–13548
Copyright © 1960 by Harry T. Moore
Copyright 1945, 1947, 1948 by
W. H. Norton & Company, Inc.
All Rights Reserved
Printed in the United States of America
First Edition

ACKNOWLEDGMENTS

Letters to MERLINE are reprinted with the permission of Editions du Seuil, Paris, and Methuen & Co. Ltd., London.

Letters to Frau GUDI NÖLKE are reprinted by permission of The Hogarth Press, Ltd., London.

The letters to BENVENUTA and the letter to Madame ELOUI BEY are reproduced by permission of Insel-Verlag, Weisbaden, and Philosophical Library, Inc., New York.

The previously unpublished letter to ELIZABETH MAYER is published with the permission of Mrs. Mayer and the estate of Rainer Maria Rilke.

Letters to ILSE ERDMANN, LISA HEISE, BALTHUSZ KLOSSOWSKI, MIMI ROMANELLI, AUGUST SAUER, RUTH SIEBER-RILKE and Countess MARGOT SIZZO-NORIS-CROUY, all previously unpublished in English, are printed with the permission of Insel-Verlag.

All other letters are reprinted by arrangement with W. W. Norton & Company, Inc., New York.

Introduction

by Harry T. Moore

Wherever he went, and he traveled often and far, the poet Rainer Maria Rilke wrote letters. Picture him, a neat little man with hooded blue eyes and a mandarin's mustache, as he sits writing in a plain hotel room or amid the rich furnishings of a château: he is fastidious in his penmanship, and will allow himself few blots or crossings out. The letters themselves are acute explorations of people, books, and places, and of the problems of Rilke and all other artists. Unlike the correspondence of many poets, Rilke's was not a weary and hasty by-product, but rather it was an important phase of his poetic activity. He wrote letters that deserve to be called great in their combination of eloquence, philosophy, and confession.

1

Some background notes will help toward an understanding of Rilke's correspondence. He was born on 4 December 1875, in Prague, which was then the capital of Bohemia in the Austro-Hungarian empire. He belonged to a German-speaking family and was brought up as a Catholic. His baptismal names were René Karl Wilhelm Joseph Maria Rilke. In his early twenties he changed his first name to Rainer, under the influence of a woman writer, Lou Andreas-Salomé, who was to be his lifelong friend.

In his early childhood, Rilke's pious, verse-writing mother dressed him like a girl, a peculiar irony because his father, a minor railway official, wanted his son to take up the career he had missed; he hoped that René would become an army officer. At the age of ten, when his parents had separated, the boy was sent away to military school for several wretched years. He often referred to this time in his later correspondence, most forcibly in the letter of 9 December 1920 to a former teacher who had become a major general. When Rilke wrote that letter, he had just turned forty-five, but his memories of the military academy at St. Pölten remained bitter.

He went for a while to still another soldiers' school, then to a business institute, and eventually to the German University in Prague. He studied law for a time, but didn't take a degree. At nineteen he removed to Munich, and so began the wanderings which can be traced in his letters: he was, in the years ahead, to go to Italy, Russia, France, Switzerland, Scandinavia, North Africa, and Spain. He showed little interest in England, which he never visited, and manifested only horror at the thought of America, which represented to him "sham things, *dummy life*" (letter of 13 November 1925). For about a dozen years before the First World War, Rilke stayed mostly in Paris between his bouts of wandering; after the war he lived in Switzerland, where he died on 29 December 1926.

2

Except for a brief period as underpaid secretary to the sculptor Rodin, Rilke never "worked." From early youth he lived intensely in his writing and his loves, which were often closely connected. When he was nineteen, the publication expenses of his first book of verse, *Life and Songs,* were paid by a girl. This was a pretty, eccentric bluestocking, Valérie David-Rhonfeld, who after Rilke's death wrote an acid memoir of their relationship. An examination of the affair suggests that Rilke, after being dependent on Valérie for a long time, left her abruptly. This was the pattern of his erotic relationships, even in the case of his marriage. The women friends he kept, such as Lou Andreas-Salomé and the Princess Marie von Thurn und Taxis-Hohenlohe, were usually mother-substitutes.

Lou, who had been rather sadly entangled with Nietzsche, took Rilke on a trip to her native Russia in 1899, along with her husband, Dr. F. C. Andreas, an Orientalist at the University of Göttingen. Rilke the following year returned to Russia, which ever afterward he looked back upon as one of the great inspirations of his work. These Eastern journeys seemed to have helped him mature as a poet, as evidenced by the verse collected in the *Book of Images* (1902).

After his second trip to Russia, Rilke visited the art colony at Worpswede, near Bremen, where he met the painter Paula Becker and the sculptress Clara Westhoff, and he seems to have been attracted to both of them. In 1901, Paula married the painter Otto Modersohn, and Rilke took Clara as his wife. The Rilkes moved into a cottage at Westerwede, near the art colony.

Soon after their daughter Ruth was born (December 1901), they learned from Rilke's father that he could no longer continue the allowance his son had been dependent upon. Joseph Rilke dangled in front of the man of new responsibilities the suggestion of a bank clerkship in Prague. But the young Rilke had long since discovered that poetry was a full-time activity, not an after-office-hours diversion. The first letter in the present collection (16 April 1897), to the novelist Ludwig Ganghofer, shows that Rilke had realized early in life that "whoever does not consecrate himself wholly to art with all his wishes and values can never reach the highest goal."

Rilke left Westerwede for Paris in 1902. He had been commissioned to write a book about Clara's old teacher, Rodin. Clara went to visit her parents and, after leaving Ruth with them, followed her husband to Paris. But their marriage had virtually reached an end; they met from time to time thereafter, but for the most part remained on terms of friendly separation. Rilke dedicated himself to solitude, out of which he would occasionally be drawn by an attractive young woman; but he always shook himself free after a little while.

He has been frequently criticized for evading his responsibilities as husband, father, and lover—and for sliding away from military obligations, after a brief taste of them, in the First World War. Yet those who knew Rilke have never blamed him for following the necessities of his poetical nature: if he sometimes avoided everyday obvious reality, he constantly sought a deeper reality. Those who have criticized his conduct couldn't have written his poetry.

Rilke was not anti-social or aloof—shy and modest though he may have been. As he had to fight against the temptations of love affairs, so he had to battle with his gregarious tendencies. He was generally quiet in social groups, yet always impressive, and when he did speak he drew everyone's attention. In a tender portrait of Rilke, Stefan Zweig says that his friends usually encountered him by chance: "In a Paris bookshop or a Viennese drawing room one would suddenly see his friendly smile and feel the pressure of his soft hand.

Then with equal suddenness he would vanish, and we who loved and honored him did not ask where he was to be found or call on him if we knew, but waited until he came to us."

As Zweig says, Rilke was that rarity in our age, a true poet. In a letter to his wife written on 4 September 1908, Rilke explained (and asked her not to consider it boasting) that he was sent among men as a gatherer of "mushrooms and medicinals among the herbs," from which he was to brew a special potion; that his mission was to see all and (in a phrase suggesting Whitman) "to reject nothing."

3

The influence of Rodin on Rilke was an important one, in its smaller way comparable to the effect upon Goethe of his sojourn amid the classical sculpture and architecture of Rome. Rilke's *New Poems* (1907) show a striving after a concreteness and objectivity not evident in his earlier work, and his letters indicate how profoundly he was impressed by the sculptor. In 1905, after knowing him for several years, Rilke undertook the burden of attending to Rodin's correspondence. The irritable old man relieved him of the joy in 1906, and Rilke must have been relieved indeed; sometime after the quarrel the two became friends again.

In Rome in 1903, Rilke had begun *The Notebooks of Malte Laurids Brigge*, completed and published in 1910. This "novel," which chronicles the loneliness of a young Dane, haunted by his past and living in Paris, is in part a reflection of Rilke's own experiences during those years. *Malte*, which influenced Jean-Paul Sartre in the writing of his first novel, *Nausea*, is now regarded as an existentialist or proto-existentialist classic;

as Walter Kaufmann says, it sounds "many existentialist motifs," particularly "the quest for authentic existence."

4

The problem of Rilke's own existence, in the sense
of day-to-day living, was attended to, beginning in
1908, by an allowance from his publisher, Anton Kippenberg, of the Insel-Verlag. The sales of the poetry
were moderate except for Rilke's one popular success,
his prose poem *The Song of the Love and Death of
Cornet Christopher Rilke;* written in 1899 from a fragment of family history and first published in 1906, the
little book began to sell widely in 1912—but this was
exceptional. Fortunately for a man without a clock-
determined income, Rilke was frequently a guest at
castles and châteaux and at the flats of city friends.
Sometimes these places were lent to him for months
at a time; or, if the owners were present, they knew
and respected the poet's habit of solitude and let him
come and go as he pleased.

Until the outbreak of war in 1914, Rilke wandered
up and down Europe, often as the guest of titled ladies.
It is obvious that in many of these cases, erotic love
was not involved—sometimes the age of the lady obviously precluded that. On the other hand, some of his
friendships with younger women were also of the type
known as Platonic. One of his tenderest relationships,
for example, was with a Parisian working girl, Marthe
Hennebert, whom he frequently mentions in the letters; yet his interest was sympathetic and protective
rather than erotic, and the girl was baffled at his un-
willingness to become her lover.

One of Rilke's admirers, the militant Swedish feminist Ellen Key, known as "the great-aunt of radical Europe," became something of a nuisance. She lectured and wrote enthusiastically about Rilke in Scandinavia, and made possible his journey to the Northern countries; but she committed the mistake of plangently trying to interfere with his precious solitude. Among other things, she tried to force Rilke and Clara to re-establish their household, with little Ruth—a condition neither of these self-centered artists wanted to cope with at the time. Ellen's visit to Paris in 1906 is ruefully described in Rilke's letters to Clara (such as the one of 21 June), which tell of the determination of "the good Ellen" in dragging Rilke about on sightseeing tours.

Early in 1914 the poet became involved with a concert pianist, Magda von Hattingberg. Benvenuta, as he called her, read his *Stories of God* (1900) at Christmastime, 1913, and wrote to him enthusiastically. He responded, writing her several long, intimate letters before they finally met. Not long after that, they were on the point of parting in Venice where, Benvenuta says (in her *Rilke and Benvenuta*), they kissed each other "for the first and last time . . . with tranquil devotion." During the war she saw Rilke once again on the street, in Munich, and they did not speak; a faded woman wearing much make-up "was limping and leaning heavily on his arm."

A Rilkean friendship that lasted was the one, already mentioned, with Princess Marie von Thurn und Taxis-Hohenlohe, which began in 1909 and ended only with Rilke's death. Twenty years older than Rilke, the Princess, as the mother of three boys, was the center of a lively family and the owner or sharing owner of several large estates: Rilke visited Princess Marie and her family frequently at their home at Lautschin, in Bohemia; at their Venetian *palazzo;* and, more importantly for his poetry, at their castle of Duino, on the Adriatic near Trieste.

Alone there in January 1912, Rilke began writing his *Duino Elegies*. On a troubled day he was walking on the wind-chafed cliffs above the sea when he "heard" the words that begin the *First Elegy*: "Who, if I cried out, would hear me among the orders of the angels?" He finished the *Elegy* on that day, and the second shortly afterward. A few more fragments came, then the power left him, to reappear only intermittently: he wrote parts of the *Elegies* in Spain in 1913, and finished the third (begun at Duino) in Paris in that same year. But he couldn't recapture the full force of the first inspiration until after the war.

The years of battle were a tormenting time for Rilke. At the outbreak of hostilities, he was for a short while the victim of nationalist fervor, as his letters of the time show; they also indicate that this chauvinism soon turned sour. He was called up in January 1916, disastrously for himself, as he wrote to Kippenberg (his publisher), in one of his most revealing letters (15 February): "I was in a rapid ascent of work. . . . I already thought the freest prospects were ahead, when the grey army cloth fell before my clarified vision." After a wretched experience of barracks life, Rilke was assigned to the War Archives in Vienna. But the hackwork involved in "hairdressing the hero" proved upsetting and frustrating. When he was released from the office at three each afternoon, he could not "give the remainder of the day its own stamp and meaning."

5

The greatest period of his poetic activity lay yet ahead. Stefan Zweig has reported how pathetically bewildered Rilke seemed in military uniform—but he was soon taken out of that bafflement and that dress. Because of the petition circulated among leading German and Austrian intellectuals by Frau Kippenberg, Rilke was given permanent leave from military service. He went to Munich, but when at the end of the war the troubles in Bavaria made daily living too hectic, he moved to Switzerland. Through all the years of "the affliction, confusion and disfigurement of the world," as he told Countess Aline Dietrichstein (from Munich, 9 October 1918), he had retained his faith "in the great, the inexhaustible possibilities of life." And before very long his writing bloomed again in Switzerland.

At Soglio, in the Val Breglia, in July 1919, Rilke met Frau Auguste (Gudi) Nölke, to whom in the next few years he addressed a number of letters whose tone contrasts with much of the rest of his correspondence. Showing a friendly interest in Frau Nölke and her three children, these are essentially family letters of a different kind from the somewhat embarrassing-to-read letters to Merline (Mme. Elisabeth Dorothee Klossowska, known also as Baladine Klossowska), whom Rilke knew from 1920 to 1922. Merline was a painter, and her son Balthusz also took up this career; as a small boy he published a collection of his drawings of his cat, *Mitsou* (1921), to which Rilke wrote a preface. Some of his letters to young Balthusz are whimsically friendly, in a rather un-Rilkean fashion.

In the fall of 1920, Rilke moved to Schloss Berg am Irchel, near Zurich, but was forced to give up this place the following spring. Then, in the summer of 1921, he discovered the towered old Château de Muzot (pronounced "Muzotte"), which his friend Werner Reinhart bought and placed at his disposal. Here, in his "great time" of February 1922, Rilke completed the *Duino Elegies* and wrote his other poetic masterpiece, the fifty-nine *Sonnets to Orpheus,* in what was perhaps the greatest blaze of inspiration any poet has known in our century. His letters written at the time he was completing these sets of poems, and after their publication, often contain important expositions of the *Sonnets* and *Elegies.*

The rest of Rilke's life is mainly a chronicle of ill health; he was in and out of sanatoria. In October 1926, his left hand was injured by the thorn of a rose and would not heal; in December, at the Valmont Sanatorium, the doctors discovered that Rilke had leukemia. As he wasted away, he told the doctors not to deaden his consciousness with painkilling drugs.

6

Rilke died on 29 December 1926 and was buried where he had wished to be, in the little cemetery next to the old church at Rarogne. "Its enclosing wall," he said in his will (written in October 1925) "is one of the first places from which I received the wind and light of this landscape, together with all the promises which it, with and in Muzot, was later to help me realize." At his funeral, without "sacerdotal intervention," a Rarogne custom was observed when young girls in Valaisanne peasant dress followed his coffin up the rocky hill. Rilke's gravestone reads, *"Rose, oh reiner Widerspruch, Lust / Niemandes Schlaf zu sein unter soviel / Lidern"* ("Rose, oh pure contradiction, delight to be the sleep of no one beneath so many eyelids").

7

Rilke's poems are included, along with prose writings other than letters, in the Insel-Verlag's six-volume *Gesammelte Werke* (*Collected Works*), which went out of print during the nineteen-thirties. Meanwhile the two-volume *Ausgewahlte Werke* (*Selected Works*) has, since 1938, gone through several editions, augmented by other volumes containing previously uncollected material.

The poetry has been extensively translated into English, most thoroughly in J. B. Leishman's version of Rilke's *Poems, 1906 to 1926* (1957), which regrettably does not carry the German texts. Leishman has also translated the *Sonnets to Orpheus* (1936) and, with Stephen Spender, the *Duino Elegies* (1939). As long ago as 1918, Jessie Lemont translated 53 *Lyrics*, followed by 154 *Selected Lyrics* in 1945. In 1938, M. D. Herter Norton brought out her *Translations from the Poetry of Rainer Maria Rilke*. C. F. MacIntyre's *Fifty Selected Poems* came out in 1940, B. J. Morse's *Poems* in 1941, Ruth Speirs' *Selected Poems* in 1943, and Ludwig Lewisohn's *Thirty-one Poems by Rainer Maria Rilke* in 1946. Babette Deutsch translated selections from Rilke's *Book of Hours* (1941), and J. B. Leishman *From the Remains of Count C. W.* (1952) and the *Correspondence in Verse with Erika Mitterer* (1953). Translations by well-known poets (including Randall Jarrell, Robert Lowell, and Hugh Macdiarmid) appear in the Anchor Book *An Anthology of German Poetry from Hölderlin to Rilke in English Translation* (edited by Angel Flores, 1960); some of the *Sonnets to Orpheus* and of the *Duino Elegies* are included with a number of the shorter poems.

There are various other translations of the *Duino Elegies* and the *Sonnets to Orpheus* besides those already mentioned. The *Elegies* were translated by V. Sackville-West in 1921, by Jessie Lemont (along with the *Sonnets*) in 1945, by Ruth Speirs (in *Poetry: London*) in 1947, by Countess Nora Wydenbruck in 1948, and by Harry Behn in 1957. M. D. Herter Norton's version of the *Sonnets to Orpheus* appeared in 1942, C. F. MacIntyre's in 1960.

Not all of the foregoing were printed in English-speaking countries, nor are all of them available now. The interested reader will find C. F. MacIntyre's *Fifty Selected Poems*, which has gone into a paperback edition, one of the finest introductions to Rilke's verse. The excellence of the Leishman-Spender version of the *Duino Elegies* is enhanced by its informative introduction and notes. Like the MacIntyre volume of selections, this one helpfully contains a side-by-side setting of the German texts.

Among the prose works, the "prose poem" of *The Song of the Love and Death of Cornet Christopher Rilke* has been translated, with varying titles, by M. D. Herter Norton (1932), B. J. Morse (1947), and Stefan Schimanski, with Leslie Phillips (1949). *The Life of the Virgin Mary* has been put into English by R. G. L. Barrett (1921), C. F. MacIntyre (1947), and Stephen Spender (1951). In 1930 John Linton translated *The Notebooks of Malte Laurids Brigge* (using the singular form, *Notebook*), later reissued in America, in collaboration with M. D. Herter Norton, as *The Journal of My Other Self* (also 1930), and finally, in a new translation by Mrs. Norton, as *The Notebooks of Malte Laurids Brigge* (1949). Jessie Lemont's version of *Rodin* was first published in 1919; this essay and others, on Rodin and other subjects, as well as the *Christopher Rilke*, are found in Rilke's *Selected Works* (Volume I: Prose), translated by G. Craig Houston and first published in 1954. This book does not include any of the *Stories of God*, translated by Countess Nora Wydenbruck (1932).

Books about Rilke in English (or translated from the German, French, and other European languages) have increased in recent years. There are important chapters on Rilke in C. M. Bowra's *The Heritage of Symbolism* (1943) and in Erich Heller's *The Disinherited Mind* (1952); this last is a study of Rilke's relationship to the work of Nietzsche. Essays by Bowra and others (including the editors of the volume) occur in *Rainer Maria Rilke: Aspects of his Mind and Poetry*, edited by William Rose and G. Craig Houston; the book contains a fine reminiscent introduction by Stefan Zweig. Another item to be noted is S. S. Prawer's *German Lyric Poetry: A Critical Analysis of Selected Poems from Klopstock to Rilke* (1952).

Other volumes on Rilke include: Federico Olivero's *Rainer Maria Rilke: A Study in Poetry and Mysticism* (1931); Eudo C. Mason's *Rilke's Apotheosis* (1938); Mason's *Rilke and Goethe* (1948); Hans Egon Holthusen's *Rainer Maria Rilke: A Study of His Later Poetry* (1952); Richard B. O'Connell's *Concepts and Symbols in the Poetry of Rainer Maria Rilke* (1952); Geoffrey H. Hartman's *The Unmediated Vision: An Interpretation of Wordsworth, Hopkins, Rilke, and Valéry* (1954); H. W. Belmore's *Rilke's Craftsmanship* (1954); W. L. Graff's *Rainer Maria Rilke: Creative Anguish of a Modern Poet* (1956); Frank Wood's *Rainer Maria Rilke: The Ring of Forms* (1958); and H. Frederick Peters' *Rainer Maria Rilke: Masks and the Man* (1960).

Three full-length critical biographies have appeared

in English: E. M. Butler's *Rainer Maria Rilke* (1941); Countess Nora Wydenbruck's *Rilke: Man and Poet* (1949), and F. W. van Heerikhuizen's *Rainer Maria Rilke: His Life and Work* (translated from the Dutch in 1952). Of these, Miss Butler's book is the most extensively critical and Countess Wydenbruck's the most extensively biographical.

8

The letters in the present volume are a fairly small selection from the vast treasury of Rilke's correspondence. They have not been specifically chosen to emphasize Rilke's involvement with his art, but inevitably they represent a great many phases of his existence both as man and as poet.

The first letter in the book, to an older writer, shows that Rilke from early youth was dedicated to his mission as a maker of poetry. Many of his early letters, including a mawkish long one to Valérie David-Rhonfeld, have been omitted, however interesting they might be as biographical exhibits. In any event, Rilke was not always at his best in love letters: if some examples of these have been included from his later life, the reason is that they are often closely bound up with his writing career and make important comments upon his work.

Besides such comments, the letters contain a good deal of valuable criticism of the works of others; despite Rilke's disclaimers to the effect that he lacked the critical talent, he often in his letters valuably explored the work of fellow-writers, not only contemporaries such as Paul Valéry and Emile Verhaeren but also authors of the past whom he admired, such as the Danish novelist Jens Peter Jacobsen. Rilke's letters are also full of word portraits of the men themselves, including some of his greatest contemporaries. The two meetings with Tolstoy are forcefully described, as well as many of those with Rodin, and there are some striking sketches of George Bernard Shaw, whom Rilke met when that most un-Rilkean figure was sitting for Rodin.

Landscapes and cities also appear importantly in these letters, which invoke the scenery of the modern world as few others have. And there are many revealing comments on love, religion, war, and other subjects of primary significance. Rilke sometimes expresses distaste for certain things, but hatred comes out only when he discusses the military schools of his childhood. Above all, these letters are a communication, to friends or to strangers with whom he would develop a sudden intimacy in letters—a communication of the experience of the poet. In correspondence, only Keats has been so eloquently intense in revealing the magic of that experience.

9

The rest of this introduction is devoted to explanations of method and to acknowledgments.

Since all but one of these letters are from printed sources—German, English, and French—I have, in the present edition, had to follow the text and style of earlier editors; their omissions of parts of letters are theirs, not mine, determined in some cases by the Rilke estate and in others by correspondents who either demanded such omissions or made them in their own editions containing Rilke letters. There are inconsistencies in the matter of salutation and signature; some letters have both, some only one, some neither—this follows earlier printings of these letters. Further, the punctuation is often not in standard English style; it suggests a translator's compromise between German and English methods.

As to the dating of these letters, this in each case either follows the European style used in earlier printed versions or, if this style is not observed in a letter, it has been made consistent. In any case, such dating (day, month, year) is the most sensible for all purposes.

In regard to annotations, the present editor doesn't believe in bottom-of-the-page footnotes to letters, and is not using them in this edition or in the volumes of D. H. Lawrence's letters he is preparing. Not that letters don't need annotation—they certainly receive it here. But notes at the bottom of the page in the text of letters are unpleasantly distracting: they gouge the eye and pull it downward, often for a trivial bit of information that merely breaks the progress of the reading. (I have an edition of Keats's letters that is full of scholarly apparatus, and while the information is necessary and even welcome, it is arranged so that it makes the reading of the letters themselves a painful ordeal.) Here, the information necessary to the fullest understanding of the letter is concentrated at the end of the letter, where a natural break comes, at whatever part of the page, as it occurs.

As to the letters chosen for this book: some of them have never appeared in English before; these will be noted later, along with the acknowledgment to translators. Many of the present letters are from the two volumes of *The Letters of Rainer Maria Rilke* (New York, W. W. Norton, 1945), translated by M. D. Herter Norton and Jane Bannard Greene. Other volumes which have been drawn upon are: *Letters to Benvenuta* (New York, Philosophical Library, 1951), translated by Heinz Norden; *Letters to Merline* (London, Methuen, 1952), translated by Violet M. MacDonald; *Rainer Maria Rilke: His Last Friendship* (New York, Philosophical Library, 1952), translated by William H. Kennedy; *Letters to Frau Gudi Nölke* (London, Hogarth Press, 1955), translated by Violet M. MacDonald. Regrettably, the editor of the present collection was not permitted to use anything from the small but valuable collection of Rilke's *Letters to a Young Poet* (New York, W. W. Norton, 1934), translated by M. D. Herter Norton. Attention might also be called to two other collections of Rilke letters in English, both of them excellent: *Selected Letters of Rainer Maria Rilke, 1902–1926* (London, Macmillan, 1947), translated by R. F. C. Hall, and *The Letters of Rainer Maria and Princess Marie von Thurn und Taxis* (London, Hogarth Press, 1958; New York, New Directions, 1958), translated by Countess Nora Wydenbruck. Thanks are due to the publishers of the volumes mentioned above, from which some letters have been taken for the present collection. Thanks are likewise due to the Insel-Verlag, Wiesbaden, Germany, from whose two volumes of Rilke's *Briefe* (1950) the letters not previously published in English have been selected. The Insel-Verlag, representatives of the Rilke estate, are also to be thanked for permission to use the heretofore unpublished letter from Rilke to Elizabeth Mayer (6 November 1916), translated by Mrs. Mayer—to whom all thanks, too.

The present editor translated Rilke's letters (from the French) to Mimi Romanelli and Balthusz Klossowski. Professor Frank Kreith, of the University of Colorado, translated (from the German) the letters to Lisa Heise; and Eva Rennie, of Carbondale, Illinois, translated (from the German) the letters to Ilse Erdmann,

Countess Margot Sizzo-Noris-Crouy, Ruth Sieber-Rilke, and August Sauer. My thanks to both these translators and to those who have given assistance to us all in making these translations: Professors Boyd Carter, Helmut Liedloff, and Douglas Rennie, all of Southern Illinois University.

As always, my wife Beatrice Moore has given technical and moral assistance to an extent for which no adequate thanks can be expressed.

HARRY T. MOORE

Southern Illinois University
11 February 1960

Selected Letters of
RAINER MARIA RILKE

TO LUDWIG GANGHOFER

from 8/I Blütenstrasse, Munich,
16 April 1897

. . . Dearest, much honored master, when one has
a very dark childhood behind one, in which the everyday resembles walking in dank cold streets and a holiday is like a resting in some narrow grey, inner court,
one becomes diffident. And even more diffident if, at
the age of ten, from these troubled and yet enervated
days one is deposited in the rough activity of a military
institution where, above the longing for love that has
scarcely come to consciousness, an icy, wild duty rages
away like a winter storm, and where the lonely, helpless heart after unhealthy coddling experiences unrea-
sonable brutality. Then comes the crisis: the child becomes either indifferent or unhappy. I became the
latter. A strong disposition toward excessive piety grew
to a kind of madness under the influence of the spiritual loneliness and the coercion of an odious duty hard
as fate. The blows I often endured from mischievous
comrades or coarse superiors I felt as happiness and
went in for the idea of a false martyrdom. The continual excitement of this almost ecstatic joy in torment,
the passing of the hours of recovery in the institution

1

chapel, the excruciating sleeplessness of nights frantic with dreams—all that together was bound finally to exercise a detrimental influence upon my resistless growing organism. After an added inflammation of the lungs, I was sent for six weeks as "highly nervous" (!) to Salzburg for a salt cure. Had I been allowed to leave then! But everybody thought it perfectly natural that, having borne it four years, I should remain for the six to come, which would be better, in order to become a lieutenant and—to provide for myself.

In the fifth year of my military training (the fifteenth of my life) I finally forced my departure. Things didn't get much better. They put me in a commercial school in Linz, where I saw a cheerless office future darkening before me.—After scarcely a year's time, I tore myself away against everyone's will by an act of violence and have since been accounted a kind of prodigal son. They wanted to try the last resort. Since in both previous institutions and in my family it was noticed with scorn and uneasiness that I "made poems," they wanted to make college possible for me. At that time it was my father's brother, who played a considerable role in Prague as lawyer and deputy to the assembly of Bohemia, who put in a good word for me and with generous financial assistance made possible the costly private study my father could never have afforded. For that I thank him far beyond the grave. After three years of serious but joyous work I had gone through the entire eight-grade grammar school so well, even after the thoroughly defective preparatory training of the military school, that in the summer of '95 I passed my entrance examination with distinction. Unfortunately my uncle could no longer look upon this success . . . and he probably took with him under the earth the opinion that I would not amount to much.

He left no stipulations of any kind in his will save that his daughters, my cousins, should allow me to study up to the entrance examination and, under certain circumstances, the university years.

Now it seems to me that all people do not give alike. And in the two years of my university study I have got the feeling rather strongly that I am a burdensome duty to the two ladies. Much more burdensome to me is the feeling of slavery in such helpless dependence at my age when others may already support their parents. And then: on this road I have *no objective at all.* For I keep costing more and more money, and if I become a doctor and do not want to pine away as a high-school instructor—then I shall be costing money again until I get some professorship or other which, however, I do not in the least desire.

With every day it becomes clearer to me that I was right in setting myself from the start against the phrase my relatives like: Art is something one just cultivates on the side in free hours, when one leaves the government office, etc.—That to me is a fearful sentence. I feel that this is my belief: Whoever does not consecrate himself wholly to art with all his wishes and values can never reach the highest goal. He is not an artist at all. And now it can be no presumption if I confess that I feel myself to be an artist, weak and wavering in strength and boldness, yet aware of bright goals, and hence to me every creative activity is serious, glorious, and true. Not as martyrdom do I regard art—but as a battle the chosen one has to wage with himself and his environment in order to go forward with a pure heart to the greatest goal, the one day of celebration, and with full hands to give to all successors of the rich reconciliation finally achieved. But that needs a whole man! Not a few weary leisure hours.

3

I do not know, dearest master, in how far you agree with me and whether you are perhaps wisely smiling at the impetuousness of this youthful resentment; then you will forgive too.—Now I am free of the university. —The time has come. Dear sir, you yourself once offered to give me help if I needed it. Now then: to-day I have come to you.

I would like through agreement with a publisher or some steady engagement on a newspaper to earn enough to be able to live soon and well on my own. I would like to spare my cousins their wanting-to-give-gladly and, by grateful renunciation of my monthly allowance, to enable my dear father, who is somewhat ailing, to allow more for his health. I cannot work in peace before that happens.—I myself, of course, need little. . . .

Full of profoundest trust I lay this whole avowal in your kind hands and sincerely beg you: counsel me, help me. . . . Be assured that I shall never and nowhere bring discredit upon your recommendation . . . and to you all the gratitude I can prove to you through deeds for a lifetime.

/ *Ludwig Ganghofer (1855–1920) was a novelist and dramatist to whom in this letter Rilke describes the agony of his military-school training (1886–1891), first at the Military College at St. Pölten and then (for nine months) at the Military High School at Maerisch-Weisskirchen; he was to describe these experiences again, notably in the 3 April 1903 letter to Ellen Key and in the 9 December 1920 letter to Major General von Sedlakowitz.*

TO LOU ANDREAS-SALOMÉ

from St. Petersburg,
[1900] Saturday morning

I have your letter, your dear letter that does me good with every word, that touches me as with a wave, so strong and surging, that surrounds me as with gardens and builds up heavens about me, that makes me able and happy to say to you what struggled stupidly with my last difficult letter: that I long for you and that it was namelessly dismaying to live these days without any news, after that unexpected and quick farewell and among the almost hostile impressions of this difficult city, in which you could not speak to me out of the distance through any thing at all. So it came to that ugly letter of recently which could scarcely find its way out of the isolation, out of the unaccustomed and intolerable aloneness of my experiences and was only a hurrying, a perplexity and confusedness, something that must be alien to you in the beauty to which your life has immediately rounded itself out again under the new circumstances.

Now I can scarcely bear it that in the great song around you, in which you are finding again little children's voices, my voice should have been the strange, the only banal one, the voice of the world among those holy words and stillnesses of which days about you are woven. Wasn't it so? I fear it must have been so. What shall I do? Can I drown out the other letter with this one? In this one your words echo, the other is built upon your being away, of which I learned nothing, and

5

now that I am informed no longer has the right to exist
. . . but *does*, doesn't it?

Will you say a word to me? That in spite of it, everything is as you write; that no squirrel has died of it and
nothing, nothing, has darkened under it or even remained in shadow behind it.

You know, I have often told you of my squirrels that
I raised in Italy, as a child, and for which I bought
long, long chains so that their freedom might come to
an end only in the very high treetops. It was certainly
very wrong to force oneself at all as a power into their
light lives (when they had already grown up, that is,
and no longer needed me), but it was also a little their
intention to go on reckoning with me too, for they
often came running after me, so that at the time it
seemed to me as if they wanted a chain.

How they will miss you, the good youngsters! And
will they be mature enough to go without you into
wood and world? High up in the firs of Rongac their
childhood will sometimes occur to them, and on a
branch that is still rocking from the burden of the leap,
you will be thought of. And though they are only three
little squirrels, in whose little eyes you have no room,
still somewhere in them it is so big that you can be in
their lives. You dear one.

Come back soon, come back as soon as you can leave
them. Lead them out into the wood, tell them with
your voice how beautiful it is, and they will be the
happiest little squirrels and the most beautiful wood.

Yes, please, be here by Sunday! You won't believe
how long the days in Petersburg can be. And at that
not much goes into them. Life here is a continuous being under way, whereby all destinations suffer. One
walks, walks, rides, rides, and wherever one arrives the
first impression is that of one's own weariness. To add

to this, one almost always makes the longest excursions for nothing. Nevertheless I already know this much, that we still have a few beautiful things to see when you come. In any case for two weeks everything I have thought has ended with: when you come.—

The moonlight night of Wednesday to Thursday I also love. I went along the Neva quite late, by my favorite place, across from St. Isaac's Cathedral, where the city is simplest and greatest. There I too (and indeed quite unexpectedly) felt peaceful, happy, and serious, as now since having your letter. I hasten to send off these lines so that what you send me Monday (and you will surely send one or two words by your brother? Only a few words, I shall understand them all!) is already an answer to *this*. Answer to the one question: are you happy? I am, behind all that bothers me, so fundamentally, so full of trust, so unconquerably happy. And thank you for it. Come soon! . . .

/ *Lou Andreas-Salomé (1861–1937), Russian-born and an important friend of Nietzsche, became the lifelong friend of Rilke and, with her husband, Professor F. C. Andreas, had accompanied him on his first Russian trip, April–June 1899; the present letter was written during Rilke's second (and last) visit to Russia, May–August 1900.*

TO SOFIA NIKOLAEVNA SCHILL

from Tula,
20 May 1900

The lovely hour with you was the last little stone in the gay mosaic of our Moscow days. Next day everything was colored by the haste of departure, and Mos-

7

cow, dear as it is to us, paled before the anticipation of
the many things ahead. We had no idea how close our
dearest fulfillment was to us. On the train, we found
Professor Pasternak who was traveling to Odessa, and
when we spoke to him of our indecision as to whether
we should after all try to see Tolstoy now, he informed
us that there should be on the train a good acquaintance of the Tolstoy house, a Mr. Bulanshe, who should
be apprised of the present whereabouts of the Count.
And it was actually Mr. Bulanshe who was most kindly
willing to advise us. We decided to remain in Tula,
and to go next morning to Lasarevo, and thence by
carriage to the estate of the Obolenskys at Pirogovo
where, in all likelihood, Mr. Bulanshe thought, the
Count must still be. Two days before, Mr. Bulanshe
had accompanied the Countess to Yasnaia, and so the
possibility was at any rate good that one of these days
he might ride to Yasnaia. Therefore Mr. Bulanshe sent
a telegram to the Countess from Serpukhov inquiring
where the Count would be on Friday. The answer was
to come by telegram to our hotel in Tula. We waited
for it in vain and went on, as had been agreed, early
yesterday to Lasarevo, completely at a loss. There we
found a station employee who informed us that the
Count had accompanied Tatiana Lvovna to the station
yesterday, and had then departed with his luggage for
Koslovka. So it became a question for us of reaching as
quickly as possible (by freight train) a place from
which Yasnaia was accessible. We drove back to Ya-
sinki, hired a carriage there, and raced with breathless
bells to the rim of the hill on which stand the poor huts
of Yasnaia, driven together into a village, yet without
coherence, like a herd standing about sadly on exhausted pastureland. Groups of women and children
are only sunny, red spots in the even grey covering

8

ground, roofs and walls like a very luxuriant kind of moss that has been growing over everything undisturbed for centuries. Then the hardly discernible street dips down, forever flowing past empty places, and its grey streamer glides gently into a green valley foamy with treetops, in which two little round towers on the left, topped with green cupolas, mark the entrance to the old, overgrown park in which lies hidden the simple house of Yasnaia Poliana. Before this gate we dismount and go quietly like pilgrims up the still woodland road, until the house emerges gradually whiter and longer. A servant takes in our cards. And in a while we see behind the door in the dusky front room of the house the figure of the Count. The eldest son opens the glass door, and we are in the vestibule facing the Count, the aged man, to whom one always comes like a son, even when one does not want to remain under the sway of his fatherliness. He seems to have become smaller, more bent, whiter, and his shadowlessly clear eyes, as though independent of his aged body, await the strangers and deliberately scrutinize them and bless them involuntarily with some inexpressible blessing. The Count recognizes Frau Lou at once and greets her very cordially. He excuses himself and promises to be with us from two o'clock on. We have reached our goal, and, minds at ease, we remain behind in the great hall in the son's company; with him we roam through the spacious wild park and return after two hours to the house. There in the front room is the Countess, busy putting away books. Reluctantly, with surprise, and inhospitably she turns to us for a moment and explains briefly that the Count is unwell. . . . Now it is fortunate that we can say we have already seen him. That disarms the Countess somewhat. She doesn't come in with us, however, throws the books about in

9

the front room, and shouts to someone in an angry voice: We have only just moved in! . . . Then while we are waiting in the little room, a young lady arrives too, voices are heard, violent weeping, soothing words from the old Count who comes in to us, distraught, and excitedly asks a few questions, and leaves us again. You can imagine, we stay behind in the little room, in great fear of having come at the wrong time. But after a while the Count comes in again, this time alert, turning his entire attention upon us, encompassing us with his great gaze. Just think, Sofia Nikolaevna,—he proposes a walk through the park. Instead of the general meal, which we had dreaded and at most hoped for, he gives us the opportunity of being alone with him in the beautiful countryside through which he carried the heavy thoughts of his great life. He doesn't participate in the meals, because, indisposed again for the last two days, he takes almost nothing but *café au lait*, and so this is the hour he can easily withdraw from the others in order to lay it in our hands like an unexpected gift. We go slowly along the long, thickly overgrown paths, in rich conversation which, as formerly, receives warmth and animation from the Count. He speaks Russian, and when the wind doesn't cover up the words for me, I understand every syllable. He has thrust his left hand under his wool jacket in his belt, his right rests on the head of his walking stick without leaning on it heavily, and he bends down now and then to pick some herb, with a gesture as if he wanted to capture a flower with the fragrance surrounding it; from his cupped hand he drinks in the aroma, and then, as he talks, heedlessly lets fall the empty flower into the great profusion of the wild spring, which has become no poorer thereby.—The talk passes over many things. But all the words do not pass by *in front* of them, along externals, they penetrate the darkness behind the things. And the deep value of each is not its color in the light, but the feeling that it comes out of the obscurities and mysteries out of which we all live. And every time something not-shared became apparent in the tone of the talk, a view opened up somewhere on to light backgrounds of deep unity.

And so the walk was a good walk. Sometimes in the wind the figure of the Count grew; his great beard fluttered, but the grave face, marked by solitude, remained quiet, as though untouched by the storm.

As soon as we had entered the house, we took leave of the Count with a feeling of childlike thankfulness and rich with gifts of his being. We did not want to see anyone else on that day. As we went back on foot to Koslovka, we enjoyed and understood the country of Tula in which wealth and poverty are side by side, not like contrasts, but like different, very sisterly words for one and the same life, jubilantly and carelessly fulfilling itself in a hundred forms. . . .

/ *Sofia Nikolaevna Schill wrote under the pseudonym Sergei Orlowski; this letter to her dates from Rilke's second Russian visit, May–August 1900, and describes his second meeting with Tolstoy; the Professor Pasternak referred to was an artist who painted Rilke's portrait—Leonid Pasternak (1862–1945), the father of Boris Pasternak.*

TO CLARA WESTHOFF

from Schmargendorf bei Berlin,
18 October 1900

Do you remember, dear Clara Westhoff, the evening in the little blue dining room? You told me then about those days that piled up before your journey to Paris.

At your father's wish you had to delay your departure and try to model his mother.—Your eyes, full of presentiment, already caught up in distances and new beauties, had to turn back and accustom themselves to the very near face of a grave, dignified, old lady, and every day go weary ways over furrows and wrinkles. The quiet work subdued your hands, already outstretched, ready for all there was to grasp. And instead of changing amid the many great chance happenings of a foreign land, you grew, rising by the daily work. Instead of your art, thirsty for the friendly strangeness of new things,—your human feeling and trust unfolded in these unexpected days, your love gathered itself together and went out to meet the quiet, peaceful face that offered itself to you, enigmatically rich, as though it were the countenance of many, having neither expression, nor head, nor hands. As though things sometimes joined together to lift a collective face as if it were theirs and hold it before a beholder . . . and before a creator! You see, I was so struck then by your humility: suddenly your eye, which was already preparing itself for larger dimensions, goes about willingly with little, hesitating, hearkening steps over the many overgrown paths of a long dead experience and stands still by all its landmarks reverently and respectfully. And has forgotten the world, and has no world but a face.

I know exactly everything you said then. The figure of the old lady who speaks rarely and reservedly, who hides her hands when a gesture of tenderness would move them, and who only with rare caresses builds bridges that no longer exist when she draws back her arm and lies again like an island fantastically re-

peated on all sides in the mirror of motionless waters.
—My eyes too were already caught up in the radiance
and bound to great and deep beauties. Your home was
for me, from the first moment, more than just a kindly
foreign place. Was simply home, *the first home in
which I saw people living* (otherwise everyone lives
abroad, but all homes stand empty . . .). That struck
me so. I wanted at first to be a brother beside you all,
and your home is rich enough to love me too and to
uphold me, and you are so kind and take me in as a
real member of the family, and initiate me trustfully
into the abundance of your work weeks and holidays.
And I am entirely devoted to the great beauty of which
I am, after all, only an enjoyer (I did not join in the
work of contemplating this beauty) . . . : So I all but
forgot it, the quiet face of life, which waits for me and
which I must shape with humble, serving hands. I was
all the time looking out beyond it into radiance and
greatness and am only now accustoming myself again
to the near and solemn sternness of the great face
which must have been shaped by me before I may receive something more distant, new. You worked for a
month; I shall perhaps have to work for years before I
may devote myself to something which down deep is
friendly, and yet is unexpected and full of surprise.
Much of the mood of those weeks of work, of which
you told, is in me. For a while now, I have felt myself
to be in the presence of the stillest hour, but only when
I resolved to stay here, to study, to make full use of all
the means Berlin offers for my plans, and merely to
serve, then only did I begin to model. I still think much
and with longing of Worpswede, of the little house in
which there will be black evenings, day in, day out,
and cold lonely days . . . of our Sundays and of unexpected hours so full of unforgettable beauty that one

can only bear them with both hands,—only behind me, my work is already growing in the great sea of the background like a wandering wave that will soon seize me and envelop me—utterly, utterly. . . .

That is what, above all, I must let happen. You will understand it, since I began with your little story and yet from the first moment have spoken only of myself, as if justifiable in a letter which comes to you in my stead. I myself cannot go away from the "face." I am arranging my whole winter to make the most of every day, and perhaps as early as January 1901 I shall go to Russia again. There all the features of life become clearer and strangely simplified for me; there I can more easily work ahead, improve, complete. . . .

I have always known that one of the events which you told me about would be especially significant for me . . . now your November days of last winter stand almost symbolically over me. And if I had not received this wonderfully beautiful picture out of your memory and out of your feeling, I should not have known *what* I am now living through, and that what I am now living through is good.

It is good, isn't it?

I am not saying farewell to you. I feel gratefully near to you, and it does me good not to have taken leave. . . . Leave-takings are a burden on feeling. Distance remains stressed behind them, acts and grows and becomes mighty beyond all that is shared, which should be spontaneous even between those who are widely separated.

How beautiful your letter was! It was very full of you and it is wonderful that you write as you are. Very few can do that, and many who only write never learn it (what a bad word "learning" is for it!) as long as they live. And with you writing isn't even the main thing. I could readily believe that it is. With your pen too, you would create people.

Before what little figure are you sitting by your warm stove? Before the stiffly standing child that you separated from the cowering girl? And the boy with the tightly drawn-up knees that I like so much,—is he all finished? Whenever you write of such things, and of everything you want to, you do me good.

I thank you so much and think of you in connection with only nice things.

(half past one at night)

/ *Clara Westhoff (1878–1954), to whose sculpture Rilke refers in this letter, was a member of the art colony at Worpswede, near Bremen, which Rilke had recently visited; he was to marry Clara in 1901.*

TO GUSTAV PAULI

from Westerwede bei Bremen,
8 January 1902

. . . In the middle of 1902, through family circumstances, I shall lose an allowance from home which is not large but on which we have lived remarkably well and are living (under various difficulties). What will happen then, I don't know. For weeks I haven't had a single moment of peace under the pressure of this colossal new fear. At first I kept hoping I could take on something that would enable me to remain out here with my dear ones in the quiet home we have scarcely established, of whose quiet I am not to be able to take full advantage for my work. The interest of a publisher who made possible for me a year of quiet work would

have sufficed to offer me the opportunity for that progress which I know I could now make if my powers
might remain concentrated and my senses within the
quiet world that has been rounded out in such a wonderfully beautiful way by the dear child. For me, marriage, which from the ordinary point of view was an
act of great foolishness, was a necessity. My world,
which has so little connection with mundane existence,
was, in my bachelor room, abandoned to every wind,
unprotected, and needed for its development this quiet
house of its own under the wide skies of solitude. Also
I read in Michelet that life for two is simpler and
cheaper than the life open to betrayal on all sides, the
exploited existence of the single person—and I gladly
believed the belief of that dear child Michelet. . . .

It is an extremely cruel fate that now, when I am
surrounded by all the conditions that were as desirable
and necessary to my art as bread,—I must probably
leave everything in midstream (for what other way out
remains!), to go away from all that is dear to all that
is alien. I am trying daily to accustom myself to the
thought of the approaching departure by taking it
every evening in stronger and stronger doses. But
where am I to go? Of what work am I capable? Where
can I be used and *so* used that that which, in the end,
remains and *must* remain my life, my task, even my
duty, is not destroyed! My father, in his remote generosity, wants to procure for me the post of an official at
a bank in Prague,—but that means giving up everything, making an end, renouncing, returning to the conditions from the proximity of which I fled even as a
child. From the spiritual point of view alone, that is a
sort of resignation, a frost, in which everything would
have to die. This my good father, who was always an
official, does not sense, and thinks anyway that beside

16

an art like mine there is room for any occupation. If it were a question of a painter, he would understand that such a position would mean the ruin of his art,— *my* activity I could still pursue satisfactorily (so he thinks) in a few evening hours. And moreover, I especially, who haven't too much strength at my disposal, must live out of a unified and collected state and avoid every hindrance and division which diverts the resultant in the parallelogram of forces from its direction,— if I want to reach my objectives (so unexplainable to others, even to my dear father). And that I want that, and that I want it although the objectives are great, is not arrogance and worldly vanity which I am choosing for myself; it is imposed on me like a task, like a mission—and in everything in which I succeed, I am, more than anyone, the willing and humble executor of lofty commands, whose device in his finest hours, may read, "I serve." And finally it would, after all, be irresponsible, at the moment when the necessity of earning my own living presents itself close at hand and energetically, to forsake the path which, obeying urges and longings of my own, I have trod since boyhood, and to leave lying on the old building site the hewn building stones of a life which bears only the traces of my chisel,—in order, with no heart for the work, to help build with manufactured bricks, in the pay of a little man, someone else's house next door, to which I am indifferent.

Wouldn't that mean jumping out of my own skiff, which will perhaps touch on my own shore after a few strong strokes of the oar (if I may be permitted to give them), and continuing on a big steamer, lost among hundreds of people, to a common place, as indifferent and banal as a coffeehouse garden on Sunday afternoon?

I would rather starve with my family than take this step, which is like a death without the grandeur of death.

Isn't it much more to the point to draw practical results from what I have already done, to make out of a poetic art a literary art-craft which would support its follower? This literary art-craft *could* be journalism, but isn't. The roads to it are closed, or at least made very difficult for me by my own disinclination. But there must be other points at which my honest powers could get started; to be sure, I am the last to find these points—I don't even know whom I could ask about such points. . . .

If nothing presents itself anywhere (a collaboration of a regular kind or something of the sort) I shall probably have to leave Westerwede in the course of this year, and I wonder if in Bremen, where as a stranger I have found such a kind and trusting reception, there wouldn't be some position in which I could prove myself useful. Doesn't the enlarging of the Art Museum necessitate any filling out of the personnel, or isn't there some other collection or an institution in which I could work? I haven't got my doctorate, and now there isn't any money to go on studying; I think that title (which I have gladly avoided like all titles) couldn't help me anyway at this moment! If I succeeded in giving a series of lectures yearly, and if my wife were to take over the school, perhaps it would then be possible to survive the first, most difficult years, as each could live on his own earnings. With the inexpensive requirements of our farmhouse, and the trifling needs we both have, an income of about 250 marks monthly would suffice us together, so that each would have to earn about 125 marks.

Shouldn't that be possible somehow?

If, without disturbing our own work, we could last out a year in this way, I am convinced that that work would have grown strong enough during this year to take us on its shoulders and carry us along.—But if you think this cannot be managed by any means, may I beg of you to give me, for some city in which you have connections, be it Munich or Dresden or another, some advice or a good word which I can use when the time comes?

Forgive me for writing this presumptuous letter. Since the fall, all my days and nights have been a continual, anxious battle with the morrow, and in the face of your generosity it seems to me dishonest to hide from you a situation which everyone really should know who wishes me well. And I know that you do, my dear doctor.

Should my disclosures be a burden to you, take no further notice of them, without therefore changing your friendly attitude toward me; I know that it is inconsiderate to take someone into one's confidence so forcibly at the eleventh hour, but I am at the point where I think that for once I may be inconsiderate of people I trust: as when one's clothes are burning, or someone is dying, one would certainly awaken a friend whose sleep one would otherwise never have dared to disturb. . . .

/ *Gustav Pauli (1866–1939) was an art historian and director of the Art Museum at Bremen; "the dear child" was Ruth Rilke (born 12 December 1901).*

19

TO PAULA MODERSOHN-BECKER

from Bremen,
12 February 1902

Permit me to say a few words about your letter to my dear wife: it concerns me very closely as you know, and if I were not in Bremen, I would seek an opportunity to discuss the matter with you in person,—the . . . indeed, what matter? Will you believe me that it is hard for me to understand what you are actually talking about? Nothing has happened really—or rather: much that is good has happened, and the misunderstanding is based on the fact that you do not want to grant what has happened. Everything is supposed to be as it was, and yet everything is different from what it has been. If your love for Clara Westhoff wants to do something now, then its work and task is this: to catch up with what it has missed. For it has failed to see whither this person has gone, it has failed to accompany her in her broadest development, it has failed to spread itself out over the new distances this person embraces, and it hasn't ceased looking for her at a certain point in her growth, it wants obstinately to hold fast to a definite beauty beyond which she has passed, instead of persevering, confident of new shared beauties to come.

The confidence you proved to me, dear friend, when you vouchsafed me a little glance into the pages of your journal, entitles me (as I believe) to remind you how strange and distant and incomparable Clara Westhoff's nature seemed to you in the beginning, how surrounded by a solitude whose doors you didn't know.

. . . And this first important impression you have been able so far to forget as to accompany only with blame and warning the entering of this person, whom you began to love because of her differentness and solitude, into a new solitude, the reasons for which you are even better able to examine than the reasons for that first seclusion, which you certainly didn't regard with reproach then, but rather with a certain admiring recognition. If your love has remained vigilant, then it must have seen that the experiences which came to Clara Westhoff derived their worth from the very fact that they were tightly and indissolubly bound up with the inner being of the house in which the future is to find us: we had to burn all the wood on our own hearth in order to warm up our house for the first time and make it livable. Do I have to tell you that we had cares, heavy and anxious cares, which might not be carried outside any more than the few hours of deep happiness? . . . Does it surprise you that the centers of gravity have shifted, and is your love and friendship so distrustful that it wants constantly to see and grasp what it possesses? You will continually have to experience disappointments if you expect to find the old relationship; but why don't you rejoice in the new one that will begin when someday the gates of Clara Westhoff's new solitude are opened to receive you? I too am standing quietly and full of deep trust before the gates of this solitude, because I hold this to be the highest task of a bond between two people: that each should stand guard over the solitude of the other. For, if it lies in the nature of indifference and of the crowd to recognize no solitude, then love and friendship are there for the purpose of continually providing the opportunity for solitude. And only those are the true sharings which rhythmically interrupt periods of deep isolation. . . . Think of the time when you came to know Clara Westhoff: then your love waited patiently for an opening gate, the same love which now raps impatiently on the walls behind which things are being accomplished of which we have no cognizance, of which I know just as little as you,—only that I have faith that they will touch me deeply and closely when they reveal themselves to me someday. And cannot your love grasp a similar faith? Out of this faith alone will joys come to it by which it will live without starving.

/ *Paula Modersohn-Becker* (1867–1907) *was a member of the Worpswede colony who, in 1901, had married the painter Otto Modersohn.*

TO FRAU JULIE WEINMANN

from Schloss Haseldorf (Holstein),
25 June 1902

. . . The last time I wrote (somewhat over a year ago) I announced to you my marriage. The person who is so fondly bound up with and indispensable to my life is a young sculptress who has worked with Rodin in Paris, a girl full of power and artistic ability, an artist, from whose growth I expect the greatest conceivable results. That and a limitless, mutual faith brought us together. Since December we have a dear little daughter, Ruth, and life has become much richer with her.—For the woman—according to my conviction —a child is a completion and a liberation from all strangeness and insecurity: it is, spiritually too, the mark of maturity; and I am filled with the conviction that the woman artist, who has had and has and loves a child, is, no less than the mature man, capable of reaching all the artistic heights the man can reach under the same conditions, that is, if he is an artist. In a word, I consider the woman in whom lives deep artistic striving the equal of the masculine artist from the moment of her maturity and fulfillment on, entitled and summoned to the same ambitious goals in which he in his best hours may solitarily believe. I am saying this only so that I may now say that the meaning of my marriage lies in helping this dear young person to find herself, her greatness and depths, in so far as one human being can help another. Clara Westhoff has for a long time been no beginner: she has proved by my portrait-bust, by the bust of Heinrich Vogeler (which was purchased by the Bremen Art Museum) and several smaller works that have been exhibited, that she can hardly be mistaken for anyone else now and can be seen beside the best.—All this, however, is not the matter about which I want to speak, although it leads me to the subject of this letter, to myself.

It is clear to me that I need help in order to continue on my way. I need the opportunity to be allowed to absorb quietly, to learn for a year or two, without having to write. The course of my education was broken by a variety of accidents, and in the end that is not a misfortune; for in those years one has not really the ability to choose one's education, which later makes the winning of knowledge and truth so precious. Now I know what I need; two great journeys to Russia which I have taken in recent years have given me wide ranges and tasks and have strengthened and confirmed me in myself. And now in the fall I want to go to Paris, in order, guided by the connoisseur of Russian things, the Vicomte de Vogüé, to work in the libraries, to collect myself, and to write about Rodin whom I have

23

loved and revered for a long time. That is the external side of what I want for the immediate future, a little portion of that deep wanting which goes toward my work and toward its continuous realization.

What can one who wants a great deal say of this wanting without betraying it and becoming a boaster? Here every word involves a false note and an affront to what it means. One can only say that one comes more and more to protect this wanting which goes toward deep and important things, that one longs more and more sincerely and wholeheartedly to give it all one's strength and all one's love and to experience worries through it and not through the little harassing accidents of which life in poverty is full. I am very poor. I do not suffer from poverty because at bottom it refuses me nothing. But this winter, for the first time, it stood before me for months like a specter, and I lost myself and all my beloved aims and all the light out of my heart and came near taking some little official post, and that would have meant: dying and setting out on a spiritual transmigration full of homelessness and madness.—I deliberated at the last moment and clung to what, even as a child, I had begun dimly and longingly to want. I am indeed no longer a beginner who throws himself at random into the future. I have worked, for years, and if I have worked out anything for myself, it is the belief in the right to raise the best I have in me and the awareness of the treasures in the sesame of my soul which I can no longer forget. And after all I know that my pen will be strong enough to carry me: only I may not misuse it too early and must give it time to attain its full growth.

My dear lady, I am speaking to you because I know of no one who could understand and feel the meaning of words like this, despite all the omissions, no one who would be generous enough to pardon them, and kind enough to see what lies behind them. I am gathering all my confidence together and begging you to accept it, because my memory of you, of your husband and of the spirit of your kindly house brings before me people who do not consider the striving for artistic fulfillment as something superfluous, but rather as a great law which awakens in those who love life most deeply.

Perhaps you remember me: perhaps one of my verses will excuse me for approaching you out of my distance, perhaps something in your heart will believe that I am not presuming too much when I beg for my best, as for a child that I do not want to let die.

In the past year I have had a little household with my wife (in a little village near Worpswede); but the household consumed too much, and so we have promised each other to live for our work, each as a bachelor of limited means, as before. That also gives to each the possibility of being wherever his work happens to require. For, since work must be quite uppermost, we are also prepared to bear a geographical separation from time to time if it is necessary. We have lost a good deal of time, but this year must take us both further along. Will you help me to my goal, dear lady? Will you and your husband make it possible for me to work on myself this year in Paris, in quiet and peace of mind, without this continual fear that insinuates itself into all thoughts and into every quiet of my heart? Not without poverty, only without fear!—And only for a year?

I have never begged from anyone; you see I don't know how it is done, nor do I know whether I can thank: but I believe I can.

My wife will probably obtain an artist-fellowship and only accept a very small subsidy from me which I can easily afford from what I earn on the side. What

I desire so ardently, however, and consider so important for my development, is what I have never actually had: a single year of quiet, fear-free work. A little peace and composure from which so much future can come.

I know of no fellowship for which I could apply, no person whom I may really ask. And so I come to you, quite unashamed, as to old friends.

Perhaps, dear lady, none of the books I have written in recent years has come to your notice. Fortunately a new book of poems is coming out in the next few weeks, so that I can at least tell you where I stand and whither I have gone in these years; that I will do at all events.

I am writing this letter in a still, lonely evening hour and not reading it over because perhaps then I wouldn't send it off. Not that I am ashamed of it; but I am afraid, dear lady, of losing or offending you the moment the picture you have of me shifts under its influence. If it could have such an effect, then—please —let it be nothing, let it not have been, for beyond everything the assurance is precious to me that you still think kindly of me and that I may kiss your hand in unaltered respect.

/ *Frau Julie Weinmann, wife of a councillor of commerce, was a friend of Rilke's in Munich to whom he dedicated a poem in the volume* Advent.

TO CLARA RILKE

from 11 rue Toullier, Paris,
5 September 1902

. . . I believe much has now been revealed to me
at Rodin's recently. After a *déjeuner* that passed no
less uneasily and strangely than the one I last mentioned, I went with Rodin into the garden, and we sat
down on a bench which looked out wonderfully far
over Paris. It was still and beautiful. The little girl (it
is probably Rodin's daughter), the little girl had come
with us without Rodin's having noticed her. Nor did
the child seem to expect it. She sat down not far from
us on the path and looked slowly and sadly for curious
stones in the gravel. Sometimes she came over and
looked at Rodin's mouth when he spoke, or at mine,
if I happened to be saying something. Once she also
brought a violet. She laid it bashfully with her little
hand on that of Rodin and wanted to put it in his hand
somehow, to fasten it somehow to that hand. But the
hand was as though made of stone, Rodin only looked
at it fleetingly, looked past it, past the shy little hand,
past the violet, past the child, past this whole little moment of love, with a look that clung to the things that
seemed continually to be taking shape in him.

He spoke of art, of art dealers, of his lonely position
and said a great deal that was beautiful which I rather
sensed than understood, because he often spoke very
indistinctly and very rapidly. He kept coming back to
beauty which is everywhere for him who rightly understands and wants it, to things, to the life of these things
—*de regarder une pierre, le torse d'une femme.* . . .

27

And again and again to work. Since physical, really difficult manual labor has come to count as something inferior—he said, work has stopped altogether. I know five, six people in Paris who really work, perhaps a few more. There in the schools, what are they doing year after year—they are "composing." In so doing they learn nothing at all of the nature of things. *Le modelé* (ask your Berlitz French woman sometime how one could translate that, perhaps it is in her dictionary). I know what it means: it is the character of the surfaces, more or less in contrast to the contour, that which fills out all the contours. It is the law and the relationship of these surfaces. Do you understand, for him there is only *le modelé* . . . in all things, in all bodies; he detaches it from them, makes it, after he has learned it from them, into an independent thing, that is, into sculpture, into a plastic work of art. For this reason, a piece of arm and leg and body is for him a whole, an entity, because he no longer thinks of arm, leg, body (that would seem to him too like subject matter, do you see, too—novelistic, so to speak), but only of a *modelé* which completes itself, which is, in a certain sense, finished, rounded off. The following was extraordinarily illuminating in this respect. The little girl brought the shell of a small snail she had found in the gravel. The flower he hadn't noticed,—this he noticed immediately. He took it in his hand, smiled, admired it, examined it and said suddenly: *Voilà le modelé grec.* I understood at once. He said further: *vous savez, ce n'est pas la forme de l'objet, mais: le modelé.* . . . Then still another snail shell came to light, broken and crushed . . . :—*C'est le modelé gothique-renaissance,* said Rodin with his sweet, pure smile! . . . And what he meant was more or less: It is a question for me, that is for the sculptor par excellence, of seeing or studying

28

not the colors or the contours but that which constitutes the plastic, the surfaces. The character of these,
whether they are rough or smooth, shiny or dull (not
in color but in character!). Things are infallible here.
This little snail recalls the greatest works of Greek art:
it has the same simplicity, the same smoothness, the
same inner radiance, the same cheerful and festive sort
of surface. . . . And herein things are infallible! They
contain laws in their purest form. Even the *breaks* in
such a shell will again be of the same kind, will again
be *modelé grec.* This snail will always remain a whole,
as regards its *modelé,* and the smallest piece of snail
is still always *modelé grec.* . . . Now one notices for
the first time what an advance his sculpture is. What
must it have meant to him when he first felt that no
one had ever yet looked for this basic element of plas-
ticity! He had to find it: a thousand things offered it
to him: above all the nude body. He had to transpose
it, that is to make it into *his* expression, to become accustomed to saying *everything* through the *modelé*
and *not otherwise.* Here, do you see, is the second point
in this great artist's life. The first was that he had discovered a new basic element of his art, the second, that
he wanted nothing more of life than to express himself
fully and all that is his through this element. He married, *parce qu'il faut avoir une femme,* as he said to
me (in another connection, namely when I spoke of
groups who join together, of friends, and said I thought
that only from solitary striving does anything result
anyway, then he said it, said: *non, c'est vrai, il n'est
pas bien de faire des groupes, les amis s'empêchent.
Il est mieux d'être seul. Peut-être avoir une femme—
parce qu'il faut avoir une femme*) . . . something like
that.—Then I spoke of you, of Ruth, of how sad it is
that you must leave her,—he was silent for a while and

said then, with wonderful seriousness he said it: . . .
*Oui, il faut travailler, rien que travailler. Et il faut
avoir patience.* One should not think of wanting to
make something, one should try only to build up one's
own medium of expression and to say everything. One
should work and have patience. Not look to right nor
left. Should draw all of life into this circle, have *nothing* outside of this life. Rodin has done so. *J'ai y donné
ma jeunesse,* he said. It is certainly so. One must sacrifice the other. Tolstoy's unedifying household, the dis-
comfort of Rodin's rooms: it all points to the same
thing: that one must choose either this or that. Either
happiness or art. *On doit trouver le bonheur dans son
art.* . . . R. too expressed it something like that. And
indeed that is all so clear, so clear. The great men have
all let their lives become overgrown like an old road
and have carried everything into their art. Their lives
are stunted like an organ they no longer need.

. . . You see, Rodin has lived nothing that is not in
his work. Thus it grew around him. Thus he did not
lose himself; even in the years when lack of money
forced him to unworthy work, he did not lose himself,
because what he experienced did not remain a plan,
because in the evenings he immediately made real
what he had wanted during the day. Thus everything
always became real. That is the principal thing—not
to remain with the dream, with the intention, with the
being-in-the-mood, but always forcibly to convert it all
into things. As Rodin did. Why has he prevailed? Not
because he found approbation. His friends are few,
and he is, as he says, on the Index. But his work was
there, an enormous, grandiose reality, which one cannot get away from. With it he wrested room and right
for himself. One can imagine a man who had felt,
wanted all that in himself, and had waited for better

times to do it. Who would respect him; he would be an aging fool who had nothing more to hope for. But to make, to make is the thing. And once something is there, ten or twelve things are there, sixty or seventy little records about one, all made now out of this, now out of that impulse, then one has already won a piece of ground on which one can stand upright. Then one no longer loses oneself. When Rodin goes about among his things, one feels how youth, security, and new work flow into him continually from them. He cannot be confused. His work stands like a great angel beside him and protects him . . . his great work! . . .

/ *Clara was preparing to leave Ruth with her grandparents and rejoin Rilke in Paris, where he was soon to write his book on Rodin (1840–1917), who had been Clara's teacher.*

TO AUGUSTE RODIN

from 11 rue Toullier, Paris,
11 September 1902

My dear Master: It doubtless seems somewhat strange that I am writing you, since (in the greatness of your generosity) you have given me the possibility of seeing you so often. But always in your presence I feel the imperfection of my language like a sickness that separates me from you even at the moment when I am very near.

Therefore in the solitude of my room I spend my time preparing the words I want to say to you next day, but then, when the time comes, they are dead and, beset by new sensations, I lose all means of expressing myself.

Sometimes I feel the spirit of the French language, and one evening, walking in the Luxembourg Gardens I composed the following verses which are not translated from German, and which came to me by I don't know what secret path, in this form:

Ce sont les jours où les fontaines vides
mortes de faim retombent de l'automne,
et on devine de toutes les cloches qui sonnent,
les lèvres faites des métaux timides.

Les capitales sont indifferentes.
Mais les soirs inattendus qui viennent
font dans le parc un crépuscule ardent,
et aux canaux avec les eaux si lentes
ils donnent une rêve vénitienne . . .
et une solitude aux amants . . .

Why do I write you these verses? Not because I dare to believe that they are good; but it is the desire to draw near to you that guides my hand. You are the only man in the world who, full of equilibrium and force, is building himself in harmony with his work. And if that work, which is so great, so just, has for me become an event which I could tell of only in a voice trembling with awe and homage, it is also, like you yourself, an example given to my life, to my art, to all that is most pure in the depths of my soul.

It was not only to do a study that I came to be with you,—it was to ask you: how must one live? And you replied: by working. And I well understand. I feel that to work is to live without dying. I am full of gratitude and joy. For since my earliest youth I have wanted nothing but that. And I have tried it. But my work, because I loved it so much, has become during these years something solemn, a festival connected with rare inspirations; and there were weeks when I did nothing but wait with infinite sadness for the creative hour. It was a life full of abysses. I anxiously avoided every artificial means of evoking the inspirations, I began to abstain from wine (which I have done for several years), I tried to bring my life close to Nature itself. . . . But in all this which was doubtless reasonable, I didn't have the courage to bring back the distant inspirations by working. Now I know that it is the only way of keeping them.—And it is the great rebirth of my life and of my hope that you have given me. And that is also the case with my wife; last year we had rather serious financial worries, and they haven't yet been removed: but I think now that diligent work can disarm even the anxieties of poverty. My wife has to leave our little child, and yet she thinks more calmly and impartially of that necessity since I wrote her what you said: *"Travail et patience."* I am very happy that she will be near you, near your great work. One cannot lose oneself near you. . . .

I want to see if I can find a living in some form here in Paris,—(I need only a little for that). If it is possible, I shall stay. And it would be a great happiness for me. Otherwise, if I cannot succeed, I beg you to help my wife as you helped me by your work and by your word and by all the eternal forces of which you are the Master.

It was yesterday in the silence of your garden that I found myself. And now the noise of the immense city has become more remote and there is a deep stillness about my heart where your words stand like statues. . . .

/ *Like the poem which appears in it, this letter was written in French.*

33

TO OTTO MODERSOHN

from Paris,
New Year's Eve, 1902

My dear Otto Modersohn, my intention of laying the monograph on your Christmas table has been badly thwarted. Two days before the twenty-fourth, I learned that the publishers of this book (because of technical difficulties unknown to me) will not finish printing before January. I am very sorry about this, for I had long been looking forward with joy to sending you the monograph for the Christmas celebration in your dear lonely country. Even to the last minute I hoped to, and now I miss the joy this gift would have given me, everywhere. I have in mind your birthday and wish Velhagen may have finished by then.

So we did nothing further on Christmas; for it was no proper, valid festival for us either,—only a kind of quiet day of remembrance that passed gently away for us in solitude. Of our dear child very good news comes to us: that made our hours bright and gave them a good confidence.—But of you two also we thought with warm wishes, on this holiday eve, and again today as a multifarious year finally dies out. We wish you and your dear wife may in these hours begin a good year well, a rich year for your art so full of future, dear Otto Modersohn, for each of you and for your life together, —in short: in every sense and by every standard a good year.

When on this last dying day I look over the past, I am impelled to say to you, dear Otto Modersohn, that to the best memories and attainments it has brought and vouchsafed belongs the close relationship I have found with your art. I have received so much that is good and great from you that my gratitude will not fade; the path through your work led me at many places nearer to myself, much became clear to me through it, much is thereby linked together for me forever, and I can well say when I recognized it in those spring days: I grew along with it for a stretch. All the blessing of my loyal trust upon your further path!

In the meantime my little book dealing with Rodin's work has also been finished. It may even come out in the first half of 1903. I was deep in work—that is why I simply haven't written. I really wanted to tell you about Paris. Dear Otto Modersohn, stick to your country! Paris (we say it to each other daily) is a difficult, difficult, anxious city. And the beautiful things there are here do not quite compensate, even with their radiant eternity, for what one must suffer from the cruelty and confusion of the streets and the monstrosity of the gardens, people, and things. To my anguished feeling, Paris has something unspeakably dismaying. It has lost itself utterly, it is tearing like a star off its course toward some dreadful collision. So must the cities have been of which the Bible tells that the wrath of God rose up behind them to overwhelm them and to shatter them. To all that, Rodin is a great, quiet, powerful contradiction. Time flows off him, and as he works thus, all the days of his long life, he seems inviolable, sacrosanct, and almost anonymous. He and his work are of the same nature and essence as the old cathedrals, as the things in the Louvre and—as the days with you, Otto Modersohn, in your big, simple, grand country that you have earned for yourself with lively love. I always feel, when I think of you, that you have everything there and that if sometime you come again to

Paris, it will be only for a short time. For whoever really has a home must care for it and love it, and he should go from it but rarely. The world is not outside for him; he must wait in patience and work for it to come to him from all distances and to fill the things of his home with all manifoldness, greatness, and splendor. . . .

/ *The "monograph" was* Worpswede, *essays on the painters of the colony, accompanied by illustrations of their work, and published in 1903.*

TO ELLEN KEY

from Hotel Florence,
Viareggio presso Pisa (Italy),
3 April 1903

How shall I thank you, dear Ellen Key, for your two so inexpressibly loving letters? I would like most to write you a long, long letter, a whole book, and tell you how everything was, how my childhood was, my difficult, difficult childhood. But I *cannot* now!—Finally after a difficult decision I have left Paris, wanted first to stay on the Riviera di Levante which, however, I found overcrowded like a full close room. So I pushed still farther to this quiet village, which lies between Pisa and the marble mountains of Carrara, by a lively, spirited sea. In the summer it is a big society seaside resort—but now nothing more than a little town with empty streets, enclosed by pine woods, and wide open before a mighty sea. I was here once five years ago, and those were days full of benefit that were given me here then, days of sun, that were the advent of many songs. That is why I trust this place and want to try to live here for a while.

You too are under way in the meantime, carrying your dear, towering and summoning word to many who hunger for it. My thoughts and wishes accompany you on this trip, and I send this letter after you and— the Rodin book that now at last has come out. May it give you joy. You won't believe how happy I am about your understanding, your encouragement, and your love, and how I return all this to you from out of my deepest depths, dear friend. I feel as if my books had never, never yet been so well off as with you. Rarely has anyone received them thus, so spoiled them with warmth.

I *thank* you!

Your second letter was sent after me here from Paris. I had already gone when it came. But my wife opened it there and conveyed everything to the Bojers that you wanted to have known. She sees the Bojers often, is very busy, and I have good news of her.

Yes, dear Frau Ellen Key, you shall have pictures of us as soon as possible; we have, I believe, a few more copies to give away, and we also want you to know us soon! Ruth's little picture will naturally come too. Should there be no more copies of the last pictures, I shall have some taken: then you must be patient a few more weeks.

It will be harder with the old books; I believe that of most of them I myself have no more copies, and the publishers no longer exist! And those of the old books that I may possess are still lying in boxes in Worpswede, and I cannot get at them. But Wilhelm Michel who wrote the article in *Zeit* has some more material; and I will look and see to it that in time you come to know everything; I am *so glad and happy* that you want to.

Oh, and to tell you otherwise who I am; that is difficult. I have a hope that we will meet sometime soon (and perhaps it will be in Italy!): then I will tell you much about myself, to make up, in a way, for what you really should have known long ago: for I feel as if you had always been close to me!

Yes, my family is old. As early as 1376 it belonged to the ancient Carinthian nobility, later it emigrated (at least in part) to Saxony and Brandenburg, and in the seventeenth and in the first decades of the eighteenth century it blossoms richly into three powerful branches. Then comes the decline, lawsuits that wipe out the entire fortune and loss of all estates and lands and: poverty, almost obscurity. After almost a century, which passed in darkness, my great-grandfather again came into power. He was lord of Kamenitz an der Linde (a castle in Bohemia, whither the family had emigrated in the anxious transition period). He collected the old traditions, he rescued from oblivion what was on the point of dying away, the family's ancient name. But immediately behind him the depths close again. My grandfather, who still spent his childhood at Kamenitz, was later steward of someone else's estate. My father began the career of officer (following a family tradition) but then switched over to that of official. He is a railroad official, holds a fairly high post in a private railroad, which he has earned with infinite conscientiousness. He lives in Prague. *There* I was born. Twenty-seven years ago. (In the Catholic baptism I received the name René Maria.) Of my mother's family I know nothing. Her father was a wealthy merchant whose fortune went to pieces on a prodigal son. My childhood home was a cramped rented apartment in Prague; it was very sad. My parents' marriage was already faded when I was born. When I was nine years old, the discord broke out openly, and my mother left her husband. She was a very nervous, slender, dark woman, who wanted something indefinite of life. And so she remained. Actually these two people ought to have understood each other better, for they both attach an infinite amount of value to externals; our little household, which was in reality middle class, was supposed to have the appearance of plenty, our clothes were supposed to deceive people, and certain lies passed as a matter of course. I don't know how it was with me. I had to wear very beautiful clothes and went about until school years like a little girl; I believe my mother played with me as with a big doll. For the rest, she was always proud when she was called "Miss." She wanted to pass for young, sickly, and unhappy. And unhappy she probably was too. I believe we all were.

Soon after she left the house, I was put in one of our big officers' training establishments. I was ten years old. After the worst coddling, I (who had never known brothers, sisters, or playmates hitherto) found myself among fifty boys who all met me with the same scornful hostility. Noncommissioned officers trained us. What I suffered in those five years (for I remained that long in spite of sickness, in spite of opposition in the place) is a life in itself: a long, difficult life. Even today, my parents still suspect nothing of it. They could not understand it. When I came out and took off the uniform, I knew that they were quite remote from me. And that now manifested itself over and over again. They put me in a commercial school, in circumstances that nearly brought about my downfall, until a brother of my father (I was already sixteen years old then) had me take school studies privately. By expending all my powers, I got over the eight classes in three years and passed the final examination. Then I was tired.

There came a time when I hated my parents, especially my mother. Over the years I got rid of this error. I see my mother sometimes and feel beyond all strangeness that she is very unhappy and very alone. And to my father I would like to show a great, great deal of love. He is of an inexpressible kindness, and my life, which he cannot understand, is a subject of touching, daily anxiety for him. I know that he has an infinite longing to know who I am and what I am doing, but, as we are poor, he sees above all only the one thing: that I cannot earn my own bread, and therefore he holds no confidence in my ability or has to keep giving it up. And I am suffering, suffering more and more from the fact that I still have to live on him, although I know that it is difficult for him: but I find no other expedient.

For what is mine no one gives me bread, and I know that I haven't powers enough to divide myself into one who earns and one who creates. And even if I had all the powers in the world, I would have to give *all* my powers to the important thing in me: it has a right to that. Isn't that so?! Tell me, my friend! The last two years since my marriage I really have tried to earn, continually, day by day: not much has come of it on the one hand, and on the other hand in so doing I have forfeited *so much*. Do you know, I am sometimes afraid that I have lost everything in the process!—I did know that I can write *only* out of deepest necessity but, when I wanted to earn by my writing, I counted on this deepest necessity coming over me *often*. But, will you believe me, dear Ellen Key: since there has been an external compulsion, this necessity has come more and more rarely, and recently it has left off almost entirely. You cannot imagine *what* I am suffering and what I have suffered all these last months; I know

I am not exhausted; but the little and continual thoughts of every day and its most unimportant things confuse me so that I can no longer recollect my own. How shall I say that to you: Before I used to hear all my voices in me; now it is as if someone had closed the window toward the garden in which my songs live: far, far away I hear something and listen and can no longer distinguish it. My head is full of ridiculous additions. And hardly have I been paid for one job and am thinking that I may now collect myself for my own work, when it is already time again to think of the *next* and of where it is to be found and by what efforts obtained. On that my nervous strength is slipping away, my time, my courage, and I fail to catch up with myself day after day, and am somewhere out of reach, full of flowers past their bloom, whose fading scents fill me with dead weight.—It isn't so new for me, indeed, this feeling. My whole art has grown up from its first day against opposition: against the laughter and scorn of the noncommissioned officers, against my father, against all about me; but this time it is more dangerous than before. For, with this idea and necessity of earning, the opposition, which until now always came from others, *from outside*, has come *into me myself*, I carry it with me everywhere, I cannot elude it, and that is why I am so fearful for everything important in me. Boundlessly fearful. Now I have journeyed here in order to recover and collect myself, in order perhaps to come to myself again in this lovely place which is protected by a good past; two weeks have now passed here, I am not yet well—and yet already I ought really to begin to think, to be concerned again about the future. . . . And the thought of money, which used not to exist so isolatedly for me, has conjured up other worries: this, for example, that all of a sudden I know

now that my education is not sufficient for a single, definite position, scarcely for a journalistic occupation. And of *that* particularly I have a nameless horror! I feel too clearly the apparent kinship between literature and journalism, of which one is an art and so looks to eternity, and the other a trade in the midst of the times: more in the times than any other. And I am so far away from the times, from all their wishes and all their successes; I *cannot* participate in them. I have nothing *in* them, not even a home. I live not in dreams but in contemplation of a reality that is perhaps the future. Only in Russia, on my two extensive journeys through that land, have I felt home; there I was somehow at home, perhaps, because there one notices so little of the times, of the temporal, because there it is always future already and every passing hour closer to eternity. I always thought I would have to live there sometime. . . .

But now I scarcely have plans any more; now it seems to me an infinite presumption to have plans, when the very next stage is so dismaying, so dark, and so full of tiniest questions. It seems as if I were in the midst of nets; I feel these nets on my hands with every gesture that would arise freely.

One day I think I must make this gesture in order at last to be able to live; the next day I believe I should somehow finish off my studies; then again I look for some person who will understand my need without taking me for a beggar: which I most fear. And finally no time is left for anything, and when an indisposition comes I have scarcely enough resistance left to avert it among all these pursuing cares, and so everything draws in about me and sets itself against the flowers in me. . . .

How is that to get better? I have written eleven or

twelve books and have received almost nothing for them, only four of them were paid for at all. The rest of the publishers took my books *without* paying. The Worpswede monograph was a commission that was well paid,—but the Rodin book, in which I have lived for months, brought only 150 marks! And still there is something in my innermost soul that does not at all want these books to become known; a longing to remain nameless fills me to the brim, and I would gladly get lost behind my songs like some bygone people. . . . But that again is—"imprudent," as my father would say. . . .

Why am I saying all this to you, dear, dear Frau Ellen Key? *To whom* am I to say it? My dear young wife knows it and is bearing it loyally with me and in addition is bearing her own lot which is similar and is bearing the separation from our little child for the sake of her serious work.—But the burden over me has become so great, and I would like so much to speak of it to a near person and ask this person, who understands and loves me: do you think there is a way out? Must a miracle happen for me to find quiet a while and hear what is mine ringing again;—and if a miracle is necessary for it: shall I live and believe that it will come? Or what shall I do? Am I wrong to be galled by longing day and night for what is important in me, since the unimportant is calling me with the voice of life? But no, I believe that is not the voice of life. For I wanted to tell you *this* too, dear friend: I love life, and I believe in it! Everything in me believes in it. You have felt that my letters lie in the shadow of some bitter sorrow, and that is why there are in your last letter those beautiful, good, bell-pure words affirming life. As a child, when everyone was always unkind to me, when I felt so infinitely forsaken, so utterly astray

43

in an alien world, there may have been a time when I longed to be gone. But then, when people remained alien to me, I was drawn to things, and from them a joy breathed upon me, a joy in being that has always remained equally quiet and strong and in which there was never a hesitation or a doubt. In the military school, after long fearful battles, I abandoned the violent Catholic piety of childhood, made myself free of it in order to be even more, even more comfortlessly alone; but from things, from their patient bearing and enduring, a new, greater and more devout love came to me later, some kind of faith that knows no fear and no bounds. In this faith life is also a part. Oh, how I believe in it, in life. Not that which makes up our time, but that other, the life of little things, the life of animals and of the great plains. That life which endures through the millenniums, apparently without interest, and yet in the balance of its powers full of motion and growth and warmth. That is why cities weigh on me so. That is why I love to take long walks barefoot, in order to miss no grain of sand and to give my body the whole world in many forms as feeling, as event, as kinship. That is why I live on vegetables, where possible, to be close to what is simple, to an awareness of life intensified by nothing foreign; that is why no wine goes into me: because I desire that only my own juices shall speak and stir and shall have bliss, as in children and animals, from deep within themselves! . . . And that is why I also want to put all pride far from me, not to raise myself grander than a stone. But to be what I am, to live what was set for me to live, to want to voice what no one else can voice, to bear the blossoms that are commanded of my heart: that I want—and surely that *cannot* be presumption.

Dear friend, I have such difficult, such difficult days.

But also it cannot become more difficult, and perhaps, when you read all this, you will find some word on which I can raise myself up a tiny bit.—My father in his dear, ready kindness, has held out the prospect, if it just won't work any longer, of procuring me an official position in Prague. Of course, he doesn't sense that it would be a new "military school" for me. But I am afraid of this rescue as of a prison. I know I shall die if I have to write figures more than three-fourths of the day in cold office rooms; I know that all, all will then be over and forever. And I am namelessly afraid of it!

So often I cannot help thinking of Ellen Ljunggren. Will she put through what she wanted? (Have you news of her?) Ought I too to do something of the sort? For two or three years, *only* earn and then . . . but it seems to me that I have already been away much, much too long from what is mine: there was so much that still wanted to come! . . .

Now you know much of me, dear Frau Ellen Key, more than you wanted to know: forgive the presumption that lies in this confidence; I didn't know, when I began this letter, that I would tell you all this; it came over me in a way, it dragged me with it; where was I to leave off?

And then, too, you would continually have felt on each of my letters the pressure, the shadow of some strange thing you didn't know about. Now you will understand everything, and that you should.

In one of your good letters, you pictured my mother as a beautiful and distinguished woman whose hands came to her child from among flowers; how often have I longed for such a woman; for a mother who is greatness, kindness, quietude, and beneficence . . . in my family's past there must have been such women, for at times I feel something of their presence, like the light of a distant star, like a dark glance, resting on me. But to you I have written as I would have written to a mother like that, or to an older sister who knows more of life and of people than I.

Accept it in your great, great kindness!

And take at the same time the Rodin book. And along with it one more request; I am putting in a second copy of the Rodin book; will you, *if it does not cause you any inconvenience at all,* see that it reaches the hands of Georg Brandes? I do not know his address, and I would like so much to have him *surely* get it. (My two last books Juncker, I think, sent him, but I do not know whether he received them.) But *only* if it is no trouble to do so. And thank you!

Are you still having snow and winter now? And how will Easter morning break then? When does spring begin in your homeland?—I think of you, full of love, full of gratitude, full of trust.

/ Ellen Key (1849–1926) was a Swedish writer, known for her vigorous feminism, who had written to Rilke, whom she did not meet until 1904; although she was unmarried, he addressed her as Frau *out of respect.*

TO LOU ANDREAS-SALOMÉ

from Worpswede bei Bremen,
18 July 1903

I would like to tell you, dear Lou, that Paris was for me an experience similar to the military school; as a great fearful astonishment seized me then, so now again terror assailed me at everything that, as in an unspeakable confusion, is called life. Then, when I was a boy among boys, I was alone among them; and how alone I was this time among these people, how perpetually disowned by all I met; the carts drove right through me, and those that were hurrying made no detour around me but ran over me full of contempt, as over a bad place in which stagnant water has collected. And often before going to sleep, I read the thirtieth chapter in the Book of Job, and it was all true of me, word for word. And in the night I got up and looked for my favorite volume of Baudelaire, the *petits poèmes en prose,* and read aloud the most beautiful poem that bears the title: *"A une heure du matin."* Do you know it? It begins: *Enfin! seul! on n'entend plus que le roulement de quelques fiacres attardés et ereintés. Pendant quelques heures nous posséderons le silence, sinon le repos. Enfin! la tyrannie de la face humaine a disparu, et je ne souffrirai plus que par moi-même. . . .* And it ends grandly; stands up, stands and finishes like a prayer. A prayer of Baudelaire's; a real, simple prayer, made with his hands, awkward and beautiful as the prayer of a Russian.—He had a long road to go to get there, Baudelaire, and he went on his knees and crawling. How far away from me he was in everything, one of the most alien to me; often I can scarcely understand him, and yet sometimes deep in the night when I said his words after him like a child, then he was the person closest to me and lived beside me and stood pale behind the thin wall and listened to my voice falling. What a strange companionship was between us then, a sharing of everything, the same poverty and perhaps the same fear.

Oh a thousand hands have been building at my fear, and out of a remote village it has become a city, a big city, in which unspeakable things happen. It grew all the time and took the quiet green out of my feeling

47

that no longer bears fruit. Even in Westerwede it was growing, and houses and streets arose out of the fearful circumstances and hours that passed there. And when Paris came, it quickly became very big. In August of last year I arrived there. It was the time when the trees in the city are withered without autumn, when the burning streets, expanded by the heat, will not end and one goes through smells as through many sad rooms. Then I went past the long hospitals whose gates stood wide open with a gesture of impatient and greedy compassion. When I passed by the Hotel Dieu for the first time, an open carriage was just driving in, in which a person hung, swaying with every movement, askew like a broken marionette, and with a sad sore on his long, grey, dangling neck. And what people I met after that, almost every day; fragments of caryatids on whom the whole pain still lay, the entire structure of a pain, under which they were living slow as tortoises. And they were passers-by among passers-by, left alone and undisturbed in their fate. At most one took them in as an impression and looked at them with calm, detached curiosity like a new kind of animal in whom want had developed special organs, organs of hunger and death. And they were wearing the comfortless, discolored mimicry of the too great cities, and were holding out under the foot of each day that trod on them, like tough beetles, were enduring as if they still had to wait for something, twitching like bits of a big chopped-up fish that is already rotting but still alive. They were living, living on nothing, on dust, on soot, and on the filth on their surfaces, on what falls from the teeth of dogs, on any senselessly broken thing that anyone might still buy for some inexplicable purpose. Oh what kind of a world is that! Pieces, pieces of people, parts of animals, leftovers of things that have

been, and everything still agitated, as though driven
about helter-skelter in an eerie wind, carried and carrying, falling and overtaking each other as they fall.

There were old women who set down a heavy basket on the ledge of some wall (very little women whose
eyes were drying up like puddles), and when they
wanted to grasp it again, out of their sleeves shoved
forth slowly and ceremoniously a long, rusty hook instead of a hand, and it went straight and surely out to
the handle of the basket. And there were other old
women who went about with the drawers of an old
night stand in their hands, showing everyone that
twenty rusty pins were rolling around inside which
they must sell. And once of an evening late in the fall,
a little old woman stood next me in the light of a store
window. She stood very still, and I thought that like
me she was busy looking at the objects displayed, and
hardly noticed her. Finally, however, her proximity
made me uneasy, and I don't know why, I suddenly
looked at her peculiarly clasped, worn-out hands. Very,
very slowly an old, long, thin pencil rose out of those
hands, it grew and grew, and it took a very long time
until it was entirely visible, visible in all its wretched-
ness. I cannot say what produced such a terrible effect
in this scene, but it seemed to me as if a whole destiny
were being played out before me, a long destiny, a
catastrophe that was working up frightfully to the moment when the pencil no longer grew and, slightly
trembling, jutted out of the loneliness of those empty
hands. I understood at last that I was supposed to buy
it. . . .

And then those women who pass by one quickly in
long velvet cloaks of the eighties, with paper roses on
antiquated hats under which their hair hangs down
looking as though it were melted together. And all

those people, men and women, who are in some transition, perhaps from madness to healing, perhaps also toward insanity; all with something infinitely fine in their faces, with a love, a knowledge, a joy, as with a light that is burning only a very little bit troubled and uneasy and could certainly be made clear again if someone would look and help. . . . But there is no one to help. No one to help those who are only just a very little bit perplexed, frightened, and intimidated; those who are just beginning to read things differently from the way they are meant; those who are still living in quite the same world, only that they walk just a little obliquely and therefore sometimes think that things are hanging over them; those who aren't at home in cities and lose themselves in them as in an evil wood without end—; all those to whom pain is happening every day, all those who can no longer hear their wills going in the noise, all those over whom fear has grown, —why does no one help them in the big cities?

Where are they going when they come so quickly through the streets? Where do they sleep, and if they cannot sleep, what goes on then before their sad eyes? What do they think about when they sit all day long in the open gardens, their heads sunk over their hands which have come together as from afar, each to hide itself in the other? And what kind of words do they say to themselves when their lips summon up their strength and work? Do they still weave real words? . . . Are those still sentences they say, or is everything already crowding out of them pell-mell as out of a burning theater, everything that was spectator in them and actor, audience and hero? Does no one think of the fact that there is a childhood in them that is being lost, a strength that is sickening, a love that is falling?

O Lou, I was so tormented day after day. For I understood all those people, and although I went around them in a wide arc, they had no secret from me. I was torn out of myself into their lives, right through all their lives, through all their burdened lives. I often had to say aloud to myself that I was not one of them, that I would go away again from that horrible city in which they will die; I said it to myself and felt that it was no deception. And yet, when I noticed how my clothes were becoming worse and heavier from week to week, and saw how they were slit in many places, I was frightened and felt that I would belong irretrievably to the lost if some passer-by merely looked at me and half unconsciously counted me with them. Anyone could push me down to them with the cursory judgment of a disparaging glance. And wasn't I really one of them, since I was poor like them and full of opposition to everything that occupied and rejoiced and deluded and deceived other people? Was I not denying everything that was valid about me,—and was I not actually homeless in spite of the semblance of a room in which I was as much a stranger as if I were sharing it with someone unknown? Did I not starve, like them, at tables on which stood food that I did not touch because it was not pure and not simple like that which I loved? And did I not already differ, like them, from the majority about me by the fact that no wine was in me nor any other deluding drink? Was I not clear like those lonely ones who were misted over only on the outside by the fumes and heaviness of the city and the laughter that comes like smoke out of the evil fires that it keeps going? Nothing was so little laughter as the laughter of those estranged creatures: when they laughed, it sounded as though something were falling in them, falling and being dashed to pieces and filling them up with broken bits. They were serious; and their seriousness reached out for me like the force of gravity and drew me deep down into the center of their misery.

What did it avail that on many mornings I got up happier and went out with more courage and capable of a quiet industrious day. . . . Once (it was rather early in the day) I came thus down the Boulevard St. Michel with the intention of going to the Bibliothèque Nationale, where I used to spend a great deal of time. I was walking along rejoicing in all that morning and the beginning of a new day dispenses, even in a city, of freshness, brightness, and courage. The red on the wagon wheels that was as moist and cold as on flower petals gladdened me, and I was glad that somewhere at the end of the street a person was wearing something light green without my thinking what it might be. Slowly the water wagons drove uphill, and the water sprang young and light out of their pipes and made the street dark, so that it no longer dazzled. Horses came by in shimmering harness, and their hooves struck like a hundred hammers. The cries of the vendors had a different ring: rose up more lightly and echoed high above. And the vegetables on their hand-carts were stirring like a little field and had a free morning of their own above them, and in them darkness, green, and dew. And when it was still for a moment, one heard overhead the noise of windows being flung open. . . .

Then I was suddenly struck by the peculiar behavior of the people coming toward me; most of them walked for a while with heads turned to look back, so that I had to be careful not to collide with them; there were also some who had stopped, and by following their gaze I arrived, among the people walking ahead of me, at a slender man dressed in black, who, as he went along, was using both hands to turn down his overcoat collar which apparently kept standing up in an annoying way. Because of this exertion which was visibly taxing him, he repeatedly forgot to pay attention to the walk, stumbled or sprang hastily over some little obstacle. When this had happened several times in quick succession, he did turn his attention to the walk, but it was remarkable that nevertheless, after two or three steps, he again faltered and then hopped over something. I had involuntarily quickened my step and now found myself close enough behind the man to see that the movements of his feet had nothing at all to do with the sidewalk, which was smooth and even, and that he only wanted to deceive those he met when he turned about after each stumble as if to call some guilty object to account. In reality there was nothing to be seen. In the meantime the awkwardness of his gait slowly diminished, and he hurried on quite quickly now and remained for a while unnoticed. But suddenly the restlessness began again in his shoulders, drew them up twice and then let them fall, so that they hung quite slantwise from him as he went on. But how amazed I was when I suddenly had to admit having seen how his left hand moved with indescribable speed to his coat collar, almost unnoticeably seized it and stood it up, whereupon he attempted with a great deal of trouble to lay the collar down with both hands, seeming, just like the first time, to succeed only with great difficulty. In so doing he nodded to the front and to the left, stretched his neck and nodded, nodded, nodded behind his busy upraised hands, as though the shirt collar too were beginning to trouble him, and as if there were work to be done up there for a long time yet. Finally everything seemed to be in order again. He went some ten steps completely unnoticed, when quite suddenly the rise and fall of his shoulders began again; simultaneously, a waiter, who was cleaning up in front of a coffeehouse, stood and looked with curiosity at the passer-by, who unexpectedly shook himself, stopped and then took up his walk again in little jumps. The waiter laughed and shouted something into the store, whereat a few more faces became visible behind the windowpanes. But the strange man had in the meantime hung his cane with its crooked handle on his collar from behind, and now, as he went on, he held it thus, vertically, just over his spine; there was nothing startling about this, and it supported him. The new position calmed him considerably, and he went along for a moment quite relieved. No one paid any attention to him; but I, who couldn't keep my eyes off him even for a second, knew how gradually the restlessness was returning, how it became stronger and stronger, how it tried now here, now there to express itself, how it shook at his shoulders, how it clung to his head to tear it out of balance, and how suddenly it quite unexpectedly overcame and broke up his walk. As yet one hardly saw all this; it was enacted at short intervals imperceptibly and almost secretly, but it was really there already, and it was growing. I felt how this whole man was filling up with restlessness, how this restlessness which couldn't find an outlet increased, and how it mounted, and I saw his will, his fear, and the desperate expression of his convulsive hands pressing the cane against his spine as though they wanted to make it a part of this helpless body, in which lay the incitement to a thousand dances. And I experienced how this cane became something, something important, on which much depended; all the strength of the man and his whole will went into it and

54

made it into a power, into a being that could perhaps help and to which the sick man clung with wild faith. A god came into being here, and a world rose up against him. But while this battle was being waged, the man who bore it was trying to go ahead, and he succeeded for moments in appearing innocent and ordinary. Now he was crossing the Place St. Michel, and although the avoiding of carriages and pedestrians, which were very numerous, might have offered him the pretext for unusual motions, he remained quite still, and there was even a strange, stiff quiet in his whole body as he stepped on to the sidewalk of the bridge beyond. I was now close behind him, will-less, drawn along by his fear that was no longer distinguishable from mine. Suddenly the cane gave way, in the middle of the bridge. The man stood; extraordinarily still and rigid he stood there and didn't move. Now he was waiting; but it was as though the enemy in him didn't yet trust this submission; he hesitated—only a minute, to be sure. Then he broke out like a fire, out of all the windows at once. And there began a dance. . . . A dense circle of people that had quickly formed, gradually pushed me back, and I could see no more. My knees shook, and everything had been taken out of me. I stood for a while leaning against the bridge railing, and finally I went back to my room; there would no longer have been any sense in going to the library. Where is there a book that would be strong enough to help me out over what was in me? I was as though used up; as though another person's fear had been nourished out of me and had exhausted me, that is how I was.

And many mornings were like that one—and evenings were like that. Had I been able to *make* the fears

55

I experienced thus, had I been able to shape things out of them, real, still things that it is serenity and freedom to create and from which, when they exist, reassurance emanates, then nothing would have happened to me. But these fears that fell to my lot out of every day stirred a hundred other fears, and they stood up in me against me and agreed among themselves, and I couldn't get beyond them. In striving to form them, I came to work creatively on *them;* instead of making them into things of my will, I only gave them a life of their own which they turned against me and with which they pursued me far into the night. Had things been better with me, more quiet and friendly, had my room stood by me, and had I remained well, perhaps I would have been able to do it even so: to make things out of fear.

Once I succeeded, though only for a short time. When I was in Viareggio the fears broke loose there, to be sure, more than before and overwhelmed me. And the sea that was never silent was too much for me and drenched me with the noise of its spring waves. But it came nevertheless. Prayers came into being there, Lou, a book of prayers. To you I must tell it because in your hands are resting my first prayers of which I have so often thought and to which I have so often clung out of the distance. Because their ring is so great and because they are so peaceful with you (and because no one besides you and me knows of them)—that is why I could cling to them. And sometime I would like to be allowed to come and lay the prayers, the others that have since come into being, with the others, with you, in your hands, in your quiet house.

For, see, I am a stranger and a poor man. And I

shall pass; but in your hands shall be everything that might sometime have been my home, had I been stronger.

/ Rilke had returned for a while to Worpswede with Clara.

TO LOU ANDREAS-SALOMÉ

from Oberneuland bei Bremen,
8 August 1903

. . . When I first came to Rodin and lunched with him out there in Meudon with people to whom one was not introduced, at the same table with strangers, I knew that his house was nothing to him, a paltry little necessity perhaps, a roof for time of rain and sleep; and that it was no care to him and no weight upon his solitude and composure. Deep in himself he bore the darkness, shelter, and peace of a house, and he himself had become sky above it, and wood around it and distance and great stream always flowing by. Oh what a lonely person is this aged man who, sunk in himself, stands full of sap like an old tree in autumn! He has become deep; he has dug a deep place for his heart, and its beat comes from afar off as from the center of a mountain. His thoughts go about in him and fill him with heaviness and sweetness and do not lose themselves on the surface. He has become blunt and hard toward the unimportant, and he stands among people as though surrounded by old bark. But to what is important he throws himself open, and he is wholly open when he is among things or where animals and people touch him quietly and like things. There he is learner and beginner and spectator and imitator of beauties that otherwise have always passed away among the sleeping, among the absent-minded and unsympathetic. There he is the attentive one whom nothing escapes, the lover who continually receives, the patient one who does not count his time and does not think of wanting the next thing. For him what he gazes at and surrounds with gazing is always the only thing, the world in which everything happens; when he fashions a hand, it is alone in space, and there is nothing besides a hand; and in six days God made only a hand and poured out the waters around it and bent the heavens above it; and rested over it when all was finished, and it was a glory and a hand.

And this way of looking and of living is so fixed in him because he acquired it as a handworker: at that time when he attained the element of his art which is so infinitely simple and unrelated to subject matter, he attained that great justice, that equilibrium in the face of the world which wavers before no name. Since it was granted him to see things in everything, he made his own the opportunity to build things; for that is his great art. Now no movement can confuse him any more, since he knows that even in the rise and fall of a quiet surface there is movement, and since he sees only surfaces and systems of surfaces which define forms accurately and clearly. For there is nothing uncertain for him in an object that serves him as a model: there a thousand little surface elements are fitted into the space, and it is his task, when he creates a work of art after it, to fit the thing still more intimately, more firmly, a thousand times better into the breadth of space, so that, as it were, it will not move if it is jolted. The object is definite, the art object must be even more definite; withdrawn from all chance, removed from all obscurity, lifted out of time and given to space, it has become lasting, capable of eternity. The model *seems*, the art object *is*. Thus the one is an inexpressible advance over the other, the calm and rising realization of the wish to be that emanates from everything in Nature. And by this the error is confounded that would make of art the most arbitrary and most vain of occupations; it is the most humble service and entirely founded on law. But of this error all creators and all arts are full, and a very powerful man had to rise up against it; and it had to be a doer who doesn't talk and who does things unceasingly. His art was from the very beginning realization (and the opposite of music, which transforms the apparent realities of the everyday world and renders them still more unreal as easy, gliding appearance. For which reason too this antithesis of art, this noncondensation, this temptation to flow out has so many friends and listeners and henchmen, so many who are unfree and bound to pleasure, who do not take increase out of themselves and are charmed from the outside. . .). Rodin, born in poverty and low estate, saw better than anyone that all beauty in people and animals and things is endangered by relationships and time, that it is a moment, a youth that comes and goes in all ages, but does not last. What troubled him was just the *semblance* of that which he considered indispensable, necessary, and good: the semblance of beauty. He wanted it to *be*, and he saw his task in fitting things (for things endured) into the less menaced, more peaceful and more eternal world of space; and unconsciously he applied to his work all the laws of adaptation, so that it developed organically and became capable of life. Already very early he tried to make nothing "on the basis of appearance"; there was no stepping back with him, but a perpetual being close to and being bent over what was coming into being. And today this characteristic has become so strong in him that one could almost say the appearance of his things is a matter of indifference to him: so much does he experience their *being*, their reality, their release on all sides from the uncertain, their completedness and goodness, their independence; they do not stand on the earth, they circle about it.

And as his great work arose from handwork, from the almost unintending and humble will to make better and better things, so he stands even today, untouched and free of intent and matter, one of the simplest among his grown-up things. The great thoughts, the lofty significances have come to them like laws consummated in something good, complete; he didn't summon them. He didn't desire them; humbly as a servant he went his way and made a world, a hundred worlds. But each world that lives radiates its heaven outward and flings starry nights far out into eternity. This: that he invented nothing, gives to his work that striking immediacy and purity. The groups of figures, the larger relationships of forms he did not put together in advance while they were still ideas; (for the idea is one thing—and almost nothing—but the realization is another and everything). He promptly made things, many things, and only out of them did he form or let grow up the new unity, and so his relationships have become intimate and logical, because not ideas but things have bound themselves together.—And this work could only come from a worker, and he who has built it can calmly deny inspiration; it doesn't come upon him, because it is *in* him, day and night, occasioned by each looking, a warmth generated by every gesture of his hand. And the more the things about him grew, the rarer were the disturbances that reached him; for all noises broke off against the realities that stood about him. His very work has protected him; he has lived in it as in a wood, and his life must have lasted a long time already, for what he himself planted has become a tall forest. And when one goes about among the things with which he dwells and lives, which he sees again every day and every day completes, then his house and the sounds in it are something unspeakably trivial and incidental, and one sees it only as in a dream, strangely distorted and filled with an assortment of pale memories. His daily life and the people that belong in it lie there like an empty stream-bed through which he no longer flows; but there is nothing sad in that; for near by one hears the great roar and the powerful flow of the stream that would not divide into two arms. . . .

And I believe, Lou, that it must be so. . . . O Lou, in one of my poems that is successful, there is much more reality than in any relationship or affection that I feel; where I create, I am true, and I would like to find the strength to base my life entirely on this truth, on this infinite simplicity and joy that is sometimes given to me. Even when I went to Rodin, I was seeking that; for I had had a presentiment for years of the endless example and model of his work. Now, since I have come from him, I know that I too may ask and seek for no other realizations than those of my work; there my house is, there are the women I need, and the children that will grow up and live a long time. But how shall I begin to go this road—where is the handwork of my art, its deepest and lowest point at which I might begin to be proficient? I shall go back over every path to that beginning, and all that I have done shall be nothing, less than the sweeping of a doorstep to which the next guest brings traces of the road again. I have patience for centuries in me and will live as though my time were very big. I will collect myself out of all distractions, and I will bring back and save up what is mine from too quick applications. But I hear voices that bode well, and steps that are coming nearer, and my doors are opening. . . . And when I seek out people, they do not counsel me and don't know what I mean. And toward books I am just the same (so clumsy), and they do not help me either, as though even they were still too human. . . . Only things speak to me. Rodin's things, the things on the Gothic cathedrals, the things of antiquity—all things that are complete things. They directed me to the models; to the animated, living world, seen simply and without interpretation as the occasion for things. I am beginning to see something new: already flowers are often so infinitely much to me, and excitements of a strange kind have come to me from animals. And already I am sometimes experiencing even people in this way, hands are living somewhere, mouths are speaking, and I look at everything more quietly and with greater justness.

But I still lack the discipline, the being able to work, and the being compelled to work, for which I have longed for years. Do I lack the strength? Is my will sick? Is it the dream in me that hinders all action? Days go by and sometimes I hear life going. And still nothing has happened, still there is nothing real about me; and I divide again and again and flow apart,—and yet would like so much to run in *one* bed and grow big. For, it's true, isn't it, Lou, it ought to be this way: we should be like one stream and not enter canals and lead water to the pastures? It's true, isn't it, that we must hold ourselves together and go surging on? Perhaps when we are very old, sometime, at the very end, we may give in, spread ourselves out and flow into a delta. . . . *Dear* Lou!

TO LOU ANDREAS-SALOMÉ

from Villa Strohl-Fern, Rome,
12–13 May 1904

Your letter, dear Lou, I have read often; it was just and good. When it came there was a great, quiet evening over the garden, and I read it slowly on the flat roof of my little house and pondered over it a long time. Perhaps, said something in me, I shall begin something good tomorrow morning, perhaps. And amid much suppressed hope there was a little bit of gladness in me—:

That was not to blossom; for the burden of my vacation time increased with every day. It had gradually grown cooler, and the disturbances had receded, and nevertheless things wouldn't begin to get better in me. . . .

With this clear experience is linked the necessity for new decisions, and before I set about making one or another, I would like to tell you, dear Lou, a few things about myself, as well as I am able in these ineffectual days. Perhaps you will say something to me in connection with this or that; which would mean a great deal to me; you know how much. (But if you are now in work, at your beloved work, put this letter aside, because it comes from a restless man; he can wait; he can wait as long as you want.)

And then see:

I have rented my little gardenhouse in the park of the Villa Strohl-Fern until fall (until October). I hoped to be able to stay on in it all summer (or at least the greater part of it); now I know that is not to be thought of. But I had the further intention of keeping the house for still a year more: for where should I ever find such another? A tiny little house, all to myself, with big windows and flat roof-terrace, containing a spacious bright simple room, and situated deep, deep in a private garden, inaccessible and secluded, and far removed from traffic and noise—a feeling advised me to hold on to this place where all that can be mine, as long as the otherwise so uncertain and intolerable external circumstances of life in any way permit it; but now this same feeling tells me that I might persist in such favorable living possibilities only if it all lay under a healthier sky, under which one may live all year without fear and dread. The fall was bad here, the winter, with so much sirocco and the long rain, oppressive, and the spring everybody extols so is only a hastening into the dangerous summer, like a descent without a stopping place. What is more, people who live here maintain that one gets along with the Roman climate best as a novice, later worse and worse from year to year, and that one becomes more and more defenseless against the seasickness-mood of the sirocco days.

And in addition (something that I already felt a year ago in Viareggio,—where I attributed it to other circumstances—) I must in the past years have got far, far away from things Italian. My feeling everything so differently now from formerly is perhaps contributed to by my being in Rome and not in the Tuscan country which, with Botticelli and the Robbias, with marble-white and sky-blue, with gardens, villas, roses, bells, and foreign girls, spoke so intimately to me—: but speak it did (and Rome speaks too), it did not keep silent and did not bluster: it spoke. It talked until my cheeks glowed—(and I sometimes wonder whether that was the good and important thing for me and

whether my first Viareggio, which closed with so great
an expenditure into nothing, with such fireworks, was
not already a proof that Italian influence is not among
the things that really advance me).

However that may be,—in any case more northern
and more serious countries have since educated my
senses to the subdued and simple, so that they now
feel what is glaring and strong, schematic and unin-
flected in Italian things as a relapse into picture-book
instruction. It came about quite of itself that I received
and learned this very obvious and showy spring from
a purely botanical point of view, with the objective
and quiet attentiveness which my observation is more
and more assuming, that its movements and voices and
the upward flight and course of its birds interested me
quite objectively, without my ever sensing it as something entire, living, mysterious, as soul alive and bor-
dering on my soul. I noted details, and since I have
heretofore observed so little and in mere looking, as in
so much, am a beginner—I was content with such occupation, making progress in it. But if once it happened
that I expected or needed something from the whole,
I opened up and shut again, empty, and hungered
deeply. As it would for a lung in a stuffy room, so it
became difficult for my soul in an exhausted world into
which nothing new comes with the spring, nothing distant and incalculable. I felt the great poverty that lies
in richness: how with us a flower, a little first flower
that struggles and comes, is a world, a happiness, to
participate in which is infinitely satisfying,—and how
here herds of flowers come without anything stirring
in one, without anything participating and feeling akin
and sensing its own beginning in other things. Here
everything is given over to the easy, to the easiest side
of the easy. Flowers come and blossoms, anemones

bloom and wisteria, and one says it to oneself and says it again, as to someone hard of hearing. But it is all so ensnaringly sham and make-believe; colors are there, to be sure, but they always subordinate themselves lazily to some cheap shade and do not develop from out of themselves. The Judas tree bloomed, bloomed, and bloomed, its redundant, unfruitful bloom welling even out of its trunk like blood-sodden mesentery, and in a few weeks everything: anemones and clover and syringas and starflowers, everything was purple with its purple, for God knows what reasons—from laziness, from accommodation, from lack of original ideas. And even now the red roses, fading, are taking on this corpselike purple, and the strawberries have it if they stand for a day, and the sunsets puff it out, and it appears in the clouds in the evening and in the morning. And the skies in which such cheap plays of color take place are shallow and as if choked with sand; they are not everywhere, they do not play about things like the skies of the moor, of the sea, and of the plains, are not endless beginning of distance, are finish, curtain, end; —and behind the last trees, which stand flat like theater wings against this indifferent photographic background,—everything ceases. It is indeed a sky over something past; drained, empty, forsaken sky, sky-shell from which the last sweetness has long ago been drunk. And as the sky is, so are the nights, and as the nights are, so is the voice of the nightingales. Where nights are vast, their tone is deep, and they bring it from infinitely far away and carry it to the end. Here the nightingale is really just a little lustful bird with a shallow song and an easily satisfied longing. In two nights even, one becomes accustomed to its call, and one notes it with an inner reserve, as if fearing to hurt one's own memories by any more interest, the memories of nightingale-nights that are quite, quite different.

Exhibition atmosphere, so typical of the city, is also the most obvious characteristic of the Roman spring: it is spring exhibition that takes place here, not spring. The foreigners indeed enjoy it and feel themselves honored like little sovereigns in whose honor everything is shined up; for these respectable Germans, Italy must always have been a kind of royal journey with triumphal arches, flowers, and fireworks. But, in a certain sense, they are right: they come down here, weary of having winter, of making fires and of darkness, and find ready-made here all that is sunny and comfortable. More they do not ask. And of this sort too was probably the effect I sometimes used to get from Arco or from Florence and the benefit connected with it. But if as a native one has seen the whole winter here (full of the morose persistence of that which cannot die), then the miracle that is supposed to come fails. One knows that that isn't a spring, for one has seen none coming, that these blossoms have had as little difficulty in appearing at this place or that as decorations, for instance, have in being put up somewhere. And one comprehends so well the illusory life of this past people, the empty phrases of its descendant-art, the garden-flower-beauty of D'Annunzio's verses.

It is good that I have experienced all this so slowly and so concretely, for Italy had still been a summons for me and an unfinished episode. But now I can leave it, comforted, for the end is here.

It will be hard for me, to be sure, because this little house stands on this spot and cannot be taken along and set up again in another, more northern garden; hard, because the new break comes unexpectedly and leads into the uncertain; hard—because I am tired anyway of breaking off and starting again.

. . . As to the question of earning a living, which bobs up again, threatening and demanding, with every change, there is this to say: that I am not closing my eyes to it and am not putting it off until it returns more urgently; I see it and always know that it is there. If nevertheless in the present choice of place I do not give it the most important voice, this is from the ever-growing conviction that my bread must one day come to me out of my work; for it is work and as such necessary, and it must be possible (or become possible) to do it and to live, if only it is done well. Art is indeed a longest life-path, and when I think how trifling and elementary is what I have heretofore done, it does not surprise me that this achievement (which resembles a foot-wide strip of half-tilled land) does not nourish me. Plans do not bear, and what is prematurely sown does not come up. But patience and work are real and can change at any moment into bread. . . .

That is why, everything else aside, I want to decide on my next place of sojourn by my work and only by it. . . .

The works I have in mind and which are to occupy me in turn are:

1. The *Prayers*, which I want to continue.
2. My new book (whose firm, close-knit prose is a schooling for me and an advance that had to come so that later sometime I could write everything else—the military novel too).
3. An attempt at a drama.
4. Two monographs:
   The Poet: Jens Peter Jacobsen.
   The Painter: Ignacio Zuloaga.

Both of these necessitate trips. The first a trip to

Thisted and a stay in Copenhagen, the second a trip
through Spain. (Zuloaga was, beside Rodin, the only
person with whom I was closely and long in contact
during my stay in Paris and whose importance and
worth I feel and can say. Or shall be able to say. Sometime I will tell you about him.)

But there is no hurry about these travels and books;
probably I shall get first to Jacobsen. You can't imagine
how necessary he has become to me; by always new
paths I have gone to him, often alone, often with my
wife (who reads him so well and so lovingly); indeed,
it is even true that when one goes anywhere in the
important one can be sure of coming out at a place
where he too is (if one goes far enough); and how
singular it is to find that his and Rodin's words agree
often to the point of congruity: then one has that crys-
tal-clear feeling one gets in mathematical demonstrations the moment two distant lines, as if out of eternity,
meet at one point, or when two big complex numbers,
that do not resemble each other, simultaneously withdraw in order, jointly, to acknowledge a single simple symbol as the thing that matters.—Singularly untouched joy comes from experience of that sort.

Besides these works, to accompany and supplement
them, I have in mind several studies. I am already
beginning to learn Danish, chiefly so that I can read
Jacobsen and various things of Kierkegaard in the
original.

Then I began something in Paris that I would like to
continue: reading in the big German dictionary of the
Grimm brothers, from which, it seemed to me, a writer
can derive much wealth and instruction. For indeed
one really ought to know and be able to use everything
that has once entered into the language and is there,
instead of trying to get along with the chance supply

that is meager enough and offers no choice. It would be good if a pursuit like this led me now and then to read a medieval poet; that Gothic, which architecturally had so much to give that is unforgettable and vast, shouldn't it also have had and worked on a plastic language, words like statues and sentences like rows of pillars? I know nothing, nothing of it. Nothing, I feel, of all that I would like to know.—There are so many things some old man should tell one about while one is little; for when one has grown up, knowing them would be a matter of course. There are the starry heavens, and I don't know what people have already learned about them,—why, not even the order of the stars do I know. And so it is with flowers, with animals, with the simplest laws that are operative here and there and go through the world in a few strides from beginning to end. How life comes into being, how it functions in lower animals, how it branches and unfolds, how life blossoms, how it bears: all that I long to learn. Through participation in it all to bind myself more firmly to the reality that so often denies me,—*to exist*, not only through feeling but also through knowledge, always and always: this it is, I believe, that I need in order to become more secure and less homeless. You will feel that I do not want sciences, for any one of them require a lifetime, and no life is long enough for its beginning; but I would like to stop being a person shut out, one who cannot read the deeper tidings of his time, that point further on and reach further back, a prisoner who senses everything but hasn't the little certainty of whether it is at the moment day or evening, spring or winter. I would like, somewhere where it can be done, to learn that which I probably would know if I had had a chance to grow up in the country and among more essential people, and that which an impersonal and hasty schooling failed to tell me, and the rest, since discovered and recognized and belonging to it. It is not art history and other histories, not the nature of philosophic systems that I would like to learn,—I want a chance to get and earn for myself just a few great and simple certainties that are there for everyone; I want a chance to ask a few questions, questions such as children ask, unrelated for those outside, but full of family likeness for me who know their birth and genealogy to the tenth generation.

13 May 1904

Up to now universities have given me so little every time; I seem to feel such an aversion to their ways. But it lies also with my clumsiness which never and nowhere understands how to take; with my not having the presence of mind to recognize what I need; and of course one thing I haven't yet had either, the most important: patience. Perhaps that has all improved now; I shall no longer lack patience, at least, in anything. And if I don't attempt as before to hear disciplines read, in which one can be of this or that opinion—words about words, conceptions of conceptions—, but hear something real said, something new, to which all that is premonition in me says yes, I shall not even notice any unpleasantness in the external conditions or shall quietly endure it for the sake of what is important. I miss a learning-time of that sort more than anything else, not only because I do not know so much that is simple and essential, but also because I always imagine that for me it must be the path on which I shall finally be able to help myself alone to what I shall later need in each case. That I am unable to do this, that I am helpless when left alone among books, a child whom one must lead out again, continually holds me up, dismays me, makes me sad, perplexed. If the pursuit of some scientific study were slowly to result in my learning to survey a subject, to sift and read the existing bibliography (not even to mention the finding), if I were to make my own the ability to study older books and old manuscripts too—in short, if I might acquire on the side a little of the historian's craft and the archivist's patience and might hear spoken a few real truths and perceptions—, then any place would suit me which would afford me such. It seems to me that without acquisitions of this kind I cannot take my next forward steps; after the Rodin monograph I thought of one on Carpaccio, later of one on Leonardo: what I lack for these is not an art historian's knowledge (which is just what I would like to avoid), but rather the simple craft of the research worker, the technical assurance and practice for which I must often envy quite young people; to the great libraries here and in Paris I lacked the key, the inner directions for use (to put it tritely), and my reading was fortuitous reading because, for want of preparation, it couldn't turn into work. With my education, over which no plan lay, and with the intimidation in which I grew up (everywhere running into laughter and superiority and pushed back by everybody into my own clumsiness), it came about that I never got to learn at all much preparatory matter and most of the technical material of life, which later are effortless for everyone; my feeling is full to the brim of memories of moments when everyone about me knew and could do something and did it mechanically without thinking, while I, embarrassed, didn't know how to go about anything, wasn't even capable of watching and copying others. Like one who finds himself in a game the rules of which he doesn't know—, I feel like a knot in the thread on thousands of occasions. Then I am a hindrance to others and a cause of annoyance—but the same deficiencies hold me back myself and disconcert me.

Once I sat a whole summer on the Schönaichs estate, alone in the family library whose archives are crammed with old correspondence and records and documents; I felt in every nerve the immediate proximity of destinies, the stirring and rising of figures from which nothing separated me but the foolish inability to read and decipher old symbols and to bring order into the unsifted confusion of those papers. What a good, industrious summer that could have been had I understood a little of the archivist's craft; something like a *Maria Grubbe* would perhaps have been given me in substance; at any rate I would have learned and gathered much from such close contact with the still untold happenings—while as it was I only got new proof every day of my unfitness, of that being shut out, which life keeps making me experience whenever I want to approach it anywhere.

And not for work on monographs alone, for every work I do, I shall more and more miss such preparation and perspective; for my plans connected with things Russian, for instance, it has always been a hindrance and the reason why I progress so slowly in them. But wouldn't a schooling such as I have in mind (without being able to picture it exactly) enable me more surely to attack and hold on to all my work, wouldn't it too be a means of reaching that *toujours travailler* which is what matters?

So in sum my study projects read thus:

1. I want to read books on natural sciences and biology and hear lectures that will stimulate the reading and learning of such things. (See experiments and preparations.)

2. I want to learn work with archives and history, in so far as this is technique and craft.

3. I want to read the Grimm brothers' dictionary, simultaneously with medieval writings.

4. I want to learn Danish.

5. To continue reading Russian and now and then to translate from the Russian.

6. To translate from the French a book of the poet Francis Jammes. And to read carefully the following books: Michelet's natural-history studies and his history of France; the Eighteenth Century of the Goncourts . . . and other things.—

I thought for a while of attempting all this in Copenhagen; of going there in the fall and working there.

But against it is

—the fact that I make my projected studies more difficult for myself if I go into a country with a foreign language, where hearing lectures has less sense and everything practical (such as the use of libraries, collections, and laboratories) also becomes complicated.

—The fact that Copenhagen is a very big city and perhaps not beneficial to my health.

. . . Do you know besides that just now in Copenhagen (in the Student Club, before a very full hall) someone spoke about my books? Yes, it really came about that Ellen Key, with a big lecture manuscript dealing only with my works, traveled to Stockholm, to Copenhagen and into God knows what Swedish cities —on my account! There she told people about me, and now, she writes me, many are beginning to buy and read my books; and through this it was that she wanted to be useful and to help me. But not satisfied with that, she wants to have published in a Swedish periodical, and (translated) in a German one, a big essay which grew out of those lectures. She is a dear and capable person and has gradually become an indispensable friend to both of us, to my wife and to me (yes, even to little Ruth). I understand well and with heartfelt gratitude the nature of her help and activity, although I distinctly feel that such intercession for me is in no way justifiable; just now, while it is going on, I am watching her undertaking (confidentially speaking) with terror—: for in reality and to less charitable eyes, nothing has actually been done, nothing demonstrable. A few things in the *Book About God,* in *In My Honor* and in *The Book of Pictures* (of the *Prayers* she knows nothing) could speak for me; but I am afraid she has presented all that as much less mixed and has given everything a semblance of conclusiveness which it doesn't possess and in which people will feel cheated when they buy my books now. Also she has based much of what she said (as it seems—I am not acquainted with the essay yet, only a small fragment of it) on passages from my letters of recent years and has found out the sort of things that cannot be deduced from my thus far published works.—And over and above all this I feel: if anybody needs seclusion, it is I. (Every line and every perplexity of this letter, but also that in which it is determined, speaks for it—.) Nevertheless, I do see that I must agree to everything that can support my existence and prolong the possibility of remaining at my work. And for that such a being named and proclaimed is surely good. Furthermore that has all come through the lips of a refined and discreet person and (even if it has happened much too early) can have no bad consequences. It also turned out in due course that there were young people here and there in Sweden who already knew about me, even some who could recite verses from my books by heart; and it came to light incidentally that one of the young Swedish writers was just in the process (independently and without knowledge of Ellen Key's intention) of collecting material for an essay on my work. . . .

Dear Lou, if it were possible to meet you this summer, do, please, let it be possible. I see for miles around no thought, no confidence, in which I believe so much that they would help me.

Meantime comes this letter, running through two days with its length and making many presumptuous demands upon you; be very indulgent toward it. The writing of it has helped me infinitely; it has been like an activity after all these weeks of immobile inner numbness.—There are, as I come to think of it, certain little animals, beetles, and insects, that fall into such states of arrested life if one touches them or comes near them; often I have watched them, have noticed that they let themselves be rolled along like things, that they do everything to be as like things as possible: they do this when they see a danger's bigness coming toward them—and want to save themselves. Has my condition like causes? Is this becoming numb and keeping still that goes to my very core, up to the very entrance of my heart's chambers, an instinctive defense by which something that can annihilate me is to be deceived? Who knows?

I will trust and not count the time and will wait for it to pass. But *then* bestir myself, for nothing has yet been done. . . .

/ *Rilke's "first Viareggio" was his visit in 1898; his* Prayers *became the* Book of Hours; *his "new book" was to become* The Notebooks of Malte Laurids Brigge; *Thisted was the birthplace (in Jutland) of J. P. Jacobsen, who wrote* Niels Lyhne, *as well as* Maria Grubbe, *mentioned in this letter.*

TO A YOUNG GIRL [EMMY HIRSCHBERG]

20 November 1904

My greeting you with only a few words, out of much occupied days, will seem ungrateful to you; since you managed to find time to tell me such nice things.

Your words were a welcome message to me. I will write you only that. I am happy to know about you, in order to imagine you sometimes and to surround you with wishes: may life open up to you, door by door; may you find in yourself the ability to trust it, and the courage to give to the difficult most confidence of all. To *young people* I would always like to say just this one thing (it is almost the only thing I know for certain up to now)—that we must always hold to the *difficult;* that is our part. We must go so deep into life that it lies upon us and is *burden:* not pleasure should be about us, but life.

Think: isn't childhood difficult in all its unexplained connection? Aren't girlhood years difficult—do they not like long heavy hair pull your head into the depths of great sadness? And it *must* not become otherwise; if for many life suddenly becomes easier, lighterhearted and gayer, that is only because they have ceased to take it seriously, really to carry it and feel it and fill it with their own entity.—That is no progress in the meaning of life. That is a renunciation of all its breadths and possibilities. What is required of us is that we *love the difficult* and learn to deal with it. In the difficult are the friendly forces, the hands that work on us. Right in the difficult we must have our joys, our happiness, our dreams: there, against the depth of this background they stand out, there for the first time we see how beautiful they are. And only in the darkness of the difficult does our smile, so precious, have a meaning; only there does it glow with its deep, dreamy light, and in the brightness it for a moment diffuses we see the wonders and treasures with which we are surrounded. That is all I know how to say and to advise. Whatever else I have known or grasped beyond all knowing is in my verses, which you read with so much affection.

It is so natural for me *to understand girls and women;* the deepest experience of the creator is feminine—: for it is experience of receiving and bearing. The poet Obstfelder once wrote, when describing the face of a strange man: "it was" (when he began to speak) "as if there were a woman in him—"; it seems to me that would fit every poet who begins to speak. . . .

/ *This letter to the translator Emmy Hirschberg (born in 1885) was first published shortly after Rilke's death; Sigbjorn Obstfelder (1886–1906) was a Norwegian writer.*

TO CLARA RILKE

from Chez Rodin, Meudon-Val-Fleury,
Wednesday, 20 September [1905]

. . . What are all times of rest, all days in wood and sea, all attempts to live healthily, and the thoughts of all this: what are they against this wood, against this sea, against the indescribably confident repose in his holding and carrying glance, against the contemplation of his health and assurance. There is a rush of forces streaming into one, there comes over one a joy in living, an ability to live, of which I had no idea. His example is so without equal, his greatness rises up before one like a very near tower, and at the same time his kindness, when it comes, is like a white bird that circles, shimmering about one, until it lights trustfully upon one's shoulder. He is everything, everything far and wide. We speak of many, many things. It is good for him to talk about many things, and though I can't always keep up with him very well, being hindered by the language, still I am doing better and better every day with the listening. And just imagine the last three mornings: we got up very early at five-thirty, yesterday even at five o'clock, and went out to Versailles; at the Versailles station we take a carriage and drive into the park, and in the park we walk for hours. And then he shows one everything: a distance, a motion, a flower, and everything he evokes is so beautiful, so understood, so startled and young, that the world is all one with the youth of this day that begins in mists, almost in soft rain, and quite gradually becomes sunny, warm, and weightless. Then he tells a great deal about Brussels where he had his best years. The model for the "Age d'Airain" was a soldier and he used to come quite irregularly, sometimes at five o'clock in the morning, sometimes at six o'clock in the evening; [Rodin's] colleague on the other works forced him out from jealousy, and so he was left with almost all his time to himself. And he spent it in the environs of Brussels, always on the move with Madame Rodin (who is a good, loyal person), in the woods, always wandering. At first he would set up his paintbox somewhere and paint. But he soon noticed that in doing this he missed everything, everything alive, the distances, the changes, the rising trees and the sinking mist, all that thousandfold happening and coming-to-pass; he noticed that, painting, he confronted all this like a hunter, while as observer he was a piece of it, acknowledged by it, wholly absorbed, dissolved, was landscape. And this being landscape, for years,—this rising with the sun and this having a part in all that is great, gave him everything he needed: that knowledge, that capacity for joy, that dewy, untouched youthfulness of his strength, that unison with the important and that quiet understanding with life. His insight comes from that, his sensitivity to every beauty, his conviction that in big and small there can be the same immeasurable greatness that lives in Nature in millions of metamorphoses.—"And if today I were to paint from Nature again, I would do it just as I do my sculptures, a very quickly sketched contour that I would improve at home, but otherwise I would only gaze and unite with and be the same as everything about us." And while we speak thus of many things, Madame Rodin picks flowers and brings them to us: autumn crocuses or leaves, or she draws our attention to pheasants, partridges, magpies (one day we had to go home earlier because she had found a sick partridge that she took with her to care for), or she collects mushrooms for the coachman, who is sometimes consulted too when it appears that none of us knows a tree. That was in the elm avenues that go around by the edge of the Versailles park outside the Trianon. A twig was broken off: Rodin looked at it for a long time, felt its plastic, strong-veined leaves and finally said: so, I know that forever now: *c'est l'orme.* Thus in everything he is receptive as a goblet, and everything becomes wellspring, wherever he proffers himself and shines and mirrors.—Yesterday I lunched in the city with him and Carrière and an author, Charles Morice; but usually I see no one but him. In the evening, at twilight, when he comes back from the rue de l'Université, we sit at the rim of the pool near his three young swans and look at them and talk of many and serious things. Also of you.—It is beautiful the way Rodin lives his life, wonderfully beautiful. We were to meet Carrière at the studio in the rue de l'Université; we were there promptly at twelve o'clock. Carrière kept us waiting, Rodin looked at the clock a few times while he was attending to some of the mail he had found there, but when I looked up again, I found him deep in his work. That is how he spends his waiting times! . . .

Soon after supper I retire, am in my little house by eight-thirty at the latest. Then the wide blossoming starry night is before me, and below, before the window, the gravel walk goes up a little hill on which, in fanatic silence, an effigy of Buddha rests, dispensing with quiet reserve the inexpressible self-containedness of his gesture beneath all the skies of day and night. *C'est le centre du monde*, I said to Rodin. And then he looks at one so kindly, so wholly a friend. That is very beautiful and a great deal. . . .

/ *The "Age d'Airain" was the Rodin statue "The Age of Bronze"; Eugène Carrière (1849–1906) was a painter and lithographer about whom Rilke once intended to write a book; Charles Morice (1861–1919) was a Symbolist poet who founded the journal* Lutèce.

TO KARL VON DER HEYDT

from Villa des Brillants, Meudon-Val-Fleury
(Seine-et-Oise), France,
Wednesday after Easter 1906

I thank you for the question. Only my father could have asked like that. And I feel that I can answer you, as I would have answered him, honestly, without hesitation. I am seriously reflecting and thoroughly took counsel in myself last night: What can you do for me? Dear friend:

What I would need, according to my feeling and my conscience, is: to be able to work for myself alone for a year or two, under conditions such as I had for a while that time in Rome; alone, with only my wife in the neighborhood, who was working too, so that we did not see each other every day by any means, yet were helping each other. Without a function, almost without outside contacts. (Then the *Notebooks of Malte Laurids Brigge*, to which I have not yet returned, came into being, and other things wanted to come. But my stay had to be cut short.) I went then to my friends in Sweden who offered me everything the most generous hospitality can give, but still could not give me this, this limitless solitude, this taking each day like a lifetime, this being-with-everything, in short, space, to the end of which one cannot see and in the midst of which one stands, circled about by the innumerable.

So the time in Sweden became more a receptive time, as Friedelhausen was later, in all its legendary beauty, and as, in still another way, Meudon is now. But after all that and after certain anxious and profound occurrences that have peculiarly linked and interpreted everything that went before, a time should, must come for me, to be alone with my experience, to belong to it, to reshape it: for all that is unconverted is already oppressing and confusing me; it was only an expression of this state that I should have been longing more than ever to take upon myself, like a vocation, this spring that reached out to and touched everything: since it would have become the highest inducement for so much that is only awaiting a start. I don't believe

I am fooling myself when I think that my age (I shall be thirty-one this year) and all other circumstances speak for the fact that, if I might now collect myself for my next advance, I could produce a few works that would be good, that would help me along inwardly and perhaps also pave the way outwardly for giving to my life a security which my so-far published books have not given, but which seems not quite excluded for later.

But: I cannot possibly leave Rodin now; that is just as clear to me. My conscience would not be light enough for work of my own if I went away from him like that, unexpectedly. Especially as he has been sick all these weeks and still feels tired and low and has need of my support, insignificant as it is, more than ever. I shall now have to hit upon some kind of compromise with my great longing. I am convinced that patience is always good and that nothing that in the deepest sense is justified in happening can remain unhappened. I shall some day take up and bring to an end the work for which conditions are now lacking, if it is really as absolutely necessary and organically demanded of me as I believe. I shall carry on this life with good will and absolute readiness to serve a while longer, as well as I can, and give it up some day when we have considered whether that is possible and in what way it is to happen. To think that out, slowly to think it out ahead of time for next fall perhaps, that is the only thing, dear friend, that you can do for me now. . . . But it will alter my life and my position very much if I can just hope to be able to return to my own work and task in the not too distant future. Then I shall at once have joy in the patience now required of me, imposed on me by circumstances, in a certain sense difficult but yet not hostile, by this great old Master

who wants it thus. I am incessantly called and interrupted and will let matters rest for today with having
spoken these few words to you: which to me has been
an indescribable relief. . . .

/ *Karl von der Heydt (1858–1922) and his wife Elisabeth
were friends of Rilke's in Rome; the previous visit he refers
to was September 1903–June 1904, when he began writing*
Malte Laurids Brigge, *which was completed in 1910.*

TO S. FISCHER

from Meudon-Val-Fleury
(Seine-et-Oise), France,
19 April 1906

. . . A few days ago Rodin began the portrait of
one of your most remarkable authors, which promises
to become something quite extraordinary.

And yet hardly ever has a portrait been so much
aided in its making by the subject it represents as this
bust of Bernard Shaw. Not only that he stands excel-
lently (with an energy in his keeping still and with
such an absolute giving of himself to the hands of the
sculptor), but he knows too how to collect and concentrate himself to such a degree in the part of his body
which, within the bust, will after all have to represent
so to speak the whole Shaw, that the nature of the man
springs over from it with unbelievably heightened intensity, feature by feature, into the bust.

This personality of Shaw's and his whole manner
makes me desirous of reading a few more of his books,
of which I think I know only the *Man of Destiny.*
Would sending me a few of his books be justified if I

say that I am hoping to write a little thing about him (though without blindly obligating myself to it)?

I would be deeply grateful to you, you may be sure, if you would send me some of his things. I could also relay something of them to Rodin; he wants to become acquainted with Shaw's books, but since there are as yet no French translations in existence, the only source for him would, for the present, be what I could tell him of them.

Madame Shaw, who brought about the making of this portrait over her husband's head in the most charming way, is a solicitous, quietly attentive good woman, full of zeal and enthusiasm for beautiful things, hovering about her husband with all this as the spring wind plays about a billy goat.—This by way of information about your remarkable author. . . .

/ *S. Fischer was the German publisher of Shaw's work.*

TO CLARA RILKE

from Meudon-Val-Fleury
(Seine-et-Oise), France,
Thursday after Easter 1906
[postmarked 19 April 1906]

. . . The summer is moving fast. Here at least it seems to be approaching with great rapidity. Can you imagine that the Avenue de l'Observatoire is thick and green, as it was that time when, returning from Viareggio, I walked up and down there. And in the Luxembourg it is all shadow on the upper terraces, the shimmer of the girls' dresses is now more subdued, with more nuances, under the full chestnuts—: no longer in

their very shiny spring-bright whiteness. And here in
the garden already yesterday a blue iris opened; the
strawberries are blooming, the currant bushes too I saw
out there in blossom. The little new light-green heraldic eagles are set up by the round fig bushes. And now,
since yesterday (after many, many summer-warm,
radiant days) there is falling, day and night, a soft,
quiet rain, thick, gentle, and full, as from the rose of
a watering can: *comme tombant d'un arrosoir,* one
would like to say, because that sounds and falls still
darker and fuller on the ear. And the green is growing
under this rain: swelling and pushing up, and here and
there opening all fresh and new. . . . (And I think of
Rome.)

Bernard Shaw comes out daily with his wife, we see
each other often, and I was present at the first sittings
and saw for the first time how Rodin tackles his work.
—First there is a firmly shaped clay dummy, consisting
of nothing but a ball set on something that supports it
like a shoulder. This dummy is prepared for him and
contains *no* armature *at all;* it only holds together by
firm kneading.—He begins his work by first placing his
model at a very short distance, about half a step from
the stand. With a big iron compass he took the measurement from the top of the head to the tip of the
beard, and immediately established this proportion on
the clay dummy by lumps of clay. Then in the course of
the work he took measurements twice more: nose to
back of head, and ear to ear from behind. After he had
further cut out the eye sockets very quickly, so that
something like a nose was formed, and had marked the
place for the mouth with an indentation such as children make on a snowman, he began, with his model
standing very close, to make first four profiles, then
eight, then sixteen, having his model turn after about

three minutes. He began with the front and back views and the two full side-profiles, as though he were setting four different drawings vertically against the clay ball, then fitted half-profiles, etc., between these contours. Yesterday, at the third séance, he seated Shaw in a cunning little child's armchair (that ironic and by no means uncongenial scoffer was greatly entertained by all this) and cut off the head of the bust with a wire (Shaw, whom the bust was already remarkably like, in a superior sort of way, watched this decapitation with indescribable joy) and worked on the recumbent head, partially supported by two wedges, seeing it from above, at about the same angle as the model sitting low down a step away. Then the head was set on again and the work is now going along in the same fashion. In the beginning Shaw *stood,* often very close to the stand, so that he was somewhat higher than the bust. Now he sits right next it, exactly as high as the work, parallel with it. At some distance away a dark cloth has been hung up, so that the profiles always stand out clearly. The Master works rapidly, compressing hours into minutes, it seems to me, executing stroke after stroke at very short intervals, during which he absorbs indescribably, fills himself with form. One seems to feel how his quick, bird-of-prey-like clutch is always carrying out only one of these faces that are streaming into him, and one comprehends his working from memory after the sitting is over. . . .

Be of good cheer and earnest confidence. Should this blessed life, which indeed never does anything twice but still might come back to letting us work side by side, give us a chance once more like the one in Rome, we shall be much further ahead and more capable and will do a lot of good things. . . .

TO AUGUSTE RODIN

[in French] from Paris,
12 May 1906

My Master, I cannot begin the unforeseen life you have prescribed for me, without having placed in your hands a short exposition of the facts as I most sincerely feel them to be.

M. Thyssen's letter was addressed to me, as your secretary; nor did I withhold it from you in speaking to you that very evening and first thing next morning and in then proposing to you to send the letter prepared several days before to M. Thyssen and to add a postscript relative to his German letter. If I was at fault in this matter, it is that I judged the letter of little importance, being built on a false supposition and therewith no longer valid. You thought otherwise, though I remain convinced that my point of view was excusable in regard to a letter that was not meant to take rather indelicate advantage of the implied mistake and of your absence.

M. Rothenstein's letter was the reply to a purely personal letter I had addressed to him; it was (I must remind you) as your friend that you introduced me to M. Rothenstein, and I could see nothing improper in accepting the little personal relation that had been established between your friend and me across our conversations, the more so as we had very dear mutual friends. But you no longer wished to remember that it was as a friend that you invited me to come to you and that the function into which you introduced me after a few weeks was at first only a means of procuring for a poor friend some quiet time favorable to his work.

It was thus that you formulated your proposition, the morning we were walking in the avenue deliberating this possibility which made me happy in the extreme.

"You will help me a little; that will not take much of your time. Two hours every morning." Those were your words.

Moreover, I did not hesitate to give you, instead of two hours, almost all my time and all my strength (unfortunately, I haven't much) for seven months. My work has been neglected for a long time; but how happy I was nevertheless to be able to serve you, to be able slightly to lessen the preoccupations that disturbed your admirable labors.

You yourself opened your intimacy to me and I entered timidly there, in the degree that you wished it; never making any other use of that unforgettable preference than to take comfort in it deep in my heart and that other use, legitimate and indispensable to accomplishing your affairs the way you wanted under your eyes. If I felt that I ought to penetrate those intentions in order someday truly to help you, by knowing your decisions in advance, that feeling need not be blamed; it was bound to waken in one who ardently wished to relieve you and to render you fully the service you had confided to him.

Nevertheless, I have all appearances against me at the moment when you see fit to shift my sincere efforts to a basis of suspicious mistrust.

Here I am, dismissed like a thieving servant, unexpectedly, from the little house where, before, your friendship had gently installed me. It was not to your secretary that you gave those familiar quarters. . . .

I am profoundly hurt by this.

But I understand you. I understand that the wise organism of your life must immediately repel that which seems to it harmful, in order to keep its functions intact: as the eye repels the object that disturbs its sight.

I understand that, and do you remember? how well I understood you often in the happiness of our contemplations? I am convinced that there is no man of my age (either in France or elsewhere) who is endowed as I am (by temperament and by work) to understand you, to understand your great life, and to admire it so conscientiously.

(My wife, from a slightly greater distance and in another way, has a similar feeling for you. I am distressed that you did not think of her in dismissing me, not a single word, although she (who has such need of your help) has not offended you; why must she share this disgrace of fortune into which I have fallen?)

You have now, great Master, become invisible to me, as though by some ascension carried up into skies of your own.

I shall not see you any more—but, as once for the apostles who were left behind saddened and alone, life is beginning for me, the life that will celebrate your high example and that will find in you its consolation, its justification, and its strength.

We were agreed that in life there is an immanent justice that fulfills itself slowly but without fail. It is in that justice that I put all my hope; it will one day correct the wrong you have seen fit to inflict on him who no longer has the means nor the right to show you his heart.

Rilke

/ *M. Thyssen was a writer who had met Rodin through Rilke; M. Rothenstein was Sir William Rothenstein (1872–1945); by November 1907, Rilke and Rodin were once again friends.*

TO CLARA RILKE

[from Paris]
Friday morning, 21 June 1906

. . . Ellen Key left on Sunday for Switzerland; I accompanied her as far as Fontainebleau and we spent some not very profitable hours there, driven by flunkies at full speed through the castle in the midst of a Sunday pack (since E. K., with her inexhaustible receptivity, must always see everything), and passing a few afternoon hours in the big forest which, with its enormous beeches, ferns, and solitary birches in quiet glades, almost made one think of Danish forests. We were in the end wholly without contact and our mutual expressions of friendship had become mere social forms and were worked with a couple of handles like a machine. In the station of Fontainebleau-Avon from which our trains went out in different directions at almost the same time, this situation rose of its own accord into a symbol and thus, having become real, lost its oppressiveness: just as in a poem, a situation taken up into a metaphor loses its transitory, painful and unstable quality, and becomes full of significance and inner validity, the moment it passes wholly into an image; so life provided us (or me: since E. K., accustomed and practiced in replacing all actuality with the "ideal" of the actual long since ready within her, must have noticed scarcely anything of all this—) with the kindly satisfaction of relieving us of what was unspoken in our situation through a complete expression of it. Just think, it couldn't be better done: two people on two opposite platforms, separated by a pair of tracks on which, in a while, two trains going in opposite directions will come in to take one away to this place and the other to that. My platform just a platform, with people, impatience, departure: nothing to stay for. Ellen's, almost exaggeratedly peaceful: wholly in the sun, with rose-beds, nice benches, and a certain imaginary happiness: like a little garden city. And then between us this legally prescribed impossibility of crossing—: so that really nothing had been left out or forgotten. And now that life had taken everything upon itself so literally, trait for trait, in the presence of this superior transfiguration, so finely developed with every means at hand, it was not difficult for me to look over in a friendly and open way now and then (the trains were a little too long in coming) and to return warmly the loyal and feeling gaze that encircled me from over there. With real warmth in my look. Now I understood how this old maid was only one of the many old maids who lay up memories in a room, memories and memories of memories and all only memories of one thing: of that love the once vague, mounting possibility of which had already been so exuberantly taken up by their hearts that the experience no longer needed to come at all. And all the accumulated things that always signify this one state and derive from it, from unlikely parents, from an error, from chance perhaps, have something uncertain in their look and something shy in their behavior, are themselves inclined to consider that they are not quite legitimate, while the old maid does nothing but weep over the indescribable respectability of her ancestry. Are certain people marked to fall into certain destinies, not to get beyond the type? And then if, as with Ellen, unusual power is added, resolution, perhaps also a certain desperate determination to grow out of the fate to which she dimly felt herself committed, then in spite of everything, doesn't just the same destiny result, as if it were lived in a larger room, with disproportionately extensive memories which make that nullity of experience even more evident? Perhaps the conventions of such wasted lives must be exaggerated like that in individual destinies in order to be noticed. Perhaps that is their way out: this once more becoming as tragic in the great and obvious as they often were in the minute. But how good life is. How just, how incorruptible, how not to be cheated: not by force, not by will, not even by courage. How everything remains what it is and has only this choice: to fulfill itself or to exaggerate itself. . . .

TO ELISABETH AND KARL VON DER HEYDT

from Villa Discopoli, Capri,
11 December 1906

I have been here a week, and that long at least I wanted to wait, so that, besides the greetings I often think in your direction, I could report to you something of what has impressed me and that not too unjust and momentary. But now I shall attempt a few impressions. There are first of all my immediate surroundings, and they are full of friendliness. The mistress of the house in a very kind way does everything for my well-being and gives me so much freedom and right to go my own way that I am able to arrange much solitude, half-days at a time and, if it becomes necessary, more. (My inner life really had been dislocated for months, I notice, and being alone provides primarily only a kind of psychic plaster cast, in which something is healing.) But nothing is so important as that; already on the long trip I felt it. There is perhaps nothing so jealous as my profession; and not for me a monk's life in the close association and isolation of a cloister, but rather I must see to it that little by little I myself shall grow into a cloister and stand there in the world, with walls about me, but with God and the saints within me, with very beautiful pictures and furnishings within me, with courts around which moves a dance of pillars, with fruit orchards, vineyards, and wells whose bottoms are not to be found. But to continue with essentials. My solitude is supported by the circumstance that the room I live in is quite separate, in a little house by itself, some fifty steps from the villa proper. For the present I am the only guest. . . . My room is simple and very congenial and already has a natural attachment to me for which I am grateful to it.

. . . no one but you knows what being completely alone, being unobserved, unseen, invisible means to me. For three days in Naples I went about with it as with a treasure in all the gloriously foreign world. . . .

And now Capri. Ah yes. I really have nothing more to learn there. Jacobsen says somewhere: "It requires so infinitely much tact to handle enthusiasm." Well, this place has got its stamp from a very ill-exercised enthusiasm; the foreigners are away, for the most part, but the traces of their stupid admiration that always falls into the same holes are so obvious and cling so fast, that even the huge storms that from time to time take the island in their jaws do not tear them away. I am always saddened in such landscape exhibitions, before this evident, prize-crowned, unassailable beauty: since it is almost too much even to pick up a stone on the path, a chestnut, a withered leaf, since even the beauty of a little, insignificant and ordinarily trivial thing (once one has recognized it) makes the heart overflow, what is one to do in such concerts of beauty, where everything is a program number and rehearsed and intentional and selected? It may be that with these picture-books of beauty one could begin learning to see and to love, but I am a little bit too advanced to say Ah and Oh before them. Rapture-spelling is far behind me and perhaps my whole life joy and life task really lies in this: that, though very much of a beginner, I am one of those who hear the beautiful and recognize its voice, even where it scarcely lifts above the noises; that I know God did not set us among things in order to select, but rather so thoroughly and largely to keep on taking that in the end we can simply receive nothing else at all but beauty in our love, our alert attentiveness, our not to be pacified admiration. And to grow in this feeling here is not the place. The name Paris must have taken shape in me under the influence of this longing, even if I had never heard it (I believe).

Truly, what people here have made out of a beautiful island is close to hideous. But that doesn't speak against them; there were in any case serious and thorough and significant people among the thousands who have collaborated here at Capri. But did you ever see that people arrived at agreeable results when they let themselves go or were active in the direction of pleasure, relaxation, enjoyment? Neither bullfights nor music halls nor any other institutions of amusement, from the dance hall to the beer garden up and down, are beautiful or pleasing or ever have been so. The heaven of which I once heard an excited preacher speak in San Clemente was replete with dubious happiness, in bad taste and boring. But in all seriousness, isn't even Dante evidence for it, whose Paradise is filled with such helplessly heaped-up bliss, with no gradations in light, formless, full of repetition, made of smiling, angel-pure perplexity, as it were, of not-knowing, of not-being-able-to-know, of pure, blissful mendacity. And the Inferno beside it. What a compendium of life. What knowing, hailing, judging. What reality, what particularization even into darkest darkness; what a meeting again with the world. From this it does not follow that suffering is more right than happiness and its surrender and expression and admission; only, so far mankind has not yet attained in bliss that depth, that urgency, that necessity which has already become accessible to it in suffering. (And therefore Capri—is a monstrosity.)

For the rest, one can see Diefenbach coming to the surface now and then, grey in grey, of those greys that old wood of wooden palings takes on under the influence of sun and rain. And Gorky has settled down here, feted by the socialists and scattering money about him. I close, dear friends, in the consciousness of having spent an evening hour with you, which I needed. . . .

/ *Karl Wilhelm Diefenbach* (1837–1913) *was a painter.*

TO CLARA RILKE

from 29 rue Cassette, Paris VI,
Friday afternoon [7 June 1907]

. . . Here I have already been to many places again. Tuesday in the little Bagatelle Palace where there is an exhibition of women's portraits from 1870 to 1900. A wonderful Manet rewards one superabundantly for all the rest. That is a painter; he is beginning to open up to me all over again after this portrait and after the incredible *Déjeuner sur l'herbe* that I saw today in the Louvre in the newly installed Moreau-Nelaton collection. That is a painter, still, and again and again and all the more. Carrière was wrong after all and van Gogh is something else, something inexorably obsessed with expression that bends painting to its will. With him the never before painted came in, but with Manet everything paintable. (That sounds strange; for by the meaning of painting everything actually must be paintable; yes, but it isn't yet, and van Gogh wanted it to be, to be, to be.) At Bernheim *jeune*, I saw van Goghs: a night café, late, dreary, as if one were seeing it with sleepless eyes. The way he has made the old lamplit air (by drawing circles concentrically about the hanging lamps, which seem gradually to dissolve in the room), is far from being painting any longer, but is forcibly won with colors, and it overpowers: one becomes positively old, wilted, and drowsily disconsolate before it. There are Maillols there too: very, very beautiful ones. The torso of a girl, still in clay (to be baked), which is indescribable. And at the same time another well-known Japanese collection is shortly being sold at auction which one should also see!

. . . But the difficult, the anxious is somehow still here too—indeed everything is again: as always in Paris.

Thank you for the notes written en route. Perhaps you are right in many respects. I thought so today at two pictures of Berthe Morisot: they were painted for Manet's sake, and Bashkirtseff painted for Bastien-Lepage—out of him, for his sake. What we do for the sake of God, do women always do for a man? But the human and the divine are equally unattainable: so their task could for that reason still become broad and personal and their own? And now a good Sunday to you. . . .

/ *The Bagatelle Palace is in the Bois de Boulogne; Bernheim jeune was a Paris art dealer; Aristide Maillol (1861–1944) was a French sculptor; Berthe Morisot was the sister-in-law of Manet.*

TO CLARA RILKE

from 29 rue Cassette, Paris VI,
19 June 1907

. . . I do not know why I am so slow this time in adapting and settling in. The neighbors are not bad, and yet it is again the Paris that consumed Malte Laurids. A student studying for his examinations for years. Then just before the tests an ailment manifests itself: his face becomes troubled over his books, the lines dance and one eyelid closes down, simply closes down like a shade whose cord is broken. This condition made him nervously miserable, and then, at the time I moved in, he was going about in his room, stamping with every turn and even late into the night, in a kind of bleary resentment, throwing things on the floor, some kind of tin things made as if for the purpose, which rolled along in order to be picked up and thrown down again and again. You know one couldn't have provided a more susceptible neighbor for this young man. How that kept me engrossed and breathless the first nights, before I knew what it meant. Alas: because I at once grasped the rhythm in that madness, the weariness in that anger, the task, the despair—you can imagine.— That ate into me a little and confirmed and occupied me in my dreadful melancholy. And a person like that, when he is at the end of his powers, takes some for himself through the wall. Instinctively,—what does it matter to him.—That is all. And now they are operating on his eyelid (the muscular exhaustion of which naturally cannot be surgically removed). But it is so in keeping with this misery to have the hospital mixing in and the clever gentlemen who for a moment are certainly taking an interest in this obstinate eyelid.—Today, I believe, he will be operated on for the second time, and then he is supposed to leave soon for home somewhere. His mother came at the worst time. To hear her step outside, ah, she had no idea how much that step had to stand by me too. One had only to hear it outside in the corridor when she came and went. One heard: a mother has a sick son—heard it as if one saw it depicted on ten bas-reliefs in various stages: that is how one heard it. . . .

/ *This letter has some of the atmosphere of, and one of the situations in,* The Notebooks of Malte Laurids Brigge.

TO CLARA RILKE

from 29 rue Cassette, Paris VI,
3 October 1907

. . . if only you were sitting in my room on this cold rainy day, which is passing unwillingly and for no one, which now at last (as I saw at Jouven's) is filling other people too with surprise and perplexity. Sitting with me before the van Gogh portfolio (which I am taking back with a heavy heart). It has done me so much good these two days: it was the right moment.

. . . You probably wouldn't have read at all the little biographical notice of at most ten lines that precedes the table of contents, relying simply on your looking. It is, nevertheless, very, very factual and yet so strangely suggestive to read. Art dealer, and when after three years he somehow saw it wasn't that, small school teacher in England. And in the midst of it the resolve: to become a clergyman. He comes to Brussels to learn Greek and Latin. But why the detour? Aren't there people anywhere who ask neither Greek nor Latin of their minister? So he becomes what is called an evangelist, and goes into the coal region and tells the people the gospel. In telling he begins to draw. And finally he doesn't notice at all how he is growing silent and doing nothing any more but draw. And from then on he does nothing else, even up to his last hour, until he resolves to stop everything, because for weeks perhaps he would not be able to paint; so it seems natural to him to give up everything, life above all. What a biography. Is it really true that all the world acts, now, as though it understood this and the pictures that come out of it? Shouldn't art dealers and equally so art critics really be more perplexed or more indifferent about this dear zealot, in whom something of Saint Francis too came to life again? I marvel at his swift fame. Ah, how he too had discarded and discarded. His self-portrait in the portfolio looks needy and tormented, desperate almost, and yet not catastrophic; as when a dog is having a bad time. And holds out his face, and one sees, in fact, that he is having a bad time day and night. But in his pictures (the *arbre fleuri*) the poverty has already become rich: a great radiance from within. And so he sees everything, as a poor man; one need only compare his *Parks*. Those too he says so quietly and simply, as if for poor people, so that they

can understand; without going into the showiness that
lies in the trees; as if even that would indicate parti-
ality. He takes no sides, not the side of the parks, and
his love for all that goes toward the nameless and has
thus become hidden by himself. He doesn't show it, he
has it. And puts it out of himself quickly into his work,
into the most inward, unceasing part of the work:
quickly: and no one has seen it! So one feels him in
these forty pages: and haven't you after all been beside
me a little and looking through the portfolio? . . .

TO CLARA RILKE

from 29 rue Cassette, Paris VI,
18 October 1907 (Friday)

. . . You must have known, while you were writing, how much good that insight of yours would do me
which sprang spontaneously from comparing the blue
slips with my Cézanne experiences. What you say now
and warmly confirm, I somehow suspected, although I
could not have indicated how far that development,
which corresponds to the immense advance in the
Cézanne paintings, is already realized in me. I was
only convinced that it is inner personal reasons that
make me more observant before pictures which a
while ago I would perhaps still have passed by with
momentary interest, without returning to them any
more eagerly or expectantly. It is not the painting at
all that I am studying (for despite everything I am still
uncertain about pictures and am only with difficulty
learning to differentiate good from less good ones, and
am always confusing the early with the late). It is the
turning point in this painting that I recognized be-

cause I had just reached it myself in my work or at least had come somehow near to it, probably having been long prepared for this one thing, on which so much depends. That is why I must be cautious in trying to write about Cézanne, which naturally tempts me greatly now. Not the person (I really ought to see that at last) who takes in pictures from so private an angle is justified in writing about them; one who could quietly confirm them in their existence, without experiencing through them more or other than facts, would surely be fairest to them. But within my own life this unexpected contact, coming and making a place for itself as it did, is full of confirmation and pertinence. Another poor man. And what progress in poverty since Verlaine (if Verlaine wasn't already a relapse), who under *"Mon Testament"* wrote: *Je ne donne rien aux pauvres parce que je suis un pauvre moi-même,* and in almost all of whose work this not-giving was, this embittered displaying of empty hands, for which Cézanne during the last thirty years had no time. When should he have shown his hands? Malicious glances did often find them, whenever he was on his way, and lewdly uncovered their indigence; we, however, are given to know from the pictures only how massive and genuine the work lay in them to the end. This work, which had no preferences any more, no inclinations, no fastidious indulgences; whose smallest component had been tested on the scales of an infinitely sensitive conscience and which with such integrity reduced the existent to its color content that it began, beyond color, a new existence, without earlier memories. It is this unlimited objectivity, which declines to interfere in any other sphere, that makes Cézanne's portraits so outrageous and absurd to people. They apprehend, without realizing, that he was reproducing apples, onions, and oranges with sheer color (which to them may still seem a subordinate device of pictorial practice), but when they come to landscape, they miss interpretation, judgment, superiority, and where portraiture is concerned, why, the rumor of intellectual conception has been passed on even to the most bourgeois, and so successfully that something of the kind is already noticeable even in Sunday photographs of engaged couples and families. And here Cézanne naturally seems to them quite inadequate and not worth discussing at all. He is actually as alone in this salon as he was in life, and even the painters, the young painters, already pass him by more quickly because they see the dealers on his side. . . .

TO MIMI ROMANELLI

from Oberneuland bei Bremen,
8 December 1907

There is an element of death in life, and I am astonished that one pretends to ignore it: death, whose unpitying presence we experience in each turn of fortune we survive, because we must learn how to die slowly. We must learn to die: all of life is in that. In preparing from afar the masterpiece of a proud and supreme death, of a death with which chance has nothing to do; of a death well realized and successful, welcomed as saints know how to welcome it; of a death patiently prepared for, which itself becomes more acceptable, being only an act that returns to the anonymous universe the recognized and redeeming laws of a life intensely fulfilled. It is this idea of death, which has painfully developed in me in experience after experience since my childhood, which commands me to endure petty death humbly, in order to become worthy of that death which renders us great.

I am not ashamed, my dear, to have wept on another Sunday in early morning in a gondola that rowed incessantly to and fro, through vaguely outlined districts that seemed to me to belong to another Venice, situated in limbo. And the voice of the *barcaiolo* who asked for passage to the corner of the canal remained unanswered, as if confronted with death.

And the bells which a moment before, heard from my room (from my room, where I had lived a lifetime, where I was born and where I was preparing to die), seemed to me so clear—these same bells dragged tatters of sound behind them that wandered over the waters and met without recognizing each other.

It is still this kind of death that lives on in me, belabors me, transforms my heart, augments the vigor of my blood, compresses the moment of life that was ours, to the end that it becomes a bittersweet drop that runs through my veins, permeating everywhere, which becomes infinitely mine.

And although I am sad, I am happy to feel that you exist, Belle; I am glad that I have surrendered myself fearlessly to your beauty as a bird to space; glad, my dear, that I have walked as a true believer upon the waters of our uncertainty unto this island that is your heart, in which sorrows bloom. In short: be happy.

Your R. Maria

(*From the French*)

/ *Mimi Romanelli and her sister Nana had become friends of Rilke when he had stayed at the Pensione Romanelli, Zattere 1471, Venice, from the 19th to the 30th of November, 1907.*

TO AUGUSTE RODIN

[in French] from 77 rue de Varenne, Paris,
29 December 1908

As for New Year's Day, I would almost like to avoid the word of greeting that is making the rounds, to speak to you more of my work. I must have told you again the other day that I am managing more and more to make use of that long patience you taught me by your tenacious example; that patience which, disproportionate to everyday life that seems to bid us haste, puts us in touch with all that surpasses us.

Now indeed I feel that all my efforts would be vain without it. In writing poetry one is always aided and even carried away by the rhythm of external things; for the lyric cadence is that of Nature: of the waters, of the wind, of the night. But to make prose rhythmic one must go deep into oneself and find the anonymous and multiple rhythm of the blood. Prose wants to be built like a cathedral; there one is truly without name, without ambition, without help: among scaffoldings, with only one's conscience.

And just think, in that prose I now know how to make men and women, children and old men. I have evoked women in particular by carefully making all the things about them, leaving a blank which might be only a void, but which, fashioned amply and with tenderness, becomes vibrant and luminous, almost like one of your marbles.

I would have to explain myself at length to anyone else. But you, my dear and only friend, you will know what that means.

Your joy and mine differ only in degree; yours having been for a long time blessed and stigmatized.

Also I am sure I am not mistaken in the wishes I bring you; there are at bottom few essential ones and on those, I believe, we are infinitely in accord. . . .

P.S. The chandelier fits in well with the ensemble, and on my New Year's gift table the candy box presides with its handsome blue which is still that of the eighteenth century.

TO GEORG BRANDES

from 77 rue de Varenne, Paris,
28 November 1909, Sunday

. . . Since receiving your letter, I have been turning over in my mind how I could contribute something to the spiritual shortening of your hospital days. Today at last something occurs to me: it is unfortunately just another book, and a sad one at that, but it is of such excellent craftsmanship that it can nevertheless be somehow gladdening.

I read very little, and so I do not know whether the impression I got from Gide's *Porte Etroite* is dependent very much upon my state of mind, upon the reading having been an opportune exception, finally upon a certain natural affinity (on account of which a close acquaintance brought the book to my house). But I shall be much mistaken if the book with its intimate precision does not give you even more pleasure than it did me, since your reading ability will doubtless reveal to you subtleties that eluded my spelling out. Gide's means, which I had a chance to admire here for the first time, have remarkable command of the world he sets up; they fulfill his intentions—it seems to me—completely, and from this there results a finely ramified assurance which nourishes the book calmly and as it were vegetatively, even to its incommensurable borders. Also one has only to imagine how one-sidedly Rodenbach, say, would have developed this conflict, in order to watch with delight the greater artist who, behind the aberration, the pathology, the fate of the individual case, allows one again and again to discern the very great task of love, which none of us has been able to accomplish.

I go so far as to conjecture that this book somehow steps out of the rotation of the French conception of love and, under the influence of a deeper force of gravity, attempts a new curve of its own into the open. But my very insignificant reading background makes me incompetent there. (Wouldn't Kierkegaard have recognized these journals and held them in honor?) . . .

/ *Georg Brandes (1842–1927) was the Danish literary critic, whom Rilke had met in Scandinavia; Georges Rodenbach (1855–1898) was a Belgian writer, the author of* Bruges la Mort *(1892).*

TO MIMI ROMANELLI

from 77 rue de Varenne, Paris,
5 January [1910]

Before I begin my day, let us make our prayers, my dear, for I feel exalted. Imagine that after so much spiritual sterility I feel the need of kneeling inwardly, like those mystic kneelers of El Greco who become greater on their knees. One might say that they have rooted themselves in the soil in order to grow up to the clouds; giant plants, they flourish on high, and their flowers blow heroically within the tempests of vision. Just think that in this Paris where people earn money day and night and where one can ruin his life in a thousand menacing and terrible ways, someone can be there who awakens thus, elevating his whole spirit. And I feel again why I live in this city where everything is possible, this city righteous as a last judgment that allows angels and devils to behave according to their inner compulsion. What the great saints retained with a constant and feverish tenacity, I absorb for a moment in my heart. I strive to keep this richness of spirit; a quarter of an hour from now I shall perform my task, which will be slight today, without any virtue. I will be lusterless, not conserving the apparent splendor, but I shall hide within me a clear conscience, with which we prayed for this morning.

Pray: to whom? I cannot tell you. Prayer is a radiation of our being suddenly set afire; it is an infinite and purposeless direction, a brutal accompaniment of our hopes, which travel the universe without reaching any destination. Oh, but I knew this morning how far I am from those greedy ones who, before praying, ask whether God exists. If He no longer or does not yet exist, what difference does it make? My prayer that will bring Him into being, for it is entirely a creative thing as it lifts toward the heavens. And if the God that it projects out of itself does not persist at all, so much the better: we will do it over, and it will be less shabby in eternity.

If I write you all this, my dear, the reason is that you have always known it. And this prayer, which I am making for us before beginning a humble day, it is still more vital in you; it arises incessantly from your loving heart, it builds and strengthens the skies that we rapidly imagine in our impatience—. I am thankful for having been able to write to you.

Your
Rilke

(*From the French*)

TO MIMI ROMANELLI

from Venice,
11 May 1910

Mon amie, write me a word to tell me that you are well. An indisposition kept me from leaving yesterday; I have had to remain another day (a sad day).

Perhaps you are suffering too much to read, but I cannot leave Venice without telling you, for the first time, that I am thinking of you in a way that can only be called bitter.

If it is my fault that this is so, it is also yours, *chère amie;* instead of profiting by my strength you count on my weakness, in acting violently toward me, you yourself destroy what I should like to give you.

There is one mortal harm that we could do to each other, and that is to attach ourselves to another, even for an instant. If it is true that I can help you, it is not by exhausting myself that I can do so. How different my life could have been recently if you had committed yourself to protecting my solitude, something which I need so very much. I am leaving here distracted, fatigued, full of self-reproach. Is this right? And how do I leave you? Believe me, the influence and the consolation that my spirit can bring to yours depend neither on the time we spend together nor upon the power with which we hold to one another: it is a fluid that must be left entirely free for it to be able to act again. I express myself poorly, but I believe that you yourself must be so close to this realization that you will understand me even against your will. It is so natural that this flaw in our relationship existed from the beginning, but it suffices, I think, for us to recognize it distinctly once, in order to avoid it absolutely.

Don't forget that I belong to solitude, that I must not need anyone, that all my strength is born from this detachment, and I assure you, Mimi, I beg of those who love me to love my solitude; without that I shall have to hide myself from their eyes, from their hands, as a wild animal hides from its enemies.

I'd find it pleasant not to leave tonight, without your understanding me, or at least to know that you will understand me some day—. Give yourself over to life, being the resolute person that you are; it will refuse you nothing, if only you believe in it.

Adieu, Mimi: I think that both of us will have developed greatly before we see each other again. *Non?*

Rainer M. Rilke

Put these pages in the fire, I beg you; in being kept, they become less real. (Adieu again to dear Nana.)

(*From the French*)

TO PRINCESS MARIE VON THURN
UND TAXIS-HOHENLOHE

from Schloss Janowič, Selčan district, Bohemia,
30 August 1910

I am all absorbed in picturing how this letter will reach you in Duino: I see your little realm up there, the world you are at home in, dense with memories, with its window on the very great; there is something definitive in this arrangement of drawing the near very near, so that the distance may be alone with itself. What is close by means much, and the infinite in this way becomes singularly clear, free of meaning, a pure depth, an inexhaustible store of spiritually usable interspace.

But well as I can imagine all that, I do catch myself hoping in every mail for a card from you, with just this much, that your trip did you good and that you found the days down there the way you like them. Is the Prince with you, and how is Prince Pasha? You must sometimes feel how much I am inwardly continuing the Lautschin life. Prague interrupted me for a few days, I arrived here almost ill, but now everything is going along, yes, I can really say things are somehow going along. Lautschin was a real watershed, now everything is flowing off in another way, I don't know whither, I don't see ahead, I am wholly taken up by springs being suddenly there that are making the most of the new declivity and driving onward. That is not to be understood at all as applying to my work, which is resting, but inside my life something is stirring, my soul is about to learn something, it is beginning with new rudiments, and to me the best thing in all this is to see it so modest. Perhaps I shall now learn to become a little human; hitherto my art has really come into being at the cost of my insisting on nothing but things; that was a stubbornness, I fear, an arrogance too, dear Heaven, and it must have been a tremendous greediness. I shudder a little when I think of all the violence I put through in Malte Laurids, how I landed with him back of everything in consistent despair, back of death in a way, so that nothing more was possible, not even dying. I believe no one has ever experienced more clearly how very much art goes against Nature; it is the most passionate inversion in the world, the road back from the infinite, on which all decent things come to meet one; now one sees them full size, their faces draw near, their movement gains detail—: yes, but who is one then that one *may* do it, that one should take this direction against them all, this eternal re-turning with which one deceives them, letting them believe that one has already arrived somewhere, at some end, and now has leisure to go back?

As for the landscape, it is much simpler here than in Lautschin, simple-minded almost, all kinds of sentiment and melancholy have got into the flowers, the blue cornflowers by the roadside want to look right into one's eyes like domestic animals, and the industrious apples want to be praised.

It is touching to see the three young orphaned children, the way they take their life, that must now be the whole of life, in hand, each in his way and yet in such charming considerateness and concord. I am by far the oldest in the house, I almost have trouble mastering the dignifiedness that is unfolding in me. Luckily there is so much superiority in the smallest and simplest of their ways, not to mention that which comes spontaneously even from the youngest. But shortly I want to read Kassner aloud to the children. Now I am reading Kierkegaard, it is magnificent, real magnificence, never has he moved me so.

A thousand greetings to you and yours, Princess, I often miss an hour of talk, a letter is no substitute at all.

/ *Princess Marie* (1855–1934), *one of Rilke's staunchest friends for the rest of his life, owned the castle of Duino, near Trieste; she had first met Rilke in Paris in 1909.*

TO CLARA RILKE

from 77 rue de Varenne, Paris,
18 November 1910

. . . I thank you, the volumes of the Arabian Nights arrived very opportunely, everything was still hanging fire, only now is it as good as certain that I will be in Algiers the beginning of next week, rue Michelet, Hotel Saint-Georges. I have been invited to go along on a lovely trip that will take me through Tunis, perhaps on to Egypt, about that I will write as things develop. It is not entirely easy for me to go away from here, although Paris during this time has been by no means easy for me; it is indeed just by the difficult that one always recognizes it again and by the difficult that one is so strongly bound to it. And yet I feel distinctly that this time I must travel, just as far as possible. I like the thought that I am leaving my little apartment behind lying open, the books are there,—how will one return?

The Seine is rising, it is up to the armpits of the

bridges, in the evening it is uncanny, this broad near-by water, now I can picture how the flood comes about, but it seems that again I am not to be in on the experience of it.

Much as I have before me, everything is in fact veiled from me by the death of Tolstoy in that little, unknown station; how much room to act there really is even in our time, how many paths to go away by, how this inner life did indeed keep breaking out again and again into the visible, passing directly into its legend. It is becoming more and more difficult to find the external action for what the soul does; Ibsen out of obstinacy carried it through within art, Tolstoy, ambitious where truth was concerned and namelessly alone, over and over again compelled life to be the degree-reading for the level of his soul. But the tremendous pressure under which this final event took place drove the fluid column of action far beyond the scale of conscience to where readings could no longer be taken; thus did he fulfill himself as a poet, *was* his own figure, which in its greatest sense, in the sense of its deepest urge and doom, he brought to its conclusion. I learned of his death yesterday morning through Rodin, who showed me the enclosed picture,—I think you know it. . . .

TO PRINCESS MARIE VON THURN UND TAXIS-HOHENLOHE

from 77 rue de Varenne, Paris,
10 May 1911

Alas, my dear Princess, my slowness is getting worse and worse, only now am I writing you. When I came here it was snowing, now the lilacs are almost over, the red and white thorn is peopled with blossoms, and tomorrow or day after tomorrow the blossoming cities and towers will stand in the full greenness of the chestnuts: how much Nature has done! And how much people do,—I don't know what they do, but for the most part they look busy or at least in love, they are on the go, I am sure they are accomplishing all sorts of things, they play their parts, they write letters, and with it all there is still time left over, stubborn time, which they set upon noisily as one would upon a clown, just to be rid of it. Everything catches up with me, time continually steals a march on me, I look at it from behind like a straggler, like a marauder; the devil, when will this stop?

Now do not think I am complaining or that Paris disappoints me. On the contrary, I find it just as full again and inwardly alive, just as one with the spring, of which it makes all that a beautiful woman can make of a dress she wears with pleasure and in a self-assured hour. If we could take a few excursions together here such as we did in Venice, you would show me much that I do not see for sheer redundance, and I would tell you things. Picture to yourself, Princess, that in addition the most important exhibitions are crowding upon one, that the most beautiful Ingres are being shown to one, glorious Rembrandts, pages with clear Persian illuminations; that out in Marly in his primitive garden Maillol is exhibiting his sculptures and that one cannot go out there without seeing countless woods in their youth beneath the skies inclining toward them and paths, on every one of which one would like to walk, they call so to one, so easy does it seem to advance on them, as if they really went and one had only to abandon oneself to them in order next moment to be far away, rustic, free. Tell me yourself, Princess, whether you should not be here? . . .

/ *After leaving Africa in March, Rilke spent a week with Princess Marie in Venice before he returned to Paris.*

TO HELENE VON NOSTITZ

from Grand Hotel Continental, Munich,
14 September 1911

A stream of business affairs, imagine, carried me away from Leipzig ahead of time and alas! far out of Auerbach's vicinity: your letter just reached me in Berlin, a few hours afterward I was traveling farther, and now I am quickly saving out this moment to thank you. The knowledge that I was almost expected at your house is dear and heart-warming to me, and even the possibility that under certain circumstances I could not be, is of so good and happy a nature that from part and counterpart I derive joy equally.

In Lautschin, shortly after my departure thence, a dear welcome grandchild also came into the summer world, and I had the feeling that this long season so assured in itself was quite particularly friendly and fitting as preparation and anticipation of that event.

We then drove in the auto from the heart of Bohemia to Leipzig, indeed on to Weimar, which I saw again still quite in the light of my former being-with-you; to be sure, I did not find it so unqualifiedly beautiful—preserved in its old essence rather than existing and quite worn out by the unyielding summer—, but, since feeling did not remain everything, I came all the more readily this time to all sorts of knowledge and insight, one or two figures seemed bright to me on their Goethe-facing side, in the Archive I read a magnificent letter of Bettina's and found that page on which Goethe in such a wonderful sudden flow wrote: *Everything proclaims Thee.* Besides this, I saw Tiefurt, the modest,—and saw Belvedere again and felt most directly in the Wittumspalais whatever echo of mutual hours of reading may still be dying away about Duchess Anna Amalia's big evening table. There a little experience befell me: as we entered the blue salon (next the ballroom) upstairs, I moved away from the group of people keeping together before a picture and had the surprise of seeing, from one of the draped, dimly shining windows, a big, beautiful, dark butterfly coming somehow significantly and expressly toward me (I instinctively turned round, no one had noticed it); it moved on slowly and complacently in the stillness, turned, lingered at a sunny spot in the air and sailed then, so very alone and adequate (heavy in its lightness as the glance of a dark eye), right through the open folding-door into the beautiful ballroom, after a time veered resolutely off there, vanished toward the left and, when we all moved around there in a while, was nowhere to be seen. All that transpired in so singularly detailed a way, passed in its bit of time so slowly, that it was as timeless as it was intimate, charming-serious, full of special tidings—, I wanted to tell you about it, perhaps Weimar is to be recognized in it and greets you in this way. . . .

I have just seen Hofmannsthal, in the old Pinakothek, in a room of indescribably beautiful Greco pictures, by the great and distinctive presence of which one was so fascinated that we rather promised to see each other again than actually saw each other. From here, in a few days, I must move on, perhaps by some little roundabout way, toward Paris, and only there will it develop how and whither, for staying does not seem very probable to me for the present, I still have much too much rusticity in me to start wintering in a city yet.

/ *Frau von Nostitz-Wallwitz (1878–1944), born von Beckwith und von Hindenburg, was a friend of Rodin's; Lautschin was the home of Princess Marie in Bohemia, where Rilke had recently visited her; Duchess Anna Amalia was the mother of Goethe's patron, Duke Karl August of Sachse-Weimar.*

TO LOU ANDREAS-SALOMÉ

from Duino Castle near Nabresina,
Austrian Littoral,
28 December 1911

Let me imagine that you are all but waiting for a letter from me, otherwise this big sheet is not justifiable at all, and I really cannot take a smaller one. There is a chance at this time that you are at home and have quiet, it was always so between the two Christmases—, so let me tell you about things for a few pages.

About you I heard through Gebsattel in the fall, but, you can imagine, he does not reflect complete pictures, he is like one of the mirrors doctors use for examinations; so nothing whole was to be learned from him, but I did understand that things are going well with you and that agrees with everything I know about you, independently of all tidings.

You see, I am still in a hurry to get to myself, I still presume that this theme can be of interest; would you like to go into it once more? Please, please, do, I will help you, as best I can, perhaps I'll be bad at it,—in that case there is a point of departure: *Malte Laurids Brigge*. I need no answers to my books, that you know, —but now I deeply need to know what impression this book made on you. Our good Ellen Key naturally confused me promptly with Malte and gave me up; yet no one but you, dear Lou, can distinguish and indicate whether and how much he resembles me. Whether he, who is of course in part made out of my dangers, goes under in it, in a sense to spare me the going under, or whether with these journals I have really got for fair into the current that is tearing me away and driving me across. Can you understand that after this book I have been left behind just like a survivor, helpless in my inmost soul, no longer to be used? The nearer I came to the end of writing it, the more strongly did I feel that it would be an indescribable division, a high watershed, as I kept telling myself; but now it turns out that all the water has flowed off toward the old side and I am going down into an aridity that will not change. And if it were merely that: but the other fellow, the one who went under, has somehow used me up, carried on the immense expenditure of his going under with the strength and materials of my life, there is nothing that was not in his hands, in his heart, he appropriated everything with the intensity of his despair; scarcely does a thing seem new to me before I discover the break in it, the rough place where he tore himself off. Perhaps this book had to be written as one sets a mine; perhaps I should have jumped way away from it the moment it was finished. But I suppose I still cling too much to possession and cannot achieve measureless poverty, much as that is probably my crucial task. My ambition was such that I put my entire capital into a lost cause, but on the other hand its values could become visible only in this loss, and that is why, I remember, *Malte Laurids* appeared to me for the longest time not so much as a going under, rather as a singularly dark ascension into a remote neglected part of heaven.

It is almost two years: dear Lou, you alone will be able to grasp how falsely and precariously I have spent them. I thought when they began I had a long, long patience; how often since then have I patched it, what all have I not shredded and tied on. I have gone through so much that was confusing, experiences like that of Rodin simply going wrong in his seventieth year, as though all his endless work had not been; as though something paltry, some sticky trifle, such as he had surely pushed out of his way by the dozen before, not leaving himself time really to get through with them, had lain in wait there and overwhelmed him easily and now day by day is making his old age into something grotesque and ridiculous—, what am I to make of that sort of experience? A moment of weariness, a few days of slackening sufficed then, and life rose up about him as unachieved as about a school boy and drove him, just as he was, into the nearest wretched snare. What am I to say, with the little bit of work out of which I keep falling completely, if he wasn't saved? Shall I wonder that life-sized life treats me downright scornfully in such interims, and what in all the world is this work if in it one cannot go through and learn everything, if one hangs around outside it allowing oneself to be shoved and pushed, grabbed and let go, becoming involved in happiness and wrong and never understanding anything.

Dear Lou, I am in a bad way when I wait for people, need people, look around for people: that only drives me still further into the more turbid and puts me in the wrong; they cannot know how little trouble, really, I take with them, and of what ruthlessness I am capable. So it is a bad sign that since *Malte* I have often hoped for someone who would be there for me; how does that happen? I had a ceaseless longing to bring my solitude under shelter with someone, to put it in someone's protection; you can imagine that in those conditions nothing made any progress. With a kind of shame I think of my best Paris time, that of the *New Poems*, when I expected nothing and no one and more and more the whole world streamed toward me merely as a task and I replied clearly and surely with pure work. Who would have told me then that so many relapses were before me! I waken every morning with a cold shoulder, there, where the hand should lay hold that shakes me. How is it possible that now, prepared and schooled for expression, I am left in fact without a vocation, superfluous? In the years when Ilya of Murom sprang up, I sit myself down and wait, and my heart knows of no occupation for me. What will you say, Lou, when you read this? Did you foresee it? I remember a passage from your last letter, which I haven't here: "You are still going so far," you wrote. And if not,—what is to be done in order not to go bad in the standstill? What is to be done?

I am thinking less than before of a doctor. Psychoanalysis is too basic a help for me, it helps once and for all, it clears out, and to find myself cleared out one day would perhaps be even more hopeless than this disorder.

On the other hand I still busy myself from time to time with the idea of pursuing a few subjects consistently at a little country university.—You smile, you are familiar with that, yes, there is little that is new with me, and the worst of it is that certain of my plans and perhaps even my best and worst qualities have sense only with relation to a certain age and beyond that are simply absurd. Indeed it is almost too late even for the university, but you know what I mean by that; the terrible thing about art is that the further one gets in it, the more it commits one to the highest, almost impossible; here enters in spiritually what in another sense the woman in the Baudelaire poem means who in the great stillness of the full-moon light suddenly bursts out: *que c'est un dur métier que d'être belle femme.*

Here, Lou, is another of my confessions. Are the symptoms those of the long convalescence which my life is? Are they signs of a new sickness? I wish I could be with you once for a week, to hear and to tell. It has been so long. I get about so much, shouldn't it be possible to meet sometime?

Do you know that last winter I was in Algiers, Tunis and Egypt? Unfortunately under conditions so little suited to me that I lost my seat and bearing and finally followed along just like someone a runaway horse has thrown off and drags along up and down in the stirrup. That wasn't the right thing. But a little Orient was instilled into me anyway, on the Nile boat I even went in for Arabic, and the museum in Cairo perhaps made something of me after all, confused as I was on entering.

This year I am enjoying the hospitality of friends here (for the time being all alone) in this strong old castle that holds one a little like a prisoner; it cannot do otherwise with its immense walls. And at least the practical disorder in my affairs will benefit by my being taken care of here for a few months. Beyond that I know nothing and want to know nothing.

Goodbye, dear Lou, God knows, your being was so truly the door by which I first came into the open; now

I keep coming from time to time and place myself straight against the doorpost on which we marked my growth in those days. Allow me this dear habit and love me.

Rainer

/ *"The two Christmases" refers to the difference in calendar date between the Western and the Russian Christmas; Emil Baron von Gebsattel was a psychiatrist whom Rilke was considering as an analyst; Ilya of Murom was a Russian singer.*

TO LOU ANDREAS-SALOMÉ

from Duino near Nabresina, Austrian Littoral,
10 January 1912

The elder Prince Taxis was here, I have been alone again only a few days, am now at last thanking you for your good letter. I have, you may believe me, read much between the words, I walked up and down in the garden with it as with something that one wants to learn by heart, what would I do without this voice: yours? I cannot tell you how intimate and comforting it was to me, I am the lone little ant that has lost its head, but you see the anthill and assure me it is intact and I will find my way into it again and make myself useful. And on top of everything came the surprise that you know this coast, so that your letter, as it were, applied not only to me but also to my surroundings, addressed itself to everything and was right for everything. You are right, it has probably always been like this with me, but, you see, I tire myself out with it; as someone who walks on crutches always rubs his coat through first under the armpits, so my one-sidedly worn nature will, I fear, one day have holes and yet at other places be like new. These last years it has often seemed to me as though many workers in art had got hold of themselves by outwitting and exploiting their own inadequacies of which they were aware, rather as they would have made use of a weakness recognized in someone else. I am too much on the side of my nature, I have never wanted anything of it that it did not dispense magnanimously and happily out of its innermost impulses, almost out beyond me. And by the other road the most that is accomplished is that one can always write; that I don't care about. What weighs upon me this time is not even so much the length of the pause perhaps, but rather a kind of dulling, a kind of growing old, if one should call it that, as though what is strongest in me had really been damaged somehow, were just a bit guilty, were atmosphere, do you understand: air instead of universal space. It may be that this continual inner distraction in which I live has in part physical causes, is a thinness of the blood; whenever I notice it, it still becomes a reproach to me for having let it get so far. No matter what is before me: I still get up every day with the doubt whether I shall succeed in doing it, and this distrust has become big from the actual experience that weeks, even months can go by in which I produce only with extreme effort five lines of a quite indifferent letter, which, when they are finally there, leave an aftertaste of incompetence such as a cripple might feel who can't even shake hands any more.

Shall I go on through all that nevertheless? Then if people chance to be present, they offer me the relief of being able to be more or less the person they take me for, without being too particular about my really existing. How often does it not happen that I step out

of my room somehow like a chaos, and outside, someone being aware of me, find a poise that is actually his,
and the next moment, to my amazement, am expressing well-formed things, while just before everything in
my entire consciousness was utterly amorphous. To
whom am I saying this, dear Lou, indeed it is almost
through you that I know it is so, you see how little has
changed,—and in this sense people will always be the
false way for me, something that galvanizes my life-
lessness, without remedying it. Alas, my dear, I do
know so well that my earliest instinct was the definitive
one, I don't want to do anything whatever against it,
but as it is I have been placed among people and have
felt real influences from them and have worked myself
into them like one of them. I am not even mentioning that in a certain year when things weren't going on
at all or rather couldn't begin anywhere (for there was
simply nothing there yet), you came—: that can be
only once, just as there is only one birth,—but I have
other single memories in the human sphere to which I
cling,—when one puts them into words, they are quite
insignificant, as to content, and yet, will you believe
me, in the long complicated solitude, often carried to
the extreme, in which *Malte Laurids* was written, I
felt perfectly certain that the strength by which I de-
frayed his cost stemmed to an important extent from
certain evenings on Capri on which nothing happened
except that I sat by two elderly women and a young
girl and watched their needlework and sometimes at
the end was given an apple peeled by one of them.
There was no trace of destiny between us, it was never
even investigated just how far *these* people were necessary in order that that should come into being which
was born there; name it has none, but I experienced
from it something almost of the mystical way of nour-

ishment that is the Communion; while it was still going on, I knew that it was giving me strength and later, in the laborious solitude, I recognized these powers among all others; it was strange, they held out longest.

Dear Lou, when I wrote recently that I was almost hoping for people, I meant that since then I have not again experienced this and need it infinitely. Can't you imagine that there is some human being who is able to give this, spontaneously, unintentionally, and who would be content to irradiate mere presence and expect nothing? There are even people who do that for the sick where all care leads at best to health, while here it would begin as it were with the healthiest and reach God knows whither. It isn't in times like these bad ones that this need of mine developed; during the immense concentration which carried through the *New Poems*, it acquired contour and in a sense I finished the writing of the *Brigge* as though on condition that this would come true. I will demonstrate it to you by something quite concrete. Imagine that I think with the same anguish of trying again in the rue Cassette with a little furnished room, or of returning among my own furniture, which in recent years has turned completely into the scenery indicated for the last act of *Malte Laurids*. Ridiculous as it is, I undergo all these things like destinies, and that is why they have once been so fundamentally gone through and cannot be begun again. Do you understand that I picture a creature who would make the things exaggerated by me ordinary and guileless once more? Is there no such person? One might think I was experiencing what happened in the fable: that I had simply sung instead of building, and was left now, when it is getting cold, without shelter. But no, you see, what I am thinking of could not have been built in any case, it would be absolutely

miraculous, and I would have no right to count on it
had not everything decisive in my life been just as independent of my provision and in no wise possible to
prepare and to lay foundations for. Perhaps everyone
who hears of this will first ask with what I, for my part,
intend to achieve such a relationship; there I must own
that I really can respond with nothing, save perhaps
with my own warmer and happier existence, as it may
possibly have revealed itself to those women too that
time in Capri. I believe in Naples once, before some
ancient tombstone, it flashed through me that I should
never touch people with gestures stronger than those
there portrayed. And I really believe I am sometimes
far enough along to express all the insistence of my
heart without loss and fatality when I lay my hand
lightly on a shoulder. Wouldn't that, Lou, wouldn't that
be the only advance thinkable within that "restraint"
of which you remind me?

It is three-thirty, I have scarcely eaten, I am spend-
ing almost all day writing to you, and yet it is so hard
to make it understandable that my head is buzzing; I
make hardly any progress, I keep wanting to begin
again and say everything over once more,—but to what
purpose, I do not want to convince you. Only you
should know what I meant by "human beings": not a
giving away of solitude; only, if that solitude weren't so
suspended in air, if it came into good hands, would it
entirely lose the accompanying tones of morbidity
(that will sooner or later be inevitable anyhow), and
I would finally achieve some sort of continuity within
it instead of carrying it like a filched bone from bush
to bush amid loud halloos.

There,—your old mole has shown you some digging
again and thrown up a lop of dark earth right across a
good road. Forgive me. To you I speak such inward

things, like the people in the Old Testament, an entire
scroll: for what stands there in the burning thornbush
of your life is exactly what shall have power over me
too.

Dear Lou, if it works, I shall probably stay here into
the spring, although neither the house nor the climate
really suits me; this continual shift between bora and
sirocco is not good for my nerves, and I exhaust myself
participating first in one and then in the other. Nevertheless when I add up the individual advantages of
this refuge, it comes to a large sum and I must count
myself fortunate in having it. In my present state any
place would have been difficult for me, but not everywhere could I have gone so to the bottom of my condition as here. It is only too bad that Nature here offers
me almost nothing, even the ocean leaves me indifferent; as if this stupid Austrian polyglottism took away
even from the landscape its unified, unequivocal expression. I can hardly say how repugnant everything
Austrian is to me. I long for Naples, or I would like to
walk for hours in the snow through woods and afterwards drink delicious coffee with you. But it will be
all right anyway . . .

/ *"The elder Prince Taxis" was Princess Marie's oldest son,
Prince Erich.*

TO EMIL BARON VON GEBSATTEL

from Duino Castle near Nabresina,
Austrian Littoral,
14 January 1912

Dear Friend, we haven't written each other at all
since Munich, I know that isn't troubling you, but now

for once I do want quickly to avail myself of the Sunday evening to ask about you and to communicate myself to you.

How have things gone since then? I would have many questions. Were you to reply with more, I could tell you that I have been here since the end of October, but only since quite recently alone, which after all was what was really intended. Over this new little while naturally I haven't yet managed to accomplish anything—, against the circumstances there is little to say; at most, that the climate, an incessant shifting between the extremes of sirocco and bora, is not exactly ideal for the inner steadiness I wish for myself. Hence not really entirely beneficial,—but on the other hand the advantages are so many that, if I manage at all well, I can still arrive at a kind of profit here. Just through the thorough solitude. The castle is an immense body without much soul: obsessed with the idea of its own firmness, it holds one by its inwardly directed gravitation like a prisoner; it is a rather austere dwelling. Along the steep cliffs, from the sea, an evergreen garden climbs up to it, otherwise any green is rare, we are in the Karst, and the hardened mountains forgo the effeminacy of any vegetation.

So much for the externals. Of what is within me there is scarcely anything yet to say—, I long for work, sometimes I think for a moment it is longing for me too—, but we do not meet. The fact that I have no plans is agreeable to me rather than disquieting. The other day the furniture at last left the memorable, the tiresome, the strange house in the rue de Varenne and is waiting for my future in a *garde-meuble* . . . Marthe, —(of her I hear only indirectly through Madame W., who, it seems, is taking a more and more lively interest in her), Marthe is learning to cook and has a talent for it, in the evening she draws and has a grasp of that too such as one would scarcely believe; occasionally she goes with Madame W. to the theater, all that is turning with her into sheer life, finds untold readinesses in her nature—, it is becoming a miracle. But I am almost too much concerned about myself and self-absorbed,—it is clear that this quiet here must bring with it some kind of decision; among all that is going through my head, there is naturally analysis too. In that connection it occurs to me that we have never talked about whether you actually consider it appropriate in my case? It still seems to me that my work is really nothing but a self-treatment of the same sort, how else would I have hit upon work at all (already at the age of ten or twelve)? My wife, from whom incidentally I only rarely have short letters, thinks, if I am not mistaken, that a kind of cowardice is frightening me away from analysis, it would be in keeping (as she expresses it) with the "trusting," the "religious" side of my nature to undertake it,—but that is not right; my very religiosity, if one is to call it that, keeps me from this operation, from this great clearing out that life does not do, —from this correcting of the whole hitherto written page of life which I then imagine all rewritten in red as in a school notebook—a silly conception and surely quite false—, but that is how it looks to me.

In a letter of some time ago, shortly after my departure from Munich, my wife expressed much concerning me so precisely and correctly that I was moved by it; it is indeed true, much of me that was simply a bad habit, through which one occasionally reached as through bad air, is solidifying, is acquiring resistance and can soon have become a wall and shut me off,—I know all is not well with me, and you, dear friend, have also observed it,—but, believe me, I am still struck by nothing so much as by the incomprehensible, incredible wonderfulness of my existence, which from the very beginning was so impossibly disposed, and advanced nevertheless from salvation to salvation, as though always through the hardest stone; so that when I think of no longer writing, practically the only thing that upsets me is not to have recorded the utterly wonderful line of this life so strangely carried through. Alas, round about me I see dim destinies and hear talk of casualties and cannot help being amazed. Can you understand, my friend, that I am afraid of disturbing by any classification or survey, be it never so relieving, a much higher order whose right, after all that has happened, I would have to acknowledge, even if it were to destroy me?

You know enough of my life to turn to examples for what I mean. You are also acquainted, better than almost anyone else, with the way I have been lying here for two years, doing nothing but trying to get up, grasping now at one person, now at another, who happens along, and living on the time and the listening of those I cause to stand still before me. It is in the nature of this state to become a complete abnormality if it lasts for long, and I ask myself every day whether I am not bound at any cost to put an end to it somehow or other. And yet, you see, it was never I who made the end,—the new beginning took it incidentally, just as it was, out of my hands.

My dear friend, with all this I have now made myself amply present to you. Write sometime, tell me about things, and if you want to bring it up, let me read what you think of this creature with regard to analysis. When I go away from here, the next thing will have its turn,—won't it? I ask myself. You ask yourself sometime. Let us be prepared, and then let us let come what can, and we shall see.

/ Emil Baron von Gebsattel was (as noted earlier) a psychiatrist; Marthe was Marthe Hennebert, a young Parisian girl Rilke had met and befriended in the summer of 1911, and about whose future he was concerned; Madame W. was Frau Hedwig Woermann-Janichen, in whose care Rilke had left Marthe.

TO LOU ANDREAS-SALOMÉ

from Duino Castle near Nabresina,
Austrian Littoral,
20 January 1912

Don't be startled, Lou, that I am already here again: it will be only a little visit, if it doesn't suit you, put me aside until tomorrow, day after tomorrow—when you will.

Chance made me find your letter this morning and the enclosed from Gebsattel simultaneously on my writing table. I beg you, read it; here quickly the few data that will make it intelligible to you.

You understand that the thought of going through an analysis rises in me now and then; to be sure, what I know of Freud's writings is uncongenial to me and in places hair-raising; but the matter itself, which runs away with him, has its genuine and strong sides, and I can conceive of Gebsattel's using it with discretion and influence. Now as for me, I have already written you that, emotionally, I rather shun this getting cleared out and, with my nature, could hardly expect anything good of it. Something like a disinfected soul results

132

from it, a monstrosity, alive, corrected in red like the page of a school notebook. And yet: dear Lou, as matters stand with me, I hardly have the right, out of mere feeling, to cast suspicion on a help that is right there and is holding itself in readiness. I knew more or less that Gebsattel was prepared to perform the whole excavation on me, but I had never actually asked him whether, so far as he knows me (and we had very detailed talks at a certain time in Paris and at, for me, a dim and wearisome period), the use of analysis seemed suitable for me. Hence the letter I sent him on the fifteenth of this month contained this question and at the same time a few of my scruples. The enclosed is his answer. It seems to me he is mistaken about some things; in any case it is time now, in view of his readiness, really to consider this expedient. The fact remains that from a purely physical standpoint I am quite unbearable to myself; certain bad habits, which I formerly always used to reach through as through bad air, are solidifying more and more, and I can conceive of their shutting me in someday like walls. The oversensitivity of my muscles, for example, is so great that a little gymnastics or an in any way exaggerated posture (as in shaving for instance) results at once in swelling, pains, etc., phenomena which are then followed by fears, interpretations, distresses of every sort as though they had just been waiting: I am ashamed to admit to what extent, often for weeks, this fateful circle dances about me in which one misery does the other every favor.

You know perhaps, dear Lou, that since sometime early in the year Gebsattel has had m[y] w[ife] under treatment,—with her it is a different matter, her work has never helped her, while mine, in a certain sense, was from the beginning a kind of self-treatment;

though, in proportion as it has developed and become something independent, it is losing more and more of its therapeutic and considerate character and is making demands; a soul that has no alternative but to find its harmony in the immense exaggerations of art ought to be able to count on a body that does not ape it in any way and is precise and nowhere exaggerates itself. My physical being runs the risk of becoming the caricature of my spiritual being. Dear Lou, if it will not be too much for you, help me with a few words to think it over. (Under certain circumstances I would go to Munich, do a few things there at the University and at the same time attempt the analysis.) Your letter I will answer soon, thank you. You see how things go up and down with me and to and fro: what to do?

Rainer

TO LOU ANDREAS-SALOMÉ

from Duino Castle near Nabresina,
Austrian Littoral
7 February 1912

Yes, dear Lou, *Dai Bog zhizn!* And what Christ manifested with so much consideration to Angela of Foligno will always be proved in the end: that he was daily so much readier to give than she was to receive. The bad thing is only that for me now, from a purely physical point of view, the receiving affects me almost like the not-being-able to receive. Alas, old calash that I am, my springs were so fine before, and now if the miracle happens to ride in me half an hour, I am amazed that it doesn't climb out: I bump and shake like the poorest *telyega* and in the process almost come apart myself.

Enough. For the third day now I have been padding about a little in the snow with the longingest bare feet; for two days indeed it has been thawing; but inadvertently such a quantity had fallen that, despite the sirocco, it still hasn't all dwindled away from the garden. (I must, I believe, sometime soon have a regular winter again, one with which to tussle.)

Today, to go back to your third letter ago, I wanted to tell you a little about Kassner. But it is difficult for me to leave the man himself out of consideration, indeed, I cannot do it at all. What I read of his before I knew him was "too difficult" for me; I have read him with real insight only since he lurks behind it for me, often directly in front of it even. Isolated, as he now is more and more, he has attached himself to me with strong confidence and considers me absolutely as his friend: wherein he is certainly not mistaken, he is really the only man with whom I can get anywhere,—perhaps better so: the only one to whom it occurs to make a little use of the feminine in me. I felt, unusually purely and directly, even when I saw him for the first time years ago in Vienna, the bright radiance of his nature which shines, which is an out-and-out light, a brightness in space. He has something which others, seen beside him, have not, he must have attained something that others do not attain. (For the rest, by descent and origin there is nothing Jewish about or in him,—you seem to take him for a Jew?—no.) He is certainly—which he too would admit—a spiritual child of Kierkegaard. Kierkegaard comes to an end in him and goes into the circle and on. I have an idea that what his "melancholy" was for Kierkegaard, Kassner's infirmity is for him. And as it was a kind of advantage for Kierkegaard always to have, instead of so many unpredictable hindrances, only this one immense, su-

perhuman melancholy before which he ranged himself
in ever new battle formations, so Kassner too somehow
prevails by the fact that all oppositions coincide for
him in one hindrance: that procures him a concentration and a tranquillity, nothing can, so to speak, attack him from behind. But this indescribable admiration for Kierkegaard may again be linked with the fact
that Kierkegaard's adversary was more mystical, more
inexhaustible, more dangerous, handed down in a way
from the Beyond through his father, while that which
he, Kassner, spiritually overcomes at every moment is
even, in a divine sense, a merit. (Kierkegaard's melancholy is still an impediment even in heaven.) Do you
know Kassner's earlier essay on Indian Idealism? I
don't know if that isn't his best. If you like, I will have it
sent you sometime by Bruckmann (where, if I am not
mistaken, it was published). In the beautiful chapter
(yes, the most beautiful in the book) about the chimeras, I might indeed be painted in down below very
small and at least kneeling, as "little originator": that
is, in Paris, in certain days when we were seeing each
other often, I advised him—without knowing what he
happened to be writing about—just to climb up once
more to the chimeras on Notre Dame, said nothing
further about them—; but that must have given the
touch-off and been strangely opportune. Furthermore,
I can imagine that what I felt in his books before I continually drew the man himself into them—is in reality
akin to what you noted in reading. But to what is it
due?—If you spoke with him, I believe you would hit
upon it in half an hour, me he prejudices in favor of
his own meaning, you would watch him quite delightedly and form your own opinion.

A few evenings ago I read the *Chamber Plays* of the
aged Strindberg; they are frightful, frightful: it is ap-

palling that old men should close thus, like the little
twenty-three-year-old dauphine whose last words
were: *fi de la vie,—ne m'en parlez plus.* The aged
Michelangelo who writes in a sonnet: what is the good
of having made so many dolls? (or something similar,
I know only the Italian text, and it is hard to translate).
But in Strindberg there must be strengths, the strength-
masses of a landslide; to have this world, and nevertheless to be, to achieve, that is beyond all conception.
For indeed he not only speaks of this despair to which
everything gives rise, he makes something out of it,
and he makes it magnificently, that one must grant
him. (Have you read these plays? *Chamber Plays*,
George Muller, Munich-Leipzig; especially the second, third and fourth plays!) . . .

But now *proshchai*, how long I have written! Thanks
for your letter.

/ *"Dai Bog zhizn!": "God give life!"; Angela da Foligno
(1248–1309) was a mystic whose Instructions Rilke had
read; a "telyega" is a Russian peasant cart; "Kassner's infirmity" refers to the fact that Rudolf Kassner was hunch-
backed; Hugo Bruckmann, of Munich, published Indian
Idealism; "proshchai": "goodbye (live well!)."*

TO PRINCESS MARIE VON THURN
UND TAXIS-HOHENLOHE

from Palazzo Valmarana, San Vio [Venice]
12 July 1912

Strictly speaking, dear friend, I haven't a single
quite clear need besides that of writing to you, and a
little too of knowing your opinion of my present life;

but it is indescribable what a ban against all activity is
in the air and in one's limbs, a season for healthy in-
fants—; as certain magicians get the idea of pulling
endless ribbons out of their mouths, so from my eyelids closed to a crack I draw meter-long strips of day-
time sleep; hardly is one finished before a new grey or
lilac starts sliding forth, and I am entangled in all these
slowly forming sleep-ribbons, so that I am living as in
a snarl that only draws together more tightly at any
attempt to escape.

This is happening oddly, my conscience is not getting better for it, and yet I don't want to cut right
through everything and break out, but am just waiting
along, letting it happen to me, and what comes takes
on the habits and has the dimensions of dream.

There is a little key lying on my table (yes, it is
really still lying there); it locks the strange, big hall in
the Casino dei Spiriti on the Fondamente Nuove;
whenever I wish myself thither, I can be there,—but
what a lavishness, what extravagance, to wish.

Duse, my having been at her house, she at mine, that
too is like a mirage in the air over-stimulated by clarity
—you can imagine, we were like two characters coming
on in an old mystery, spoke, as charged by a legend,
each his gentle part. A meaning arose immediately
from the whole and at once transcended us. We were
like two basins one above the other forming a fountain
and showing each other only how much was continually slipping from us. And yet we could scarcely be
prevented from somehow agreeing on the magnificence of being so full, and perhaps at the same moment we thought too of the living, vertical ray that
rose above us and fell (ever and again) and filled us
so full.—Cowardly as I now am, I hardly dared look

at her; it caused me a kind of pain to find her so broad and robust, that stoutly grown body, like a setting from which at some time the stone has already fallen. The fear of seeing a distortion, or simply something that is no longer there, is to blame for my remembering almost nothing but her mouth, that heavy mouth that looks as though only a fate unfeeling and not its own could still move it, as for certain swords the hero must come, the half-god, to raise them. And the smile indeed, surely one of the most famous ever smiled, a smile that needs no space, that retracts nothing, conceals nothing, is transparent as a song and yet so full of added being that one is tempted to stand up when it enters.

More staggering almost than the event itself was to me the fact that suddenly, without my lifting a finger, this meeting came about which for many years was almost my greatest wish. For some time now I have lost the precision necessary for wishing (wishing is target-shooting and I am under heavy fire before an invisible foe)—, but, as at several times in my life, I unconsciously took the quiet realization as proof that I am, despite everything, on my path, otherwise this village, so often sought out on the map, could not have come.

The experience with Rodin has made me very timid toward all changing, all diminishing, all failure—, for those unapparent fatalities, once one has recognized them, can be endured only so long as one is capable of expressing them with the same force with which God allows them. I am not very far off work, perhaps, but Heaven forbid that I should be called upon (right away at least) for insight into anything more painful than I was charged with in *Malte Laurids*. Then it will be just a howl among howls and not worth the effort.

Yesterday I wrote without premeditation in my notebook:

Alas, as we waited for help from mankind, angels
stepped over soundlessly, in a single stride,
over our prostrate hearts.

Here Moissi walked in on me, suddenly, coming from Duse, I knew she was already expecting him yesterday; he rushed, burst, broke in, at first I thought it was his tempo, an inner, absolute one,—but now, now I am almost afraid it is the tempo of Reinhardt enterprises: Heavens, what an actor he has become, I saw him shortly thereafter with Duse, we were standing by the window, she came by with her friend, Mme. Poletti (who is writing the *Ariadne* for her), we climbed into the gondola beside her and rode slowly toward the Lido. Duse was quite magnificent today, of a sadness such as cloud formations can have, one interprets it as sadness, but in reality it is nothing but immense space, not gay, not disconsolate,—great. Later we dropped Moissi off, but we remained together, I ate with them in their house on the Zattere, it was intimate, full of friendship, full of nearness, and again much meaning came out of the simplest things and passed into the great. Now it is late, with this I close a letter that would otherwise have continued quite, quite differently, but as it is, is more complete, for today we looked at each other really without fear, seriousness for seriousness, melancholy for melancholy: it seems we can do each other no harm. (And the world is so different from Moissi.)

This must suffice; we have telegraphed Placci he must come tomorrow; a thousand greetings to everyone, especially to the Prince and you, my dear friend,

how often I think how you are in everything that befalls me, now again here,—how without you nothing
would have come.—

Yours

D. S.

*/ Rilke here mentions the names of several actors: Alexan-
der Moissi (1880–1935), Eleonora Duse (1859–1924),
Carlo Placci, and the producer Max Reinhardt (1873–
1943); his signature, D. S., stands for Princess Marie's name
for him, "Doctor Seraphicus."*

TO PRINCESS MARIE VON THURN
UND TAXIS-HOHENLOHE

from Ronda [Spain],
17 December 1912

I long for a letter from you, dear friend, God
knows where it is wandering about—and the last I
wrote you seems quite vague in my memory; what was
thoroughly alive in it was merely like warmed-up food
from the one written only in thought in Córdoba, furthermore it bore no mark but that of my discontent
with Seville, with myself, with myself and ten times
with myself. Again there came a series of really irksome days, pains physically and the spirit so little at-
tuned to endurance, if I had happened to have a
"home," I would by all means have gone home, since
for every journey, especially one through Spain, a certain equilibrium is required, the certainty of being able
to rely on oneself, but for me the world collapses completely every moment, inside in my blood; and if then
an entirely strange world stands all about outside, it

is a strangeness beyond measure. I have it in mind, Princess, I must track down the cause of this malaise, discover the source whence evil keeps welling up; scarcely have I a little boat somewhere before this misery rises and overflows it and leaves it desolate behind. And I know that there a doctor can help, not I, if only he were the right one,—with me everything is too much of a piece for me to be able to suffer at some place and accomplish at another, really I am not at all addicted to suffering, a pain takes the world from me, that is why I am so completely unfitted to be a saint and haven't the slightest prospect of ever spreading abroad this good odor. (Instead you recognized and expressed it, that was inexhaustibly right.)

For the rest you must know, Princess, since Córdoba I have been of an almost rabid anti-Christianity, I read the Koran; to me, in places, it takes on a voice that I am inside of, as it were, with all my strength, like the wind in an organ. Here one thinks one is in a Christian country; well, even here it is long since outlived, it was Christian as long as one had the courage to kill people a hundred paces before the city; thus the many unassuming stone crosses increased which read simply: here died so and so,—that was the local version of Christianity. Now there is a boundless indifference here, empty churches, forgotten churches, chapels dying of starvation,—really one should no longer sit down at this cleaned-up table and hand out as nourishment the finger bowls that are still standing about. The fruit is sucked dry, so now, to put it crudely, one just spits out the rinds. And then Protestants and American Christians keep making another infusion with these tea dregs that have steeped for two millenniums, Mohammed was in any case the next stage; like a river through a primeval mountain, he breaks his way through to the one God, with whom one can speak so magnificently every morning without the "Christ" telephone, into which people continually shout: *Hello, who's there?*—and no one answers.

Now just imagine, Princess, I am three hours from Gibraltar, five, when the weather is good, from Tangiers—, tempted like anything in this mood, to sail over sometime to the Moors; on the other hand, I am afraid a whitewash of light would then lay itself over dark, clay-red Spain.—For the present I am here in Ronda (since a week ago), I at once sent P. a few pictures, it seemed to me so very probable that the incomparable phenomenon of this city piled up on two steep rock-masses divided by the narrow, deep river gorge would confirm his dream picture; it is indescribable, surrounding the whole a spacious valley, busied with its expanses of meadow, its evergreen oaks and olive trees, and beyond again there rises out of it, as though well rested, the pure mountain range, mountain behind mountain, forming the stateliest distance. As for the city itself, in these conditions it cannot but be odd, rising and falling, here and there so open toward the abyss that not one window dares look that way,—little palaces behind crusts of yearly white, each with a portal set off by color, and under the balcony the coat of arms with crest slightly flattened, but in the shield distinct, detailed and full as a pomegranate.

Here would of course be the place to live and to reside quite Spanishly were it not for the season, were it not for my tiresome disinclination to let myself in for any but the most necessary hardships (innate and zealously assumed)—, to crown it all the devil prompted the English to build here a really excellent hotel, in which I am naturally living now, neutral, expensive and as this person and that would desire it, and still I am shameless enough to spread it abroad that I am traveling in Spain.

I tell you, Princess (no, no, you must believe me), things must become different with me, from the ground up, from the ground up, otherwise all the miracles in the world will be in vain. For here I see once more how much is lavished on me and just plain lost, the Blessed Angela had a similar experience—, *quand tous les sages du monde*—she says—*et tous les saints du paradis m'accableraient de leurs consolations et de leurs promesses, et Dieu lui-même de ses dons, s'il ne me changeait pas moi-même, s'il ne commençait au fond de moi une nouvelle opération, au lieu de me faire du bien, les sages, les saints, et Dieu exaspéreraient au dela de toute expression mon désespoir, ma fureur, ma tristesse, ma douleur, et mon aveuglement.* This I marked a year ago in the book, for I understood it with all my heart and, I cannot help it, it has since become only the more valid.

Today, when I saw these mountains, these slopes, opened up in the purest air as if one were to sing from them, I had to tell myself to what joy that would have incited me even three years ago, how it would have transformed me into just sheer joy—, now it is as if my heart had moved miles away, I see many things that start off and go in its direction—, but I do not learn of their arriving. Alas, I am not quite over expecting the *nouvelle opération* from some human intervention, and yet to what end, since it is my fate, passing the human by as it were, to arrive at the ultimate, at the rim of the earth, as recently in Córdoba where an ugly little bitch, to the highest degree prematernal, came to me; she was not a remarkable animal, and certainly she was full of accidental young ones about which no fuss will have been made; but since we were all alone, she came over to me, hard as it was for her, and raised her eyes enlarged by care and fervor and sought my glance,—and in hers was truly everything that goes beyond the individual, whither I don't know, into the future or into the incomprehensible; the situation resolved itself in her getting a piece of sugar from my coffee, but incidentally, oh so incidentally, we read mass together so to say, the action was nothing in itself but giving and accepting, but the meaning and the seriousness and our whole understanding was boundless. That after all can happen only on earth, it is good at all events to have gone through here willingly, even though uncertainly, even though guiltily, even though not at all heroically,—one will at last be wonderfully prepared for divine conditions.

How the tiniest bird voice outside affects and concerns me, dear heaven, would that it were spring and I were approaching Nature somewhere with all my senses,—I have discovered for myself such a singular valley, a kind of hunting park of the Marqués de Salvatierra, scarcely laid out at all, only so rearranged that rabbits don't quite know their way any more,—something out of a dream or out of the *Elective Affinities*; I take long, long walks—, but still recognize myself most truly in the fateful coincidence of the first excursion in each city,—even in Seville, where nothing else went right, I began, God knows how, with the Old Men's Home of the *Caritad*; it was morning, in the long, cheerful halls the old men were sitting around the brazier or simply standing about finished like toys, two lay in bed resting from life as though they didn't at all need the extravagance of dying for that purpose; but on the other nicely made beds, everywhere at the same spot on each of the flowered bedcovers, lay two of the enormous, pale Spanish loaves of white bread, peaceful in their evident superfluity, pure recompense and no longer to be eaten in the sweat of the brow.

Here the church of San Francisco, outside in the southern suburb, was the first thing I discovered, I shall tell you about it another time; anyhow it is time for me to close and say Merry Christmas, I shall think many thoughts in your direction—, newspapers I haven't seen, but let us hope you have no more war misgivings; from the Prince's kind, good letter, which reached me by the first mail that caught up with me in Ronda, I see that he has hope and that no one really sees what good a war would do.

Princess, your letter! That is what I call coming in the nick of time. I shall go right on writing without reading or discussing the poems now (I must first get hold of the German text in my memory in order to be able to compare), for I saw that with the little delay in Seville your lines really took six days, and, festive or not, I still have the ambition that this may be with you for Christmas. It is frightful that the danger of war is still not out of the air, politics usually makes a point of being swift, it is a bad joke when it gets as slow as God.

As for Seville, to the last we did not get together, not at all, although the Sevillians take the festival of Mary very personally and a whole octave of ceremonies was impending, in the beginning of which I was just able to participate. The cathedral was so fundamentally repugnant to me, even hostile, nowhere does it become serious, there is something vague, evasive about these ambitiously upward-built spires, a spirit of out-trumping that would like to out-trump even God and, as it were, manage to take him from above. And the infamous organ made the air so sweet with its pampered voice that the colossal pillars felt quite weak, it was a matter of indifference to one, this softening of stone, a conjuring trick, however far it might go.

Have you been seeing books, Princess? In the evening sometimes (I have such congestion in my eyes that I cannot read much) I read *Don Quixote* in German translation and find it rather childish; from an artistic point of view this book has no limits at all, except perhaps those that a witty, ingenious disguise would have in reality—, and they are frivolously far overstepped. But Christmas: Christmas greetings to you, to the Prince, to the Mzell family with all my heart. Do you know that exactly on the night of Christmas it will be full moon: how that will go with your white world in its silver dress. Everything that is affectionate and grateful—

Yours

D. S.

/ *"The blessed Angela" was Angela da Foligno; Elective Affinities is the novel by Goethe; "the Mzell family" refers to the family of Princess Marie's eldest son, Prince Erich, who lived at Mzell castle.*

TO ANTON KIPPENBERG

from Hotel Reina Victoria,
Ronda [Spain],
7 January 1913

. . . I have behind me a few very bad weeks; nevertheless I have remained here, for air, lodging and diet could nowhere be more pleasant. My indispositions are not due to the climate, are only a new chapter in this singular overcoming or renewal which my entire nature, I must believe, is having to accomplish in these years; my most hopeful insight is more or less this, that in the physical as in the spiritual, the same thing has been going on since the *Malte,* a digging-up process in the entire soil of my being whereby the uppermost gets to the very bottom: times, when it would be most propitious to have no consciousness whatsoever; for the continual revolution of such processes cannot there express itself otherwise than as torment and a being exposed. The appearance of the *Elegies* last year has drawn me a little into the confidence of that which, unutterably slowly, under pretext of such great devastation, may be ordering itself, and in the worst days I do still keep finding a remnant of patience, not patience with myself (that is long since used up), but patience toward God, if one can put it that way, a quiet resolute desire for his standard of measurement.

It is indescribably much, dear friend, that you, on the grounds of I know not what trust, are in these difficult enigmatic years putting me in a position to be patient in this sense, to require nothing of my nature, so that it can pursue, where I myself do not disturb it, its inner and averted activities in all their disguises. If I am destined to reach the next phase of my existence, I shall be, thanks to this protection, more sound and more complete in it than I ever was. As concerns the present journey, it actually has difficulty in distributing itself over inner conditions so disturbed and uneven, nevertheless I am not for a moment in doubt that it is the very thing to do the most urgent service to these changes, in that it draws certain regions, lying there as of old, into the realm of these movements. . . .

/ *Anton Kippenberg* (1874–1950), *director of the Insel-Verlag, was Rilke's publisher.*

TO PRINCESS MARIE VON THURN UND TAXIS-HOHENLOHE

from Paris,
Good Friday, 21 March 1913

Your letter was an elixir of life, your beautiful letter (and thanks for all its news), but everything works slowly on me now, I shall reread it often; for the present, *à quelques exceptions près*, I am going about really depressed, somehow amazed that the new beginning, new as it is, fits so exactly on to the old end on which a year and a half of absence has settled merely like a little patina.

What, now what would have to happen to me, to make me feel it? Duino, Venice, Toledo that gripped my heart so violently, all that is past now, like any interruption, like a bit of deep sleep in the open. God knows: is it due to the vehemence with which Paris takes me in again, takes possession of me, sucks me into itself, into the midst of its existence; though sad, though bewildered, though not to be envied, outside in walking I occasionally feel a smile on my face, a reflection of this wide and open air, just like one of the houses shimmering at the end of the street, brightly, brightly, notwithstanding perhaps that the saddest thing is happening in it. What reality in this city, I marvel again and again at how pain stands there, misery, horror, each like a bush, blossoming. And every stone in the pavement is more familiar to one than a pillow anywhere else, is a stone utterly and entirely, hard to the touch, but yet as though descended from the stone that Jacob pushed under his head. *La mort du pauvre qui expire, la tête sur une de ces pierres, est peut-être douce quand-même.*

You ask about Marthe: I have seen her only twice, the first time however for a whole night. It was *mi-carême*, two days after my arrival, I went out to Sceaux, Frau W. was away, so I went into the park and knocked at the studio of the Russian. He himself appeared at the door, a little, blond, Christlike peasant, surrounded by the vague immensities of his already darkened studio; we didn't know each other, I said my name, a pure smile fought its way through his face, he called my name breathlessly upward as a bird does his soul, a high curtain to the right was clutched from within and impatiently thrown open, Marthe rushed out, forward inclined like a deer, a golden headband about her temples, in a quaint, Tanagresque garment—, but quite swallowed up in the bigness of her own eyes—. It turned out that she wanted to go in to Paris, to dance; all day she had done nothing but wash and comb and dress herself, and always, as she told me, with the presentiment that it was not for the ball —for much more. The night was sad, I took her to the Bullier, we missed the last train to Sceaux, my rooms were not in order, so till morning we loafed about in the streets and in inhospitable cabarets, in barbarous surroundings (my maladroitness in knowing nothing better!). She had insisted on going barefoot in her sandals in order to be properly Grecian: that gave her something improbable, touching (something as of a beggar-girl in Heaven); at the Bullier and on the street where, enveloped and draped in her tunic, she stepped with strangely little steps over the confetti lying there and whirling like colored snow, they looked at her surprised, embarrassed,* I would even say with a kind of timid respect. So different was she from all this world

150

of obstinate and cheap amusement. Among all those more or less scabrous girls she looked like a little dying maiden who will be a saint a few years after her death. They took her for a little woman, they scarcely dared speak to her, she seemed to have fallen from a very high nest that she will never find again. She was not much troubled at dancing so little, she needed only to talk and to eat endlessly. She was hungry, she ate with difficulty and effort, with despair, like a ghost that is materializing. And at the same time she wanted to leave that world and enter completely into my eyes and into my ears; she bent over me like a little girl on a lake, desirous of finding her image there even at the risk of drowning in it. She spoke much of her life, of her so provisional life, so incomprehensible, and that no event causes to advance. She lives with this Russian like a sister, she says, immensely relieved not to love him, for "the woman who loved him he would drag about by the hair." He is a savage, a Mordvin, a Siberian, good and terrible, who makes the people he loves decidedly unhappy. The Mordvin language, his own language, possesses only a few words for the most elementary objects; speaking rather little Russian, he has created for himself, since he had to leave his country for political reasons, a mixture of his idiom and Italian (having lived a few years in Milan), an imaginary language with which Marthe seems very well acquainted. His vast studio, a part of which serves as sleeping quarters, is in such disorder that one would doubtless call it a landscape if it happened to be out of doors. One sleeps on pallets among piles of things strewn there and forgotten.—Marthe, very proudly, showed me hyacinth bulbs that have begun to sprout among the covers in the innocent warmth of her poor feet. For the moment, the Russian has a few amateurs who are interested in his work (I remember having seen a Christ on the Cross, gigantic, expressing, with that musical disquiet the Slavs introduce into sculpture, the final agony),—he has some money, but his kindness and his negligence cause the pennies to disappear with the rapidity of running water,—days and nights, they use them without any organization whatever, they sleep from time to time, they eat rarely, only he smokes all the time since he has lived abroad in exile,—from nostalgia. Marthe, while profiting by this irregularity that must seem ideal to her, nevertheless perceives that it is difficult to walk in the mire of liberty. I think she suffers a great deal, that she is using herself up, also she told me she no longer wants to accompany the Russian if he goes to Ialy now as he proposes. She sees no existence for herself, for the moment she goes about on the back of this other life like the little heron of Egypt that lives on the backs of cows. Having worked since she was four, doing all the little tasks that fall between the chinks of professions, she sees no further work to broach and all roads seem closed to her by the heavy shadow of the "boss" which one has to pass through with closed eyes if one wants to arrive at profitable and lasting jobs.*

And I, you understand, Princess, know nothing to advise, can just simply let it go along and from time to time go there; I am neither the man of experience who can with composure be helpful, nor yet the lover overtaken by the inspiration of his heart. I am not a lover at all, it moves me only from without, perhaps because no one has ever shaken me utterly, perhaps because I do not love my mother. Very poor I stand there before this rich little creature, in whom a character less cautious and not quite so imperiled (as I have been for a while) could have found endless delight and unfoldment. All love is exertion for me, something achieved, *surmenage*, only in relation to God have I any ease, for to love God means to enter, to walk, to stand, to rest, and to be everywhere in the love of God.

Marthe has been here for five minutes, she knocked softly as though this writing about her had attracted her; she was sick, had been lying somewhere at one of her sisters', since at Erzia's no one gives her anything to eat; she has quite lost her voice, *pretend que "le sang lui était monté à la gorge."* I have the impression that she was pretty sick. I have put in her hands Claudel's *L'Annonce faite à Marie;* she is reading, quite far off, as always when after a long time she gets to a book. She must read a while longer before I take her with me to lunch, for I must quickly tell you further: that Monday I lunched with my good and great Verhaeren and with Romain Rolland—I accepted (by way of exception) because Verhaeren is already leaving—, well, Romain Rolland made such a sympathetic and humanly significant impression on me, that I strongly urged him to visit you sometime in Duino. He is just now going to Italy again, to Rome, but to work, wants to see no one, it seems, so it will not be this time, unless Placci (who also happens to be in Rome and who naturally knows R. R.) stages a visit. One must not expect an artist, but even without being told his name one would be strongly and particularly struck, wherever one met him, by this man who looks up so clearly out of a courageously achieved sincerity. I had the impression of sitting opposite a tireless reader, whose glance, every time his scholar's eyes became exhausted and worn out in his books, God, by some special favor, freshly painted with the purest blue of his childhood; we took to each other with some warmth and curiosity; Verhaeren was magnificent, it was a by no means superfluous lunching, you would have enjoyed it.

Now I must close. Rodin is sick at the moment, otherwise better, and the frightful Mme. de C. [Choiseul] is no longer around; unfortunately the end came about for quite a miserable reason, I had hoped it would come more from within and would be more convincing and more real for him. This fantastic Paris, everywhere in the house the opinion persists that this American woman had operated with some Indian poison with which she spiced Rodin's milk! Now with God's help, she's over.

Farewell, Princess, remember me cordially to the Prince, to P., etc. Today and yesterday I am hearing old Italian music by the singers in St. Gervais. Vittoria, Palestrina, Ingegneri. . . .

/ *In the original, the passage between * and * was in French; Bullier was the Bal Bullier, a Latin-Quarter dance hall; Mme. de C. was the American-born Duchess of Choiseul; Erzia was the Russian painter whom Marthe loved; Emile Verhaeren (1855–1916) was the Belgian poet whose work Rilke had translated.*

TO ILSE ERDMANN

17 rue Campagne Première, Paris,
last day of November [1913]

Your letter has been in my hands since day before yesterday noon; I reproach myself for not having written immediately. But I find, to be honest, that the further life progresses, the more difficult it is for me to find an immediate valid reply for words like yours.

And not only that it becomes more difficult for me, I make it also more difficult for myself by asking myself where, in the end, would lie my justification to attempt such an answer at all. Those elements of success and insight that in a poem or some other work of art come happily together actually are not to the same extent mastery and command of everyday life—, and if it were the problem to determine which of us both is more helpless, perhaps the scales might tip over on my side.

Of course, in all trouble the artistically creative person has his confirmation in the great power that at times makes use of him and then achieves so much with him that he, distressed as he may otherwise be, musters the patience to preserve himself for it.

Where might there be, for others whom the sorrow inundates, the profound, fruitful source of patience—: I have often asked myself this, without having achieved an explanation. Meanwhile we have to admit that hardly anything presents itself to our view in such manifold aspects, from the banal example to the most memorable shape, as the fact that life has been accomplished under the most insulting, most tormenting, even most deadly circumstances; that one has been able to love it even at those points where it was dreadful at each turn. Indeed, [we have to admit] that people who bore a magnificent fate indifferently, without much enjoyment and interest, after a sudden reversal of their condition into one of despair, sick, maltreated, in the depths of darksome dungeons, were permitted to unfold the joyfulness and confidence in their hearts; indeed, for the first time to realize and enjoy them.

I have followed with zeal the courses of such lives, where I could, and although in none did I see the secret itself flashed before me, which makes possible such immense endurances, nevertheless I live in constant conviction that they occur continually. I can read your letter, too, only in this light; it will even seem to me that it could not have been written at all if somewhere an inner "being-in-order" did not keep account of that which befalls you. If it does not tire you too much to write down for me the two occurrences which you mention, I would consider them a desirable complement to your letter and inform you of my impressions. If this is shorter than I like it to be, I ask you to forgive me because of the fact that I am forced this winter to a special concentration on certain plans and works, and must restrict all externally directed things to a minimum.

Rainer Maria Rilke

/ Ilse Erdmann (1879–1924) had in 1913 moved to Laubach (upper Hesse); she was in Munich, later (1917), when Rilke was there.

TO ILSE ERDMANN

17 rue Campagne Première, Paris,
21 December 1913

The pages you wrote in Bonn I have read today with special sympathy, enveloped, so to speak, by the good spirit of kindred experiences through which we might be connected. With what facility you have made vivid for me those people, each in his way striving to fit something greater to the narrow circumstances with which the ordinary day is satisfied. If it were to be our task to develop in ourselves God's awareness in an incomparable and immeasurable way, then, considering the weakness of each one of us, every agreement which men enter into in such exalted dispositions would be justified—of course only in so far as every participant remains able to expend the whole productiveness of his heart.

Is there anything more unfathomable than this, our heart? What shall we think of it or say, if such a thing is possible, as that reunion related by you with the old woman thought to be an imbecile? What might the one, in such indescribable moments, recognize deep down and smile at in the other? Is it not like the passage from the *Fioretti,* where one of the brothers, summoned without, on the threshold of the cloister, without knowing him, embraces St. Louis, holding him close, imparting and receiving blessed knowledge and then, when an eternity of happiness has passed, letting him go again, depart, without a single word?

I must admit, it is all these fabulous circumstances that, in spite of all the grief, render my being here precious for me—and the longer I live, the more necessary it seems to me to endure, to copy the whole dictation of existence to the end; for it might be that only the last sentence contains that small, perhaps inconspicuous, word through which all the laboriously learned and not understood orients itself toward glorious sense. And who knows whether we are not somehow dependent, in the circumstances of the beyond, on having reached here that end which, after all, was prepared for us; also, no certainty is given that we, fleeing away, out of too great an exhaustion, from here, shall not be faced in the beyond with new achievements, in the face of which the soul, confounded and unqualified though it may arrive, would find itself all the more shamed.

"Not cold and not warm"—you write—indeed, who does not think to be so at times and for years, for years?

But if I, called upon as someone impartial, may write down my impression, then I admit that already your first letter permitted a certain innermost glow to shine through, how much, even more, this beautiful one, wherein so many of the outward shows are mirrored clearly, if darkly.

Do not think me fainthearted if again I answer with so little. These past days I have just been wondering which were the dates of my three last Christmases: three years ago Tunis, the following year a lonely castle on the Adriatic coast, in the past year Ronda, a small old southern Spanish town. When you imagine how much room there is between such sojourns for external impressions, then you will understand that now, almost fearfully (not seeing a soul), I maintain an inward orientation, only to achieve a balance against the so much powerful external world.

Be assured that I am grateful for your letters, as for something humanly rich which comes to me undeservedly.

Rainer Maria Rilke

/ Fioretti: The Little Flowers of St. Francis.

TO AUGUST SAUER

17 rue Campagne Première, Paris,
11 January 1914

Most Admired Sir and Friend,

I find it genuinely agreeable that it is yet again necessary for me to make a request (and this request is the irrepressible, bold motive for writing this letter to you), so that I can at the same time use it as a pretext to offer you and your esteemed wife greetings and best wishes as the year begins: May it turn out to be a prosperous and enjoyable one for you, in work as well as in experience, whose role it is to cultivate the soil from which may rise accomplishment and joyousness. Concerning my request of today, I must make a few remarks in advance.

Since last winter, Stifter has become for me a most special object of affection and edification: never shall I forget how I, there in southern Spain—attacked, so to speak, from all sides by an unexplainable feeling of strangeness—felt a most decided need to escape toward something familiar; how for such assistance there seemed to be no book really sufficient; how finally, by and by, I took up in the evenings from the volumes which the Insel publishing house had sent me the beautiful collection of *German Writers* and, occupying myself with it, eagerly looked forward to a pleasant association, which might help make [the experiences of] the next few weeks easier and help me to assimilate them, but how then suddenly on such an evening, sitting opposite my small fire in the fireplace, I was snatched from the incomparable "Counterpart" to the "Bachelor" and, following such an inclination of my nature, I rushed toward these pages until I flowed into and merged with their current as it were. And from then on it really was Stifter who evening after evening withdrew me from the influences of a scenery of surpassing grandeur, in order to offer me in his relative world perfect shelter and sustained delight. I had ordered the *Studies* (again from the Insel publishers), and they occupied me for a long time. And now, exactly one year later, an aquaintance sent me from London the *Late Summer* (in the old edition of 1857, Budapest, published by Gustav Heckenast—the first edition?). And although this rambling work, which is spun out at great length, does not carry with it the thrill of certain pages in the *Studies*, I nevertheless owe to it, also, so much composure that I feel a definite inclination to own Stifter's other works and not to leave acquaintance with the rest to chance, which seems prepared to occur once a year. Of greatest importance to me would be the letters (with a biography, three volumes, Budapest, 1869) and the two volumes of *Colored Pebbles* (1853, the same). However, my London friend wrote me that these old editions are fast becoming rarities. Then yesterday, for my elucidation, I open Meyer's *Encyclopaedia* and find, to my great joy, a notation that the Society for the Advancement of German Science, Art and Literature in Bohemia is concerning itself with the edition of Stifter's *Complete Works*. And from this now arises the request contained by this long preamble: write me, esteemed friend, whether this edition is actually in progress or even completed. And whether there would be a possibility for me to acquire it—perhaps by means of installment payments. It is true that for this I will not give up completely my desire to hunt up old copies, but it is likely that this desire may be fulfilled only with difficulty and perhaps very slowly. Then, I admit openly that I am also tempted to possess this new edition, on the assumption that its arrangement will be the fruit of your care and experience—and finally, it might even have been provided with a penetrating introduction by you (because without a doubt Stifter above all others touches your heart).

Am I mistaken, or is he really one of the few artistic figures who compensate and console us for the fact that Austria, in which complete permeation of all its parts with its essence was in no sense achieved, was unable to attain a language of its own? The older I become, the more painfully I carry forward this disadvantageous entry, it is figuratively entered as a debit at the top of each new page of my achievements. Having grown up within the language I am now using, I was nevertheless in a position to abandon it ten times, since it was necessary to build it up for myself independently of early language memories and even by suppressing them. The unhappy contact of disharmonious language units results in our countries in the progressive deterioration of the language at its fringes. It follows further from this that whoever might have grown up in Prague has been nurtured from infancy with such tainted language scraps that in later life he cannot restrain himself from developing an antipathy, even a kind of shame, toward all the earliest and most tender things he has been taught. Stifter, in the purer conditions of the Bohemian Forest, may have perceived less of this fatal environment of an adverse language-world, and thus he naïvely achieved through nature and nurture the structure of a German language, which I would like to claim, if any, as an Austrian language, except those parts which are merely a characteristic and peculiarity of Stifter's and nothing else. Amazing, however, is the authenticity with which it succeeds, even where it only stems from a most personal need, in establishing a clear model for the experience, wide in its limitation, of this mind. If, on the one hand, one may gauge the worth of the poet by how truly his words express the most secret depths of his soul, then one will have to count Stifter, in this sense, among the happiest and thus among the greatest figures. . . .

Finding myself at the end of the eighth page, I hastily end requests, reports, and questions with the old conclusion of gratitude and respect, which I never repeat without building it anew and feeling it stroke by stroke.

Your

Rilke

/ *August Sauer (1855–1926) was a literary historian at the University of Prague; Adalbert Stifter (1805–1868) was an Austrian novelist with a Wordsworth-like gift of mediation between nature and man.*

TO HELENE VON NOSTITZ

17 rue Campagne Première, Paris,

27 January 1914

. . . As I telegraphed you, Gide, whom I saw yesterday, knew of a newspaper report which was immediately afterward retracted. Besides that, I saw at an acquaintance's a letter of R[odin]'s written on the 21st, in which he told them that he felt *"malade un peu"* and would remain a few days in his room (there was no talk of going to bed).

I experienced, even now again, a real compulsion to go straightway to Meudon, and you mustn't think that any petty touchiness is keeping me from it; a feeling like that I would easily overcome, if I were able to entertain it at all toward Rodin. But that in itself really unimportant incident of last spring seems to me, when I think back, like a place at which the actually existing sickness of our present relationship clearly emerged, so that one could see how no real benefit was to be gained from it at present. Our intercourse was in fact unhappy and unfruitful, at least measured by that powerful necessity out of which it had formerly arisen and out of which it seemed always to shoot up into new healthy sprouts. This too is one of the curious limitations within human approaches, that it seems denied us, or at least surpasses our strength, one day to experience half, conditional, lesser things with someone with whom we have known how to get on in the greatest.

To this is added a kind of cowardice or perhaps merely caution: since I am now maintaining myself on so narrow a rim of calm and on it trying, sleep-walking rather than walking, to reach a place in my inner being on which I might quietly settle down to all kinds of confident achievement, every diversion into the external is fateful for me: fateful to see again places like Meudon, or even just the rue de Varenne, which I cannot glimpse without everything in me, disintegrated by sharp memories, assuming another structure, stopping, stiffening and, if at all, only slowly taking shape again in other forms.

Where feeling determines, one should not raise such misgivings, but I have behind me so many years that are lost or at least have almost eluded me, that I am now ruthlessly living toward a certain inner ownership and feel equal to drawing into my obstinate isolation *only* what I can immediately resolve and turn to use and nourishment for myself.

Beyond this I hope that after all there is no cause at present for real concern; haven't you tried writing a word to R. himself, perhaps you will receive the most reliable reassurance by a line from his own hand.

The cold which had the mastery here for two weeks seems since yesterday to have broken, perhaps this too will be to the good.

I was at Gide's yesterday, though I don't go out otherwise and don't see anyone, because I translated his *"Retour de l'enfant prodigue"* some time ago and

needed a few bits of information on passages doubtful
to me. The translation is to represent Gide in the Insel-
Bücherei, that work is beautiful and characteristic of
him (long a favorite of mine).

*/ Meudon was the location of Rodin's studio; the "incident
of last spring" refers to Rodin's refusal, for political reasons,
to go through with a promise to Clara Rilke that she might
do a bust of him; the Insel-Bücherei was Insel-Verlag's
series of paper-bound volumes.*

TO ILSE ERDMANN

17 rue Campagne Première, Paris,
the last day of January 1914

In the end it would still be for me like coercion,
were I to decide not to write you at all; could we not,
quite independent of one another, let ourselves go in
such a way that for either of us a letter is possible at
anytime, and that when it arrives, there be no challenge
for or even suggestion of a reply to either of us. This is
all the more easily conceivable, as the questions that we
give to one another to read are not at all arranged for
an actual answer; still they also include for me those
questions that move me the most, the most deeply, and
you may believe that for me, since the way exists, it
is natural to write to you in the same manner as it was
simply understood that you should have written to me.

About your last letter but one I would have to say
this to you: that an overestimate between us cannot
actually exist; we know much too little of each other to
attribute explicitly to one another the things that we
sense in each other; how far these things themselves lie

within our power, how far we may act familiarly with them in the rarest hours—what does it matter? We have still experienced these things—, and were it only the most momentary and most exceptional relation which they would permit us, that we know them is true, and this rich truth let us, where it comes to light, admire in one another calmly and without suspicion.

The joy that your beautifully descriptive letter gave me at the time could by no circumstances be taken from me by disappointment; for the reality of any joy in the world is indescribable, only in joy does creation happen (happiness, on the contrary, is only a promising and interpretable pattern of things already existing); joy, however, is a marvelous increasing of what already exists, a pure addition out of nothingness. After all, how lightly must happiness actually concern us, since it immediately leaves us time to think of its duration and to worry about it: joy is a moment, unobligated, from the first timeless, not to be held but not truly to be lost again, because under its impact our being changes chemically, so to speak, and does not only, as may be the case with happiness, savor itself and revel in a new combination.

Filled with this experience, I have protected myself from disappointment to a great extent, especially since the greater thing always has the right to be unexpected, to come and go, and I have long since ceased to expect it to arise as a consequence out of something previously great. As far as I am concerned, it does not stand in line, it steps forward, so to speak, always especially out of the unrecognizable and immeasurable depth, and therefore I never cease to feel it as a possibility, even there where it fails to appear.

Now let these lines convince you as much as possible that you may write me "completely freely," as to no one and to all, as one lifts one's gaze and, looking with the inner self, believes himself looking at the scenery in no other way; only so that the distance may be there which is necessary for writing.

Rainer Maria Rilke

TO BENVENUTA

from Paris,
8 February 1914

Oh, Benvenuta, what have I done, that the burden of *achievement* has always fallen to me in love, that, by my nature, I have never borne its sunny fruit, as an orange tree bears its innocent, blissful wealth? That I have had to go to and fro with it, like a slave in the marketplace, weighed down, carrying provisions which I could not see, which some god purchased over my head to use for his feasts, to which I was not bidden?

Children *rest* in love (has this been ever granted me?), but then, they are unsullied in their illusion that it is possible to belong to someone; and when they say "mine," they make no claim to ownership; they grasp and let go, and when they do not, they cling to God, with whom they retain a subtle connection, who draws even others to himself through their guiltless open arms.

Can *you* explain why it is that people always become my undoing? I shall confess to *you* that if at this moment my neighbor were to enter—a young Hungarian painter whom I scarcely know, and to whom I bring no more than the sympathy one feels for young people when one is no longer quite convinced of one's own youth—no more than that—if that young man were to enter here now, having no conceivable inkling of *what* preoccupies me—I should yet put aside my pen and for two hours on end, until I ran out of breath, relate impressions and memories to him, with the warmth (can *you* conceive of such a thing?)—with the warmth that belongs to *you*, that is of rights *yours* in this place— with that self-same suppressed warmth—what in the world is this? Surely not kindness, weakness, sickness, vanity, a crime? And I do the same thing with my work. The innermost tension that exists for its sake, to which it alone has a claim, is released in some less worthy cause, is spent, vanishes into thin air. Must I then not keep myself well-stoppered, as the merchants do their attar of roses? And, dear, am I not right in doing so? Why should I not say that I prefer to be alone? My friend, believe me, this is my sole desire. In the same breath with which I implore God to *let* me love you, I beg him, I implore him to strengthen my will for militant solitude, for such is the destiny of every fiber of my being. Oh, do you not feel it in my heart? —do you not feel it when you hold your hands against it—that ineffable urge to push everything aside, all tenderness, to stride irresistibly from deed to deed, down the hard and splendid path of action? Can you feel it? Is it not true that, in the end, there may be no need for anyone to lay my funeral pyre, since I myself have touched the torch of ecstasy to my unblemished heart, that it consume itself utterly and flare up in a single flame to God? But here I am under lock and key, you see, behind barred doors, yet I do not act. Once, unless I am mistaken, it seemed to me each morning, or now and then at least, as though each beginning were the first, the only one. Long since, now, it has been very different. The least and the greatest that I undertake —even ventures that are dear and familiar to me (and these perhaps most of all)—are burdened in advance

by such an indescribable weight of experience and suspicion of incapacity. In the morning, when I lay out
my work—sometimes, indeed, start on nothing more
than a letter—a sense of foreboding sweeps over me:
You shall not be able to do it!—and often enough I cannot. True, the crucial element in art—what people have
long called "inspiration"—is not within our power; but
that I have always understood—it could not be otherwise, because we are so fickle—and it has never troubled me; nor have I ever used the slightest means for
conjuring it up. To be patient in the face of the divine
is natural, for it is governed by standards of its own.
The difficulty arises from another side and has but
slowly spread its infection to the point where my real
certainties lie. A young and rather eccentric author (I
should like to send you his book—his name is Marcel
Proust—the pencil-marked copy over which I have
spent my evenings) speaks of a peculiar fear that
haunted his childhood and exerted great influence on
him. In the later course of his life, when there should
have been no more question of such a fear, he nevertheless thought he still recognized it in different guises,
c'est cette angoisse qui revient dans l'amour. If that be
true, mine is the next phase, *l'angoisse de ne pouvoir
pas aimer qui revient dans la travail.*

(The suddenly inspired familiar address does not
mean that I forgo the earlier form. I want to say everything to *you*—call *you* by every name—and thus keep
mindful that to me *you* are both nearness and distance,
that you are both an open door and refuge from it.)

My dear friend, I see *you* are familiar with *Brigge.*
There is no identity, of course, but it is true that he
absorbed much of my own life, some of it almost completely—yet what a different record it would be, if the
ineffable sorrows of the three or four years that have

elapsed since then were suddenly to be precipitated in words! The rift in my heart dates only from certain other events—that rift that must be the reason why my heart flutters so fitfully when it is touched by nature, by the stars, by lofty things. (You should have heard it before—the exalted purity with which it sounded forth, when purely touched!) That was on a great journey to another continent, when I had laid open my mind to the most powerful things; and since it lay wide open, fatefully distorted circumstances overwhelmed it at the same time. Deeply receptive, surrendered to grandeur, I was yet steeped in guilt and torment; I lost all my bearings, all self-assurance, but for that one spot in my heart which has retained its inborn stability in every vicissitude. I recall a night in a small hotel room in a Tunisian town—the nightmarish atmosphere in which I dwelt had infected my innermost being so frightfully that the very hands with which I touched myself seemed like strangers to me. There was no electric light, and I lit a candle. I sat on my bed—friend, sister, try to understand: That simple little flame, into which I must have so often drowsily gazed as a child—will you believe it, it was the first thing in a long time that I knew and recognized, a cherished survivor from an earlier, lost world—my world! Can you understand that? I was touched to the heart, felt a swelling sense of gratitude—something like the feeling that now joins me to you. . . .

You who are full of love—

. . . My life was never given a foundation. No one was able to imagine the direction of its growth. In Venice there stands the so-called Ca' del Duca, a princely fundament, on which subsequently the most wretched tenement came to be built. With me the case is opposite—the fine arches to which my spirit soared rest on the most tentative beginnings, on a wooden scaffold, a few flimsy boards. . . . Is that why I feel thwarted in rearing the nave, the steeple to which the burden of the great bells is to be hoisted (by angels—who else could do it?)? . . . How wonderful are great lives, how wonderful is *yours* to me, dear friend!—a life to which I suddenly speak as though I were talking to the clouds and the depths of my sky, to settle when there are to be showers in my nature and when the weather is to be clear.—How overwhelming is the impact night after night, from sky to earth! I sleep by open window, and when I open the bedroom casement (it adjoins the lofty studio where I live and work)—when I open it, I must first compose my face, that it be equal to the nearest star. How feeling overwhelms the spirit! What freedom in the soul! How overpowering the fellowship of man!

Tomorrow night *you* will be in Berlin. Perhaps my letter will be waiting for *you* there, the letter I wrote yesterday afternoon, still dispatching it to Vienna. This one I shall not be able to post until early tomorrow—my little post office takes Sunday seriously and will not be receptive again until tomorrow.

Farewell, dear true friend, champion on behalf of my future, fine, joyful heart, dear one, farewell! Tell me soon how it is with you in Berlin—I know many of your errands. . . .

R

(Here are three little pictures of me—may I soon have one of *you*? There are no others, for I have not allowed any to be taken for some ten years. In part, because I do not like self-conscious modern photographs (*old* ones all the more)—in part, because the indiscreet publicity of our age too readily broadcasts a picture, making it a fatuous article of commerce. As for Busoni's book (*Outline of a New Esthetics of Music*), I should like to devote some quiet hours to it, if I may have it from you; and if you have time for Proust's *Swann's Way,* I shall send it to you shortly).

/ *Benvenuta was Rilke's name for Magda von Hattingberg (who later became Frau Graedener), a concert pianist who had written to Rilke after reading his* Stories of God; *Rilke wrote the present letter, and several others, to Benvenuta before meeting her.*

TO BENVENUTA

from Paris,
Friday, 13 February early [1914]

The postcard from Berlin: how glad I am it is here—everything seemed so distant, so silent. I am abysmally ignorant of geography, which troubles me little, but I do not even know: are *you* now farther away, nearer at hand? Never mind, you are inconceivably close, in any event. Thus I shall swiftly dispatch these many sheets—the *femme de ménage* has already arrived. Good God, what will *you* have to read! I think it should be Sunday down *your* way.

Oh, love.
R

[With a long letter]

Joyous one, my familiar, how much there is that I would make real for myself within you, within your heart, Benvenuta! . . . Friends of my childhood, girls—what has become of them!—Blessed Theresa of Avila, could love's arrow have pentrated into thy heart more imperiously than the dazzling silver point of fulfillment into swooning foreboding? One saw them coming down the street, recognizable from afar in all the guises of their grace—in truth, sensed them with one's whole body before they even turned the corner in company of their Frenchwoman.

Was there one who had an inkling? . . . One of them did know. I shall not forget it—it was of a summer, in a little watering resort, her name was Hueber, Fräulein Hueber (of course I knew her first name as well); and her family name, which I only just realized I remember, had its own peculiar charm, in that it must on no account be pronounced Hüber, as might have seemed natural, but only Hu-eber, whether that was agreeable or not: I found it enchanting. I cannot recapture her image, by the way—a slender, fair-haired figure, half-averted, flits through my memory; and just how she behaved during that certain scene has utterly slipped my mind (a trace of laughter haunts my ear, but it may not even be hers). Yet I can visualize the noonday promenade at the spa, the crowds, though I cannot recall whether I happened to follow her, nor just what fuss I did make over her. This much alone is certain: My extravagant sentiments had been discovered and this is what took place: I was seized by both arms from behind, below the shoulders, and before I knew what was happening, I was pushed through the crowds and in the bright sunshine planted foursquare before Fräulein Hueber, who was thus prevented from proceeding; and while the vise in which I was held grew ever more unyielding, a loud, merry voice over my head related my secret story, rather accurately, I believe. I do not understand what further use I could have had for all the blood that shamed my face. . . . But now I think of the man, and try to fathom what it was that had prevailed upon him. Did he perhaps love her?

Good God, if I were now to tell you, my familiar, how I withdrew time and again from such upheavals, how humdrum was my life, compared to these extravagances—why, it seems to me I never properly knew love at all.

Not that we did not arouse each other, nor lacked endearments, nor failed, in saying good-night, to undergo all the turmoil of parting and hope for another meeting—all this was present (almost too much so, I am inclined to think); but it did not necessarily flow from an inner richness and generosity. We might even have saved ourselves the trouble, had it not been unceasingly exacted from us by a certain suspicion of life. Just as some dogs eat only when someone makes a gesture as though to take the food from their dish, we reached for each other only because there was disease in the world and incalculable danger, because someone was always dying, and because there were so many strange ways of drifting apart over all this. What joined us in this fashion must have been, above all, a kind of fear—yes, that is what it was!—we were mutually afraid of one another and for ourselves. We exhaled a dreadful fear of life and death, and then inhaled it again, diluted with only a tiny amount of real air. It was clear, moreover, so far as I was concerned, that the future was altogether unknown, and one sought to get that future into one's power, while it was still quite small, that it might grow up under restraint, as it were, never coming to know its own untamed character. . . .

You, you (what shall I call you, what carefully chosen name, what name dear enough for my heart which sweeps toward you?)—behold: all this I consider for the first time, you make it real for me (for what knew I thereof?). I must take my own good time in writing you, the words coming like the first heavy drops from the charged wine-press of my past. I sense it, somewhere back there, in the legendary sphere, I must begin with my love for you—I, the beginner.

R

13 February, toward evening

You must know, I read no newspapers, though every day I buy two of them, that I may occasionally keep informed about exhibitions and the tireless foreign literary life. There is also another reason, for were I suddenly to cease calling for my two journals, the newsstand woman, rather than surmising that I had suddenly lost all interest in current doings, would be persuaded that her *Figaro* was not late enough for me and insist that I was buying it elsewhere. (Is not, I sometimes ask myself, love wrongly lived the reason why, even in the most superficial human affairs, the very *act of cessation* is in such bad odor, as though, of rights, it should never occur?) As for the times—our own—one should keep one's eye on them, quite true; well, even though I scarcely read about them, I do see on occasion what goes on and wonder to myself. . . .

In yesterday's *Figaro* there was a prominent article entitled *"De l'amour"* and signed "Foemina," which is to say, Madame Bulteau. I read Madame Bulteau occasionally, and if I muster the necessary resolve, it has to do with the fact that Mme. B. was the best friend of the late Countess de la Beaume, and that this Mme. de la Beaume left two rather strange books that strike a note of great intensity (the second surprised even those who had been close to this unusual and modest woman). It is for the sake of these striking books by another woman that I occasionally read Madame Bulteau who, on her part, is quite accomplished (you can see how everything with me arises cunningly and surreptitiously—are you beginning to feel uneasy?). So I began to read *"De l'amour"* too, yesterday, but did not get very far. What is this curious mixture of virtuosity and incapacity they call by that name here (and cannot mention often enough)? On the one hand the most exquisite skill, on the other everlasting frustration. Do you know what I felt like?—leafing through Plato's *Symposium* for the first time in a long while. When I first read it, I dwelt alone in Rome in a tiny house deep in an ancient park (the same house where I began *Brigge*, as yet unaware of what was to become of it). My friend, I grasped one thing then, predisposed as I may have been—there is no beauty in Eros; and when Socrates said so and in his cautious way waited for his younger and more volatile conversational antagonist to block all other paths, one by one, leaving but the one way open—that Eros is not beautiful—Socrates himself then walking that path toward his god, serene and pure in heart—how then my innermost nature took fire that Eros could not be fair! I saw him just as Socrates had invoked him, lean and hard and always a little out of breath, sleepless, troubled day and night about the two between whom he trod, to and fro, hither and yon, ceaselessly accosted by both: yes, that was Eros. Truly, how they mistook him who thought he was fair, envied his soft life. Ah, he was slender and tanned and covered with the dust of the road, but there was no peace for him amid the two of them (for when, I say, is there not distance left between them?); and when he came he spoke with fervor of the other's beauty, teasing each heart to grow fairer, goading it on. Surely there is much in the book—we do not grasp it yet: once upon a time it *was* grasped—who lost it? How do we spend the centuries? Where is he among us who dares speak of *love?*

Verily, nature speaks not of love; nature bears it in her heart and none knows the heart of nature. Verily, God bears love in the world, yet the world overwhelms us. Verily, the mother speaks not of love, for it is borne for her within the child, and the child destroys it. Verily, the spirit speaks not of love, for the spirit thrusts it into the future, and the future is remote. Verily, the lover speaks not of love, for to the lover it comes in sorrow, and sorrow sheds tears. Hush, hush—oh, it is music, then, that would speak! But when music speaks, she speaks not to us. The perfect work of art touches upon us only in that it survives us. A poem enters into language from within, in an aspect forever averted from us. It fills the language wondrously, rising to its very brim—but it never again thrusts toward us. Colors are congealed in a picture, but they are broidered into it like rain into the countryside; and all that the sculptor shows his stone is how it may most splendidly hold itself aloof. Music, indeed, is closer to our heart . . . but how much of her is beyond our reach, pushes just past us, carries right through us—and we comprehend it not! . . .

Benvenuta, you yourself, have you not at times sought to halt her, your heart filled with perplexity—and failed? Or would have failed, but for the angels that descend on you?

(Tell me much about your present good surroundings—above all, tell me much.)

TO ANNA BARONESS VON MÜNCHHAUSEN

> from Hotel Marienbad, Munich,
> Ascension of the Virgin, 1914 [15 August]

Who: who would have thought it! And now one thinks nothing but this, and everything former has become as it were immemorial, separated from one through abysses and heights of no longer feelable feeling. . . .

The high heart of all those who are out there must sustain us over the still water of not-knowing and not-grasping which sometimes threatens to engulf even me.

/ Rilke, who thought the war was glorious—for a little while —also wrote an enthusiastic letter on the same day to the Baroness's son, Thankmar, a lieutenant in the Hussars.

TO ANNA BARONESS VON MÜNCHHAUSEN

> from Pension Landhaus Schönblick,
> Irschenhausen—Post Ebenhausen,
> Isartalbahn, Bavaria,
> 29 August 1914

. . . If I could only send him something soon again from a more uplifted heart; he is riding forth there so bold and gloriously-young, really it is wonderful, this ancient knight's destiny upon a young man of today, unawares.

Gradually I am beginning to find my having stayed behind in the rear of so much break-up bewildering and vexatious: in the first days my spirit went along with the general current, could in its own way join in; then, as one unspeakably isolated, I remembered myself, my old heart as it had been hitherto (which I cannot give up), and now I am having a very hard time finding, by myself, across this span, the valid and if possible somehow fruitful attitude toward the monstrous generality. Happy those that are in it, carried away by it, drowned out by it.

Until now I have, in spite of circumstances, lived according to my plans; was in Munich to confer with and be treated by my doctor, came out here Monday on his advice; but this is now the most unendurable of all, to side with unsuspecting Nature and take care of one's self. While I am trying it, an impatience and a discontent are growing in my breast which I shall not long be able to stand. Probably I shall go back to Munich after all and then to Bohemia to my friends there: to see if I can't make myself somewhat useful from there and leave "convalescing" and "getting strong" for later, until we (when?) are across the terrible mountainrange in the unforseeable future which no one can picture to himself.

The Hölderlin volume is a comfort now; wonderful, that these poems live and reach to one's heart through all the tangle of apprehension. I read the *Hyperion* too with keenest participation: how much it sounds like what is happening to us, and yet from the start goes far beyond it, forming pure clouds above the war and above love. . . .

/ *The friends in Bohemia were the Prince and Princess von Thurn und Taxis;* Hyperion *is a novel by Hölderlin.*

TO LOU ANDREAS-SALOMÉ

from Landhaus Schönblick, Irschenhausen,
9 September 1914

How often, dear Lou, in this monstrous August, have I known that there was just one place where one might really survive it: with you, in your garden; for if one can imagine two people to whom this unsuspected time brings exactly the same suffering, the same daily horror, we are they—how could we help it?

Thus I felt your telegram and understood it more deeply than I can say, but still I don't at all know how to answer its questions right away,—so little have I yet considered what one might go on to do on one's own initiative. Since this fortnight out here in the country I have really been hesitating, from the very beginning, only between two decisions: going back to the city, or, if it is really a matter of recuperating, taking the cure at Ebenhausen, where at least baths, sunbaths, etc., would be at my disposal. Just staying in the country is, this year particularly, a halfhearted business, since one lacks the simplicity of mind to be with Nature; her influence, her quiet penetrating presence is outweighed from the start through the mere thought of the nameless human doom that is happening irresistibly day and night. I would almost have gone back to Munich; but then Clara wrote that she wanted in any case to come back with Ruth for the opening of school, which would be around the end of this week—and so I hesitate, for she hasn't much money and if I am to help her I can most easily do it from here, where I need little for myself and each week exactly the same. My arrangements with Insel-Verlag, which looked so comforting, are not exactly canceled, but, as Kippenberg told me in the end, they hold only "when possible." That of course is already a good deal, for how much has not become simply *im*possible. Freiburg, for example: a gleam of probability finally fell upon the plan, when we were considering everything in Leipzig, that I should attempt certain studies there in the Schwarzwald air, not too far from Paris, near Colmar and other lovely places. I would like, even now, to choose my next abode with these intentions in mind—which incidentally, imagine it, greatly surprised and pleased Stauffenberg, who in the back of his mind wanted and planned something very similar for me. The good man had prepared himself for me as honestly and fully as it is possible to do through my books and from his own most sympathetic attitude,—so that what we said seemed merely the continuation of all the inner intercourse with me which had long been natural to him. Against this background it was not easy, in the continually disturbed present, to find the composure for our talks, but the time he always found, whole hours, even when work in the hospital was piling up around him on all sides; then he would come to me or we would quickly arrange for a walk together.—The result? He kept trying to get to the region in which he believes he has particular authority, and we did walk across it now and again, only that all digging and hoeing and real work there remained out of the question. With terror I sometimes felt a sort of spiritual nausea which he was trying to bring on; it would be awful to throw up one's childhood like that in fragments, awful for a person who is not committed to resolving the unconquered part of it within himself but exists quite particularly for the purpose of using it up in converted form, in discoveries and feelings, in things, in animals—in what not?—if need be, in monstrosities.—At one of his thorough examinations Stauffenberg discovered an old pulmonary lesion, harmless and unimportant in its way, and from then on there was at least something definite to warrant his dealing strictly physically with me, which made things easier for both of us. . . .

Dear Lou, this is about how things stand with me. Write me about yourself, what you may be thinking. Herewith a few pages written in August, chiming in with the universal theme. How one's *own* looks in with it, what it will become because of it, I am but slowly understanding—I keep thinking, as with approval, of those who have died in these last years, and that they no longer had to grasp all this from here.—Write me; meanwhile I shall see better what is to be done.

/ *The mention of Freiburg refers to Rilke's intermittent plan of studying at a small university; Emil von Stauffenberg was his physician; the "few pages written in August" were* Five Songs, *war poems which appeared in the 1915 Insel-Almanac.*

TO FRAU HANNA WOLFF

from Munich,
29 January 1915

. . . I would have been so glad to see you . . . but: I must consistently and strictly sequester myself, after a month and a half of Berlin have brought me much strain and confusion; physically exhausted and unprecise in mind I came back here to be silent, to keep myself absolutely hidden, nothing else. My sequestration is still too new to bear an exception so soon, so it is safer for me to decline and go to bed, following my rule, at 8:30.

The uncertainty out there, this flickering world in which one can place no object, no word even, without its casting most unquiet shadows, quite unconditionally obliges me to draw myself in; perhaps thus one may arrive at some further inward place, where one has never oneself been, and from there out be stable. . . . Who would have thought, when in the beginning of August we strolled from the Englischer Garten through the excited city, that for so many months the anomaly then beginning would still be unresolved over us and in the right. In the right for how long—and so much that is wrong! . . .

TO THANKMAR BARON VON MÜNCHHAUSEN

from 2/IV Finkenstrasse, Munich,
6 March 1915

. . . The *Cornet* was being performed in Leipzig with music . . . I could not positively advise [your mother] to go, for this reciting to music is a running-along of one art beside the other as though it depended on which won: and only one does actually win. . . . So, my dear boy, I quite unexpectedly find myself among the authors of this exceptional year, my voice of fifteen years ago speaks into the attentive ear of the people who have been frightened for months—mine? The voice of that one distant night of my youth in which I wrote the *Cornet*, stimulated to it by clouds passing in strange flight high across the moon. . . .

But from the fact that Christopher Rilke is thus being turned to account today you may notice again and again how dumb we have grown here. I am sure everyone is so at heart; even if a few must hear themselves and pluck their strings with this thought and that, there is no one who can draw sounds from the air that sweeps through him, not even to lament,—it is a silence of halted, interrupted hearts. I am certain no one loves in these days; however much one or another heart may achieve, it acts out of some sort of universal stores of human kindness, warmth, willingness and devotion, it does not give what is its own, but behind every act primeval store-rooms of human need are opened up; even you out there act and struggle out of such strengths as were hoarded up in some sort of barns of involuntary fellowship. It seems to me as though the heart in each of us were only passing things on, confined to gazing in astonishment at the store that is going through its hands.

What we are doing here, so far as reading still counts as doing (for who could achieve a contemplative mood?), is to read Hölderlin (over and over), I for my part Strindberg, Montaigne, Flaubert, the Bible. . . . There are some new Werfel poems, one tries them and yet is elsewhere and cannot get back into the tone of day before yesterday. . . .

/ *"The* Cornet" *refers to* The Song of the Love and Death of Cornet Christopher Rilke (*based on the experiences of a 17th-century Rilke*), *which was a prose poem written in 1899, first published in 1906, and then, with astonishing success, in 1912; the musical setting Rilke refers to here was by Kasimir von Paszthory.*

TO PRINCESS MARIE VON THURN
UND TAXIS-HOHENLOHE

from (c/o Koenig)
32/III Widenmayerstrasse, Munich,
9 July 1915

. . . Thank God, I said, thought, felt at the news
about Duino and still dared not answer Thank God
aloud to you, for so long as havoc is in the world, who
may breathe freely, who may consider anything safe,
spared, rescued? In personal matters as well as in general it is a giving up, an offering of all possession, at
what cost? At what cost; if only there were not that
question, who would not cast off everything that was
his and himself into the bargain, if he but understood,
if he but guessed, that, sheerly surviving, a thing needs
such underpinnings in order to rise up further?—We,
some of us, have long been feeling continuities that
have nothing in common with the course of history;
even over the present vicissitude the furthest past and
the furthest future will come to an understanding, but
we, constrained between yesterday and tomorrow,
shall we ever again simply, quietly, serenely take part
in the swing of great affairs? Or remain frightened below with the stamp of a period on our shoulders, co-
knowers of unforgettable details, co-responsible for the
big as for the merely fearful, used up by this endurance
and performance and persistence—; and shall we not
then later, forever, as we are learning to do now, defer
all understanding, hold what is human to be inextricable, history to be a primeval forest to the soil of which
we never reach because it lies, layer on layer, unend-
ingly, upon tumbled stuff, an apparition on the back
of destruction—?

Are you reading, and what? I have been busy with
Hermann Keyserling, also with Strindberg, the Strindberg of the truly incredible *Ghost Sonata* (very mov-
ingly performed here), the most important thing in the
theater besides Georg Büchner's *Wozzek,* which the
Hoftheater . . . generously came out with. A monstrous affair, written more than eighty years ago . . .
nothing but the fate of a common soldier (around
1848) who stabs his faithless sweetheart, but power-
fully setting forth how, around the most trivial existence, for which even the uniform of a common infan-
tryman seems too wide and too much emphasized,
how even around the recruit Wozzek all the greatness
of existence stands, how he cannot prevent, now here,
now there, before, behind, beside his dull soul, horizons
from being torn open onto violence, immensity, the infinite; an incomparable play, the way this misused
person in his stable-jacket stands in universal space,
malgré lui, in the infinite relationship of the stars. That
is theater, that is what theater could be like . . .

/ *Duino Castle was later severely damaged, and in 1918
the Princess found it "but a phantom"; Wozzek was the
Büchner play subsequently made into an opera by Alban
Berg.*

TO HELENE VON NOSTITZ

from (c/o Koenig)
32/III Widenmayerstrasse, Munich,
12 July 1915

Yesterday, Sunday, came your letter. I should
have answered it that same evening, but before I can
persuade my pen—writing now means somehow pre-

vailing over oneself, for what to write when everything one touches is unspeakable, unrecognizable, when nothing belongs to one, no feeling, no hope; when an enormous provision, gotten I know not where, of suffering, despair, sacrifice and misery is used up in large amounts, as though everybody were somewhere in the whole mass, and the single person nowhere; nowhere any longer is the measure of the individual heart applicable which used to be the unit of the earth and the heavens and all expanses and abysses. What used the cry of a drowning man to mean—even if it was the village idiot, who with a suddenly sharper cry reached out of the water, everybody flew to the scene and was on his side and against his sinking, and the swiftest risked his life for him. How immemorial everything has become, Heiligendamm, times, like childhood itself, so remote and innocent—who will ever feel them again!? You say that "one now feels Beethoven and the stars more deeply and more overpoweringly"; that is perhaps because (as you write) a personal sorrow has come to you out of the continuously common lot—perhaps that helps. It is not so with me; for me all that, all that is biggest and most stirring, remains attached to the other world, the earlier, the former world, in which I had long been a sufferer, but never a numb person, never an emptied-out person, never a person shouted at who does not understand. The longer it lasts,—the disturbing thing is not the fact of this war, but that it is being used and exploited in a business-ridden, a nothing but human world, that the god himself, once someone has flung it into that world, cannot call it back, because people cling to it greedily, with all the weight of their heavy conscience. Man-work, as everything has been man-work in the last decades, bad work, work for profit, save for a few painful voices and pictures, save for a few warning figures, a few zealous individuals who clung to their own hearts, which stood against the stream. Rodin, how often, as always, repeated words of disapprobation, mistrust for the course of things; it was even too much for me that he always did it with the same expressions. I took it for weariness and yet it was judgment. And Cézanne, the old man, when one told him of what was going on, and he could break out in the quiet streets of Aix and shriek at his companion: *"Le monde, c'est terrible . . ."* As of a prophet one thinks of him, and longs for one who will cry and howl like that—but they all went away beforehand, those old men who would have had the power to weep now before the peoples. . . .

/ *Heiligendamm: in July and August of the summer of 1913, Rilke had visited this old spa near Mecklenburg with Frau von Nostitz and her husband.*

TO PRINCESS MARIE VON THURN UND TAXIS-HOHENLOHE

from c/o Koenig,
32/III Widenmayerstrasse, Munich,
2 August 1915

How should I not constantly with all my heart be with you, when participation in what you suffer and hope is so thoroughly natural to me. I do not understand the present hell, but how you bear it and go through with it I do understand. There are few constants in human affairs, and how many have changed, have become incomprehensible—have taken on the color of a time that could not itself say whether it has a color, a time that I believe is going on at some still undiscovered point of the spectrum, in an ultra-red that goes beyond our senses. . . .

Munich is getting empty, I imagine it has just about its usual summer appearance. I have outwardly the most even days, but inwardly it's an abyss, one is living on the edge, and below there lie, perhaps in pieces, who knows, the things of one's former life. Was it that? I say to myself a hundred times, was it that, which in these last years has been lying upon us as a monstrous pressure, this frightful future that now constitutes our cruel present? I have to think of how I one day said to Marthe: *Marthe, il n'y aura devant moi que des désastres, des terreurs, d'angoisses indicibles; c'est avec vous que finnessent les bontés de ma vie—*, it came out of me just like that, as though in the midst of a calm the impact of a storm had torn it out of me. I pricked up my ears as I heard myself say it, I was thinking only of my own curiously collapsing destiny and did not guess that the world as a whole would be bringing forth destruction. And Marthe made an unforgettable gesture of taking-me-under-protection. Now for the first time do I realize, it was just like that that those two powerful old men went around, Tolstoy and Cézanne, and uttered warnings and threats, like prophets of an ancient covenant that is soon to be broken—and they did not want to live to see that break. Whatever comes, the worst of it is that a certain innocence of life in which after all we grew up, will never exist for any of us again. The years ahead of us, many as they are —what will they be but a descent, with trembling knees, from this mountain of pain, up which we are still being dragged ever farther. . . .

You are reading Balzac, I have always stuck to Flaubert, read a wonderfully fresh early version of the *Edu-*

cation Sentimentale which has scarcely anything in common with the later novel: for the latter is highly deliberative, spontaneous sentiment occurs in it only as in rich savory translation. And then Strindberg. They are giving the *Dance of Death* here, after the incredible *Ghost Sonata,* and these dramas have almost reconciled me to the theater, which for years has given me nothing. At first it seems so hopelessly obstinate to present humanity's disconsolation as its absolute condition, but when someone like this has power over even the most disconsolate, there hovers above the whole, unspoken, a concept of illimitable human greatness. And a desperate love. . . .

TO ILSE ERDMANN

[from Munich]
11 September 1915, Saturday

. . . I am beset by circumstances that constrain me within my most private perceptions and concerns; my being is at almost no point able to lift itself up to more general matters; were I to have to speak of the times, the war, indeed of any phenomenon of the outer or inner existence, I should have to do so in the most subjective form—that is, in the most agonizing form; in the end I would prove to be the one who is basically most awkward, indeed almost the one who seeks help, while you instead are determined to address me as the helper. And I know that it is no presumption and direct untruth, if I let you act as if I were actually helping. This is a supposition between us, the proof of which we disregard—, and in the end no one among the lonely knows anyway whether, in his own misery, he was even then consoling to the other, whether the gestures of his own helplessness were not effective signs and nods in the realm of the incalculable.

Only this much: whatever you have found of security in my books are no longer the securities upon which I live. Spiritually as well as often physically, I have at this time been deprived of all support, I maintain, so to speak, an impossible position, but since I maintain it, a power is probably acting upon me which I perhaps gradually make my own, since after all it proves itself in me. The fact that, enveloping this internal affliction, the world, now also afflicted, has been shattered, surrounds my troubled heart with indescribable gloom. In order to know how badly these times affect me you have to realize that I do not feel "German,"—not in any way; although I cannot be a stranger to the German essence, because I am imbued to my marrow with its language, nevertheless its present application and its present angrily remonstrative self-consciousness have, as far as I can think, caused me only abashedness and insult; and to be completely at home in the Austrian spirit, which has remained throughout the times a superficial compromise (the untruth as a state), to be completely at home in the Austrian spirit is for me totally inconceivable and incomprehensible! How should I, I whose heart Russia, France, Italy, Spain, the desert, and the Bible have shaped, how should I have accord with those who brag around me! Enough.

I have thought much about your attitude to physical pain and have noticed that a mere honesty in it may not necessarily lead to complete poverty, since actually it is not itself a lack, but a display (in the body). And about the profound sharing in the experience of death: is it not the same as with the ugly in art, which precisely by being overcome by art loses its stigma?

—thus in life it becomes primarily a matter of experience and with it our tension becomes dead with the
dead, a cause for accomplishment, something of our
own: A greater richness through death.

RMR

TO ELLEN DELP

from 32/III Widenmayerstrasse
[Munich],
Sunday [10 October 1915]

. . . I must leave these rooms tomorrow, as the
owner is returning from the country, and with them
the glorious big Picasso beside which I have been living for almost four months now. Four months—what
times are passing and how? For me with always more
dismal insight into the in-sanity and non-sense into
which everything is incorrigibly pressing on, using
man's energy and man's existence, which were there
for what is beyond all naming, as names for something
arbitrary and imposed and overdone. What a helplessness this will make afterwards, when all the accepted
orthodox concepts are taken off the pedestals upon
which they have been exhibited, and the bewildered
survivors will want to attach themselves again to the
abandoned laws of innermost being. Can no one, then,
check and prevent it? Why are there not a few, three,
five, ten, who stand together and cry in the public
squares: enough! and who will be shot down and will
at least have given their lives that it should be enough,
while those out there are now succumbing only so that
the frightful thing shall go on and on and there shall
be no taking account of destruction. Why is there not

one who cannot endure it any more, will not endure it
any more; did he but cry out for one night in the midst
of the untrue, flag-hung city, cry out and not let himself be pacified, who might therefore call him liar?
How many are holding this cry back with difficulty,
—or no? If I am mistaken and there are not many who
could cry like that, then I do not understand human
beings and am not one myself and have nothing in
common with them.

Forgive me, Ellen, but I have felt like this for nearly
a year, I storm it out against you because you are a
girl and looking towards high things and moreover in
your inmost feelings full of equilibrium after your rides
through the radiance of autumn into its new open-
nesses. . . . So you will be able to stand it all right if
one's bitterest heart overflows. . . .

/ *"The glorious big Picasso" was* Saltimbanques (*1905*),
the inspiration of the fifth of the Duino Elegies *and later
bought by the Art Institute of Chicago.*

TO ELLEN DELP

from 11 Keferstrasse, Munich,
27 October 1915

Were you, Ellen, happy Ellen, not so secure in
having gone through and come through the almost impenetrable present, I would have to reproach myself
for having brought up again, in my recent letter, the
vast impending doom in all its strength and persistence. But it has not done you any harm, I feel, since
"through the thick of it" (as you say) you have come
on to open ground again, in the deep surviving world

of Nature, with which your whole being is in harmony.

Was this way possible for me as well? I also am pushing on, but I linger all too much on my way through, Nature behind things does not draw me enough, "tree, beast and season," all that no longer has the immediate magic for me which at times, like a sheer decree to be happy, could still prevail over my heart, however much entangled. "Working after Nature" has in such a high degree made that which is into a task for me, that only very rarely now, as by mistake, does a thing speak to me, granting and giving without demanding that I reproduce it equivalently and significantly in myself. The Spanish landscape (the last I experienced to the utmost)—Toledo—drove this attitude of mine to its extreme: since there the external thing itself—tower, hill, bridge—already possessed the incredible, unsurpassable intensity of the inner equivalents through which one might have been able to represent it. External world and vision everywhere coincided as it were in the object; in each a whole inner world was displayed, as though an angel who embraces space were blind and gazing into himself. This world, seen no longer with the eyes of men, but in the angel, is perhaps my real task—at least all my earlier experiments would come together in it; but to begin that task, Ellen, how protected and resolved one would have to be!

TO ANTON KIPPENBERG

from 11 Keferstrasse, Munich,
15 February 1916

. . . To add a brief account of personal matters: [In Vienna] from December 13th on, I finally achieved, shortly before enlistment, not having to go to Turnau (even that was very hard to achieve!). Called up on the 4th [of January], I joined in almost three weeks' duty and training in barracks; my physical inability to go on fortunately coincided with a new summons to the War Archives; thither I was ordered the end of January. My situation there (office hours from nine to three) is now outwardly better and more comfortable, but probably untenable if I do not succeed in being transferred to purely mechanical copy or registration work; for the fiction-service at which these gentlemen have been practicing for a year and a half is utterly impossible for me. I cannot describe it, it is very paltry and ambiguous in nature and the stoppage of all intellectual functions (as was the case in barracks) seems enviable alongside this crooked and irresponsible misuse of writing activity. The gentlemen themselves call it "hairdressing the hero"; for a long time they shuddered at the thought, but now they have overcome their objections and turn it out with a flick of the wrist. There will certainly be lots of difficulties, —for the moment, they do not know what to do with me and are keeping me in that incalculable idleness which belongs to the most intense military experiences. The being spent and weary, as it came over me in the period in barracks, has understandably enough not been removed by the new position; at three I get out of the office, eat, go home by trolley-car (i.e., Park Hotel, Hopfner, Hietzing, Vienna XIII) and yet am not in a condition to give the little remainder of the day its own stamp and its own meaning. For that I am too full of rolling stones from the mountains of strangeness that have fallen over me. I taste, if I try myself for a moment, nothing but patience, patience in which nothing is dissolved, pure, colorless patience. . . .

You ask about my work. Almost—no, certainly—the most provoking thing is that a fortnight before the muster here, in which my lot was drawn, I was in a rapid ascent of work, a fore-storm of work, some curious single poems, the *Elegies,* everything mounted and flowed, and the stores of Michelangelo increased from day to day in a manner indescribably surpassing myself. Never before have I written down such strong and accurate and clean translations. I already thought the freest prospects were ahead, when the grey army cloth fell before my clarified vision. . . .

/ Rilke, at this time, after "the grey army cloth" had obscured his "clarified vision," was at a depth of discouragement that made him consider giving up his poetry for a medical career; his reference to Turnau concerns the place where, as a native of Bohemia, he would probably have had to take his military training; the present letter was written during four days' leave from the Vienna military duty it describes, and four months before Frau Kippenberg's petition, signed by leading intellectuals, helped Rilke obtain a leave of absence that proved to be permanent.

TO HUGO VON HOFMANNSTHAL

from Hopfner's Park Hotel, Hietzing,
Vienna XIII,
28 March 1916

You cannot know (or do you feel it?) how I reproached myself—that same afternoon—for having been so talkative about a lot of my own affairs, old ones in part, wholly worth forgetting—, this having let myself go really calls for a special apology. But I have so often in the last months wished for a talk with you and imagined, in feeling, that no one could understand my position better than you yourself—so that my tongue at last just ran away with me and I couldn't stop it.

Not to continue this outpouring, on the contrary to relieve you of the last afterthought concerning it, I will just tell you what happened yesterday. The most important seems to me that Lieut.-Colonel V. sent for me, asked about my situation and finally instructed me to have the Munich Headquarters release sent to the War Archives. It would have been called in already had they known exactly where to ask for it. Once the document was there, he would see what could be done with it, and he hopes in this way to get me entirely free. So from this side everything possible will surely be done. This interest of my superiors is extraordinary and it goes without saying that I no longer complain of remaining idle here either, since it is only an expression of this same tendency to eliminate me from the whole apparatus until I am fully discharged.

So I beg you, my dear Hofmannsthal, not to worry about me, also not to tell anyone of my complaint, for now that this extremely well-intentioned effort is impending I must of course admit that my position is bearable, no worse than any time of waiting. I am still not yielding to too great confidence, to be sure—who knows how far the Munich decree is still alive—but if the War Archives administration's plan doesn't suceed, one may be sure nobody's would have.

Troublesome as I may have made myself the other day, to me the hours with you were extraordinarily delightful and at a distance so pleasantly linked with those first ones years ago. It was all most enjoyable and of your Picasso I think with amazement. . . .

/ *Hugo von Hofmannsthal (1874–1929) was the Austrian poet who, upon hearing of Rilke's conscription, had exclaimed, "The poor child, the poor child!" "Your Picasso" refers to an early self-portrait of the artist, with a blue background.*

TO ELIZABETH MAYER

from 11 Keferstrasse, Munich,
6 November 1916

To save Hanns Holdt the trouble, I shall myself answer your question regarding the *Cornet Rilke;* but first of all I must reproach myself for having so long delayed my answer. The reason for this is partly that, after having spent half a year in military service, I have to work off the very large arrears of my correspondence; partly because I hoped from day to day to be able to give you a more precise and more definite reply to your question. Namely, almost at the same time with your letter, I received a letter from the Insel-Verlag, informing me that Herr von Pásztorý has now made all possible efforts to obtain the authorization to have his composition printed. To this day I do not know if the publishing house had to give in to the wish of the composer; they would only comply unless they could prove their right of refusal. The editor of the Insel-Verlag knows well that I would not be greatly in favor of the musical use of my youthful work, and he is, of course, bound to be afraid, as I am too, that a publication in print of the music to the *Cornet* would also remove the last obstacles for performances, which now take place already too frequently and too emphatically. Therefore I have still hope that the work of Pásztorý will remain in manuscript. Should, however, destiny decide otherwise, I shall inform you of the publication of the music, as you wish it. With regret: since I should like to preserve my *Cornet,* particularly for its friends, as it was felt and was given once (about twenty years ago).

Though not knowing you personally, but with reference to Hanns Holdt, I am, with respectful greetings:

Rainer Maria Rilke

/ *Elizabeth Mayer, a friend of Hans Carossa, was married to a psychiatrist; now a translator, she lives in New York City; the present letter, previously unpublished, is of particular interest because Rilke's break with Magda von Hattingberg (Benvenuta) was caused by her insistence upon playing at her concerts a musical setting for the* Cornet *(with someone else reading the text aloud).*

TO ELISABETH TAUBMANN

from 11 Keferstrasse, Munich,
18 May 1917

. . . How long I have left you without an answer. By this I clearly see the degree of my numbness and apathy. The present time with all its hindrances and its activity gone to the most frightful ruin is like lead poured around me—, I cannot move, not outwardly and not far inwardly. And should there still be some life in my inmost being, I am too blunt and too untransparent to feel and recognize myself in it. . . .

After our meetings in Paris I completely absorbed only Cézanne's work; later paintings, with the exception of a few Henri Rousseaus, did not claim my full attention, on the one hand because Cézanne still seemed to me the biggest and most modern, then also because long journeys had, as is their way, filled me with pictures and demands which, without the misfortune of the war, I would have developed and worked up within myself. Only in the "exile" in which I live here did I begin, more out of *désœuvrement* than receptivity, to look about me again, and here I began to get a feeling for Picasso (as certain pictures chanced to come through here, and other important ones are privately owned in Munich). Among the Germans it was Franz Marc, who fell in the war, that interested me particularly; sculptors none—and if you ask me how I feel about these artists, I am really embarrassed to give an answer that would be useful and to the point; for how much else forces itself upon our eyes that purports to be art and often in fact carries a certain strength and conviction. Directions and individuals, of yesterday and today—no, I could not say how many of them are in the right, within the law—I do not know. I must assume that our experiences are shifting always further into the invisible, into the bacillary and microscopic: and thus it is possible to understand the absurd violence with which painting, like the stage, comes to display its magnified and wrenched-out objects. What violence here too, how little Nature, how little peace.

Ah, I would counsel you, Frau Elisawetta, to work heart and soul from the stores of life, out of the savings of only subjects you yourself have experienced without trying to orient yourself too much with regard to other contemporaries, at most in connection with a few reliable experiences with the really great. Too bad you did not stick to painting. . . . But now you are a sculptor. And at the same time hold livable life in your sure hands. Do let me sometimes watch and listen, even should I prove unfit as an advisor, cut off as I now am from everything.

/ *Elisabeth Taubmann was a painter whom Rilke had known in Paris.*

TO CLARA RILKE

from Hotel Esplanade, Bellevuestrasse,
Berlin W.,
19 November 1917

I was about to write you a little birthday letter yesterday when I got the news of Rodin's death, and then all my thoughts, you may imagine, were switched in that direction and rearranged. My wishes now stand before that background, which you and I still immeasurably share—like me you will be steeped in memories and sorrow and, with Paris and all we have lost in it, will have to go through this now so final loss. I do not know what Rodin's death would have meant to me in normal circumstances—perhaps something after all reconcilable—; for the present, I am dominated by perplexity that something so close should come to pass without standing out at all sharply defined against the chaos of the time, that behind the unnatural and terrible wall of the war these clearly known figures sink away from one, somewhere—Verhaeren, Rodin, those great wise friends—their death becomes indistinct and indiscernible . . . I only feel that they will not be there any more when the horrible vapor clears away, and will not be able to stand by those who will have to raise the world up again and nurse it. Yesterday and today I received a few deeply moved letters about Rodin—if I could only still properly believe in the power of human emotion, in the midst of this predominating inhumanity.

But now the heartiest wishes, dear Clara. Have a good birthday as a new landed proprietress; may you, together with the growth of a life that is awaiting its peaceful time, set yourself up a dear little house on your home soil. I do hope Grandmother has seen to providing the materials for about the right (white flour) sort of birthday cake. I can't send anything of the sort from here, only occasionally in a private house is one surprised by such desserts. . . .

/ Rodin had died on 17 November at Meudon; "Grandmother" was Clara's mother.

TO BERNHARD VON DER MARWITZ

from Hotel Continental, Munich,
9 March 1918

At how many times in my life I would have been able to reply in full measure to a letter of the cordiality of yours. To let you take even the smallest part in my life now would mean plunging you into a poverty so great that I have not sufficient means to describe it. What might, under the violent and extraordinary conditions of your present life, make you desirous of getting letters, is surely only the assurance which flows from them that intellectual and spiritual continuity has not been given up in this land of ours. And it is just that for which I cannot produce the least evidence. On the contrary, where I am concerned, all general circumstances and the most difficult personal ones have worked together to interrupt all flow in me and to separate me from the nourishment that otherwise, even in the worst days, rose up to me imperceptibly from unerring roots. The more I felt this fatality, the more I began to look about in the disastrous events of the time, but this very orientation made me more and more miserable. For where for us here is the visible in this desperate world? Doesn't one think one should, laden with the years-long consciousness of whatever of evil is fulfilling itself therein, finally come to some place where people are on their knees and crying out—, this I should understand, I should throw myself down among them and might then have my outcry too under the shelter of theirs. Taking part in the visitation means here in our country reading the newspapers—stuffing oneself with the ambiguous sham-happening they are daily piling up, and being able at last to think of pain and worry only in the transposition which they impose upon everything. Fearful as the war is in itself, it seems to me still more dreadful that the pressure of it has nowhere contributed to bringing man out more distinctly, to forcing him—the individual or the mass—face to face with God, as great tribulations in earlier times had the power to do. On the plane meanwhile cultivated, on which the newspapers are able to give a conscienceless verbal cross-section of all that happens (a scrimmage in which what is beyond us and conjectured stands beside the factual, what is most commercial beside the most incalculable): on this plane an incessant equalizing of all tensions is created and humanity becomes accustomed continually to accept a world of news in place of realities which no one has time or is minded any more to let grow large and heavy within them.

I never was and cannot any longer become a newspaper reader. . . .

/ Bernhard von der Marwitz, of Friedersdorf (1890–1918), was a poet who was to die of wounds at a field hospital in France in September 1918.

TO JOACHIM VON WINTERFELDT-MENKIN

from 34/IV Ainmillerstrasse, Munich,
16 September 1918

Again and again since your letter came, my dear Herr von Winterfeldt, I have taken up my pen and tried and have no command of the words the moment calls for. Which are they? Have we not long since dispensed all those adapted to the various demands of grief? Anything there might still be to say we would have to break off with a piece of our heart—, it lies beyond exaggeration, beyond any extreme ever possible to words, and the excess of mourning for the dead that threatens to break out presupposes, in order still to be kept within bounds at all, an infinite extension of soul in us which again cannot have developed in such a tangled and chaotic time.

What shall I say: I know, I feel, you have lost a young friend, the best, the biggest, the incomparable thing that in essence these two words can stand for. Among the thousands of young men who have sacrificed their own, specially intended lives in the impenetrable destiny of the war, Bernhard von der Marwitz will remain, to those who knew him, one of the most unforgotten.

The memorial you are gathering for him in your heart will have more than personal significance. For the "being young" and the "being friend" of this young man of fine culture and large capacity for emotion was a more than personal manifestation, was in a certain sense standard for that German youth which, without the interruption of such fearful disturbances, would have assured our future in a wide-open spiritual world. The continued and inextricable wrong of the war has called up more and more young people of contradictory mind, who think to deduce the future more cleanly out of the negation of the past. In Marwitz, on the contrary, tradition functioned together with a perfect readiness for intellectually responsible freedom: if a future is to come out of German youth, it must be an attitude very closely related to his that would be determinative for it. So the thought of his survival, it seems to me, is linked with those most intimate hopes that we have yet to direct toward life which is altogether to be rescued.

I cannot at the moment, dear Herr von Winterfeldt, do more to comfort you than admit with entire conviction the great and unique worth of your friend.

How indescribably, furthermore, I hold myself a loser you may understand from the circumstance that one of Marwitz's magnificent letters (written the 9th of August) has not only occupied me continually all these weeks, but (to be truthful) contained association for a long time. After that letter (the answering of which I incomprehensibly, tired and frustrated as I am, put off to a more favorable hour—) I was certain of having in young Bernhard von der Marwitz a friend, a close friend, and I regarded this relationship as a possession not yet entered upon, the future productivity of which seemed to me the more precious in that men have seldom sought my intimacy. Thus the number of my hopes, with which I have been left in the lurch, is at least as great as the quantity of your orphaned and uncontinuable memories: may this maintain a sort of lasting understanding between us, my dear Herr von Winterfeldt.

Had you not expressed the wish to let me have a look (advisory) into the writings your friend has left, I should have come out with it as a request: in the feeling that this reciprocal, almost unexercised friendship would entitle me, with gentle affection still, to retrieve intimacy I had in a way neglected.

And now to add to real request. If there was any-one in his immediate family (it seems to me he spoke particularly of a sister) with whom he had a really close understanding, I feel I would like to write that person a few words of sympathy and sorrow, perhaps even a certain assurance of devotion such as would be comprehensible in one left behind with a quite unex-pended affection. If you know such a person and ad-vise my writing the letter, I beg you to give me the name and address.

When we meet again, as I now the more sincerely wish we may, I shall be unable to repress many ques-tions about his last days, as indeed I shall always be grateful to you for everything through which you con-nect me with his memory, which I love and honor.

/ *Joachim von Winterfeldt-Menkin (1865–1945) was* Landesdirektor *of the Province of Brandenburg.*

TO COUNTESS ALINE DIETRICHSTEIN

from 34/IV Ainmillerstrasse, Munich,
9 October 1918

. . . I do not want to complain again (and certainly not at this moment) of my indescribably benumbed and inhibited state of mind; but this it is with which the time has stricken me—as it has thwarted and interrupted everyone in some way—and through just this condition of inwardly turning to ice, which makes my heart almost inaccessible to me, I am continually shut out from everything: from friends, from Nature, and (most baffling of all) from the happiness and the fullness of my own work. You, my dear Countess, did not know me when this oppression was not yet upon me, when I lived in an open world and more than anyone else (I may well say) was borne along by the currents that carried the great inspirations of a common humanity across all lands and skies. When I now imagine that the day might come again when I could use my natural self, made for gazing and marveling, for acquiescing, for infinite worship, then I rejoice in this future for your sake too. You shall (this too I promised myself that day on the balcony, in the face of the rising thunderstorm), you, Countess Aline, shall always be among the few people who may claim a direct share in my being happy and clear, in my growing powers, as something that belongs to you as naturally as the sun of an open-hearted day, as the feel of a free wind, as a view over the clear valleys of the serene and harmonious landscape.

All these years I have not asked myself (it would

have been imprudent to do so) how much, with all the affliction, confusion and disfigurement of the world, I still believe in the great, in the consummate, widely inexhaustible possibilities of life; may your wedding-day be an occasion for me to test myself. And so I confess to you, dear Countess, that I hold life to be a thing of the most inviolable preciousness, and that the entangling of so much doom and horror, the prostituting of such countless destinies, everything that in these last years has been unconquerably growing for us into a still augmenting terror, cannot dissuade me of the fullness and goodness and congeniality of existence. There would be no sense in coming to you with wishes did not the one conviction *precede* all wishes, that out of subversion and destruction the goods of life spring clean and unspoiled and most deeply desirable; but that I (although myself sad, dejected and bound to a heart I can scarcely unravel) can hold this conviction —may this give my wishes the greatest and truest validity. And if on the one hand I thus vouch for the wonderful provisions of life, on the other I am inwardly convinced that you of all people will know how to value what it bestows at its most fundamental worth.

The happiness and confidence of a courageous love fills your richly-endowed heart. Amid superficiality and chance you unerringly recognized your destined companion and humbled yourself before the law that is related to those laws by which the stars move. And already this natural honesty and sincerity of yours has rewarded you, in that at one stroke not only was he who loved you loved, but the whole world turned a different face to you and was yours. And so on your beautiful wedding-day celebrate the doing right and the being right of your heart!—Celebrate it confidently, even though external confusions and tribulations still

surround everything that is personal and of one's inner
world. The moment for an awakening and a turning
no longer seems quite out of reach and the happy new
beginning and progress of your own life will perhaps
soon be borne along by a current of universal awakening and good will. . . .

/ *Countess Aline (Alexandrine) Dietrichstein, who in 1918
was to marry Count Wolfgang von Küenburg, had become
acquainted with Rilke in Vienna in 1916.*

TO CLARA RILKE

from 34/IV Ainmillerstrasse, Munich,
7 November 1918

Your letter (of October 28th) with its great free
breath blew in ahead of the events. We here in the city
have now to go instead through all the ups and downs
and the many newspapers, the hundred repugnant
rumors—and at every hesitation in the strife of that
which finally has come, one's heart stops as though this
future, still going on foot through the crowd, might
stumble or turn back again.

I was so busy watching and listening, and above all
hoping, that I overlooked how long it must have been
since I had written you both. Now, in face of your telegram, I reproach myself for having made you uneasy
by this silence: there was no reason whatever for that.

. . . In the last few days Munich has given up some
of its emptiness and quiet, the tensions of the moment
are noticeable here too, even though between Bavarian
temperaments they don't act in an exactly spiritually
elevating manner. Everywhere gatherings in the beer-

halls, almost every evening, everywhere speakers, among whom Professor Jaffe is of the first prominence, and where the halls aren't big enough, gatherings of thousands out of doors. I too was among thousands Monday evening in the Hotel Wagner; Professor Max Weber of Heidelberg, national economist, who is regarded as one of the best minds and as a good speaker, spoke, after him in the discussion the anarchistically overstrained Mühsam, and then students, men who had been four years at the front,—all so simple and frank and of-the-people. And although they sat around the beer-tables and between the tables so that the waitresses only ate their way through the human structure like wood-worms,—it wasn't at all stifling, not even for breathing; the fumes of beer and smoke and people did not affect one uncomfortably, one hardly noticed them, so important was it and so above all immediately clear that the things could be said whose turn has come at last, and that the simplest and most valuable of these things, in so far as they were to some extent made easily accessible, were grasped by the enormous multitude with a heavy massive approval. Suddenly a pale young worker stood up, spoke quite simply: "Did you, or you, or you, any of you," he said, "make the armistice offer? And yet we ought to do that, not those gentlemen up there; if we take possession of a radio station and speak, we common people to the common people yonder, there will be peace at once." I can't repeat it half so well as he expressed it; suddenly, when he had said that, a difficulty assailed him, and with a moving gesture towards Weber, Quidde and the other professors who stood by him on the platform, he continued: "Here, these professor gentlemen know French, they will help us to say it right, the way we mean it . . ." Such moments are wonderful, and how we have had to do without them in this very Germany where only invective found words, or submission, which in its way was after all but a sharing in power of those who submitted. . . .

Enclosed is a not uncomfortable letter from Grandmama Phia; it speaks for the Czechoslovaks that she feels comparatively calm and protected in the new state . . .

P.S. Friday morning early.

We have a remarkable night behind us. A soldiers', peasants' and workers' council has now been set up here too, with Kurt Eisner as first president. The whole first page of the *Münchener Neueste* is taken up by a decree he has issued, through which the Bavarian Republic explains that peace and security are assured the inhabitants. The night's enterprise was preceded by a gathering on the Theresienwiese attended by a hundred and twenty thousand people. Now it only remains to be hoped that this unusual insurrection will engender sense in people's heads and not go on beyond to fatal intoxication. So far everything seems quiet and one cannot but grant that the time is right when it tries to take big steps.

/ *Professor Jaffe was Edgar Jaffe (1866–1921), an economist at the University of Munich and the brother-in-law of D. H. Lawrence; Max Weber (1864–1920) was the Heidelberg sociologist and political economist; Erich Mühsam (1878–1931) was a writer; Professor Ludwig Quidde (1858–1941) was a historian and pacifist; "Grandmama Phia" was Rilke's mother, still living in Prague, where the republic of Czechoslovakia was being formed.*

TO THE PRESIDENCY OF THE NORTH AUSTRIAN GOVERNMENT, VIENNA

from Munich,
17 December 1918

The undersigned respectfully begs to call attention to the following:

When in May of this year he learned through the newspapers that an honor had been most graciously bestowed upon him, he immediately decided to decline it; for it has always been his intention never to accept any decoration that might be designated to him. At that time informed friends called his attention to the fact that since he was still in the army he had no right to exercise such a refusal.

The official notification of the bestowal of this honor, as well as the order itself, have only now reached the undersigned, at a moment when he is free to act according to his conviction: may he therefore be permitted to return the order together with all the accompanying papers to the office which conferred it.

It would certainly be unfair to attribute this action of the undersigned to any lack of respect; he declines simply in order to remain personally inconspicuous, as his work as an artist unconditionally obliges him to do.

R. M. Rilke

TO ELISABETH BARONESS SCHENCK
ZU SCHWEINSBERG

from 34/IV Ainmillerstrasse, Munich,
5 January 1919

If I were to say what binds me to people in the
most touching way, it is these tokens of steadfastness
that are sometimes, richly as they are undeservedly,
given to one: the happy perenniality of a memory that
apparently without any care still goes on and survives
in the manifold and distracting (alas, in the so indis-
criminate) congestion of life and, in the midst of loss,
brings a subtle sure permanence to mind in him who
a moment ago was still bewildered by a surface of transiency. How one's thoughts collect at such moments of
being remembered as you, charming Caprese of long
ago, were able to prepare for me in a few lines, a few
pictures! Alas, I too need to remain connected with that
past; the longer the exceptional period of the war
lasted, the denser and more impenetrable it grew, the
more did I take pains not to be separated by it from
all that had been, the more did I insist on keeping what
was happy, open, guileless in my past, indeed, on nourishing and continuing myself, across the terrible interruption, out of this very past. Practically my only
achievement in these dreadfully annihilated years was
to believe in what once in the past was mine, in Capri,
in Rome, in Paris, in Russia, in Egypt and Tunis—in
all the marvelous sheer happenings of my life, to which
a different future seemed to belong. Tell me yourself,
how else should I have survived, I especially, to whom
the onset and course of all that has happened since

1914 could mean nothing after all but revocation and insanity? But I do not really know whether I have survived. My inner self has shut itself up more and more. As though to protect itself, it has become inaccessible even to me, and so I do not know now whether in my heart's core there is still the strength to venture upon world-relationships and realize them, or whether only a tombstone of my former spirit has quietly remained there. I still do not know, and have not been able (for how long) to give myself the slightest proof of inner activity; the intersection point of my forces has lost its starriness, has fallen out of the great constellations that used to shelter and support it in spiritual space.

And with us it is not at all to be taken for granted that we survive years of unproductiveness, of hindrance —years that somehow leave one out of use. With women it is different. Do you know the letters of Caroline Schlegel-Schelling, two volumes—shall I send them to you? They should become a reinforcement for you in moments when you yourself incline to doubt the fruitfulness and meaning of your own life just because for a few years perhaps it may not lend itself to any entirely gratifying use. Today as formerly, Elisabeth von Schenck, I believe *wholly* in your riches: if you cannot make full use of them now, that cannot lessen them and ought not to lower their value in your own mind. . . .

/ *Elisabeth Baroness Schenck zu Schweinsberg (born in 1875) had known Rilke in Capri when he was a guest of her aunt, Frau Alice Faehndrich; Caroline Schlegel-Schelling had been in turn married to two leaders of the German Romantic movement, Wilhelm Schlegel and F. W. J. Schelling.*

TO ILSE ERDMANN

from 34/IV Ainmillerstrasse, Munich,
20 March 1919

Both your letters, dear Ilse, the last one and the last but one, have occupied me a great deal, in so far as that degree of self-reliance and independence which you approach in them has never been considered by myself; how many such attachments have I allowed myself, and even in the future I am not certain that I will not come further under their spell.

Giving importance to and elevating a small object unimportant in itself, the [superstitious] faith in it—is for me an indescribable experience, and I have never thought, when giving in to such urges, that it thereby concerns the misuse of one's own nature, although I knew how easily, with the slightest solidification, it might become fixated as something morbid. Now that I consider it, I have to acknowledge that you are right; it is naturally the freer thing to press forward past all similar temptations to complete independence, and that is probably one's intention, so long as one makes use of such aids, each of which has the stigma of the provisional and of weakness (besides its Godlike character). I have always considered as such a little thing the emotional spark that illuminates a milestone of an otherwise still unexplored field, toward which one grows, and that one involuntarily retains when at some point one gets past it. Should we really be judged so very severely, if we still feel some inclination toward this formulation of myths, which has been reduced to something bourgeois and homely? Since almost all conditions of our inner, invisible experience surpass us by their very nature, it seems to me rather innocent if once in a while we draw a willing object into confidence, in order to presuppose in it a carrier of powers ready to develop within us. How much sheer audacity might such a small precaution have presupposed? And do you not believe that superstition (as long as it actually helps one and does not ask instead to be served by us as something morbid) is just a piece of fore-faith, a move toward genuine faith?—oh, it all just has to be vivid, then there is no danger. We shall never get over the pretexts anyway, and if we commission some insignificant object to be, momentarily, something more, then, exactly because of its insignificance, it has to return this power to us: and will this power, when it is returned, in the end not seem slightly greater by dint of the simple virtue of the object? Savings banks: yes, that was what I meant from the beginning, that is how all these talismans always appeared to me, they collect like small batteries of vitality, charged by us with that which we otherwise give off into the air to be randomly scattered. . . .

But your sternness again makes me feel wary, and in the future each one will have a more difficult time in becoming idolized . . .

TO ANTON KIPPENBERG

from 34/IV Ainmillerstrasse, Munich,
22 May 1919

. . . The embargo on mail, externally long since lifted, still continues in me; for who would not rather remain silent about the experiences we had here in

April, and particularly about those other infringements
and interferences that have been going on since the
first of May. "Poison" and "antidote"; but the right
deeper therapeutics is nowhere being used, sore
though the moment confesses itself to be.

From a purely domestic, housekeeping point of view
we have not had to suffer much, thanks to Rosa's foresight, but one's spirit has been damaged. Since my lin-
gering cold I have not gained much in health either,
my body longs for helpful change and everything suspended and watchful in me is indescribably ready to
think that it is right. So I grasped the friendly hand,
offered me again yesterday in a telegram from Switzerland, with an affirmative answer. It now seems possible to get in through the Hottingen reading circle,
perhaps the permission will follow in a few days. . . .

At present I doubt whether later, on my return, I
shall keep my Munich quarters; one hears and sees
nothing but departures; many of the most permanent
residents are giving up their houses, here and there
great moving vans spend the night before their gates;
for most people believe that from now on innocent
Munich may continue to be a bad and uneasy spot, and
that, worse luck, not because of the temperament, but
because of the sluggishness of the mass now that it has
been set in motion. Who knows, dear friend, but I may
choose Leipzig for next fall and winter; I turn over the
idea often. . . .

/ *This letter signals Rilke's departure from Germany, where
he is said to have been called "a Czech perverting the German language"; during the Communist and anti-Communist
régimes of April and May 1919, he was subjected to other
abuse, and once had soldiers stamping at his door at five in
the morning to accuse him of being a Bolshevik.*

TO LISA HEISE

from Soglio, Graubünden, Switzerland,
2 August 1919

I believe, dear lady, that I cannot reply to your lines better and more accurately than by assuring you that I deeply understand the impulse from which they arose. The art-object cannot change or improve anything: once it is there, it stands before man in the same way as nature does, in itself fulfilled, occupied with itself (just as a *Fontane* does)—well then, if you want to call it that, unconcerned. But, after all, we know that this second, restraining, and by its determining will restrained, nature is also made up of things human, of the extremes of sorrows and joys—, and herein lies the key to that treasure chest of inexhaustible consolation which appears collected in the artistic work and to which, precisely, the lonely may lay a special, an inexpressible claim. There are, I know, moments in life, years perhaps, in which living alone among one's peers reaches a degree that one would not have admitted if it had occurred during a time of involuntary, easygoing intercourse. Nature is unable to reach one, it is necessary to have the strength to interpret and woo it, in a way to translate it into the human realm in order to relate to it in the smallest part; but this is precisely what, as a complete recluse, one is unable to do: one wants to receive, unconditionally; one cannot reciprocate, as a man at a certain low point in his vitality hardly feels like opening his mouth for the proffered food—it is necessary that the thing which strives, and should reach one, must overtake one as though it were yearning, as though it wanted nothing short of taking possession of this existence, to transform every atom of its weakness into devotion. Even then, strictly speaking, nothing is changed, it would be presumptuous to expect of a work of art that it could help; but that the human tension a work of art carries within itself without interceding externally, that its inner intensity, without becoming extensive, by virtue of its mere presence, can produce a deception, as though it were striving, demanding, courtship—, courting and devouring love, uproar, calling: that is the good conscience (not the calling) of the art-object—, and this deceit between it and the abandoned people becomes similar to those priestly deceits on the basis of which the godly has been promoted since the beginning of time.

I am immodestly detailed, but your letter has really spoken to me—to me, not just to anyone who happens to be the writer of this letter and bears my name—and so I wanted to be no less detailed, and reply not simply with phrases but, rather, with real, factual experiences of this concern.

Your mentioning your child at the end gives the letter a turn into a confidence I can reply to in no other way than with a complete willingness to accept this trust. If it helps you, tell me about your child, even if it takes many pages. I belong to those old-fashioned people who consider the letter a means toward a most beautiful and fulfilling relationship. Naturally I must say that this concept multiplies my correspondence at times beyond what I am capable of, that further—often for months—the work and, more so, a *sécheresse d'âme* that I cannot overcome leaves me mute; but I do not reckon human relationships with the measures of precarious human existence, rather with those of nature—

Let this from now on be, if you like, a pact and agreement between us; I shall be silent for long periods of time, but if you agree, I shall always be here, knowing, partaking, just as I was permitted to be today.

Rainer Maria Rilke

/ *Lisa Heise (born in 1893) was from Kassel; her letters from Rilke were originally published as "Briefe an Eine Junge Frau," in the 1930 Insel-Almanac.*

TO COUNTESS ALINE DIETRICHSTEIN

from Soglio (Bergell, Graubünden), Switzerland,
6 August 1919

You wrote me on the 14th of June—three days earlier I had gone to Switzerland, an undertaking long hoped for, finally realized when I hardly thought of it any more, and which I am now in the midst of. Well, you can imagine that I needed to get away from Munich: really and actually one did not have to suffer too much, the newspapers, in their way, exaggerated a lot—, but emotionally it was an indescribable and, worst of all, in the end a futile tension in every direction. For behind so much upset, racket and malicious crowding there was after all *no* will to real change and renewal, to share and to take part in which one would have been only too ready. The intellectual would of course have to be from the start an opponent and disavower of revolutions; he of all people knows how slowly all changes of lasting significance are accomplished, how inconspicuous they are and, through their very slowness, almost imperceptible, and how Nature, in her constructive zeal, hardly anywhere lets intellectual forces come to the fore. And yet on the other hand it is the same intellectual who, by reason of his insight, grows impatient when he sees in what miscarried and muddled conditions human things are content and persist: indeed, we are all continually experiencing the fact that this and that—almost everything—needs changing (and that at the root): life, this infinitely rich, infinitely generous life, that is permitted to be cruel only by very reason of its inexhaustibility: life itself—in how many instances it simply cannot make itself effective any more, pushed aside as it is by a lot of secondary institutions, grown lazy by their continuance,—who would not often wish for a great storm that would tear down everything obstructive and infirm, to make room for the again creative infinitely young, infinitely benevolent forces. There is no doubt that many such clean and forceful impulses collaborated in the birth of the revolution: for the only thinkable counterweight to the dreadful war would have been if a new state of mind on humanity's part, prepared to be different, had here and there arisen and penetrated various parts of the shocked and bewildered world. For a moment one hoped. But the preponderance of material aspirations and inferior, if not indeed evil and vengeful impulses, almost in its first hours destroyed the cleaner future of this forward drive, joyful at first, but later desperate and finally totally senseless—in the whirlpools of which many innocent persons went under and almost all *those* who thought to carry ahead a vision of humanity, impatient indeed, but noble. Strictly speaking, the unswerving intellectual could side with neither party in this chaotically confused struggle which the poison of the stagnated war—turned back as it was into the country —further and further provoked; neither with those who drove ruthlessly ahead nor with those who met the often criminal outbreaks of this insanity with old and no less unjust and inhuman means: the future lay with neither, and to *it* the intellectual is after all allied and sworn, not in the sense of the revolutionary, who would presume to create from one day to the next a humanity freed (what is freedom?) and happy (what is happiness?), but in that other patient understanding that he is preparing in people's hearts those subtle, secret, tremulous transformations out of which alone will proceed the agreements and unities of a more clarified future. If now, my dear Countess, you will measure against these thoughts of mine the sad and from day to day more hopeless events that have taken place since November, and take into account also with how little foresight and reflection, how witlessly they have been combatted—, then you will understand how much I am likely to have suffered. Not so much under privation and uncertainty as under this very disappointment and worry that reaches out beyond one's own life and its realizations. But finally I did have to think once more about this life too, mine, and the tasks that have, after all, been set it, and before which it has stood for five years hampered and paralyzed, without collecting itself for its own inmost function. And so from day to day the wish grew for some influence on me—for a journey into some foreign country not directly affected by the war, for its landscapes, cities, streams, bridges, woodlands: since what I have suffered most in losing during these painful last years has been just this very contact of mine with Nature, usually so close, I could no longer succeed in making it. The human being of this war, and every one of his contemporaries, I myself, seemed to me so far removed from the world of Nature—, it seemed to me arbitrary and untrue to have recourse to a tree, a field, the clemency of evening, for what did the tree, the field, the evening landscape know of this hapless, devastating, killing human being? It is true that neither have these things fundamentally any share in one kindly disposed, constructive, blessed, but still there is an inexpressible connection between a person peacefully working, creating, and Nature busying herself in holy and thorough fashion.

. . . so here too (for my consciousness) a rift had become apparent, to which I was the more sensitive since that secret unison, that being in tune with the natural, as I know better all the time, somehow belongs to the premises of my productiveness, even of my daily life itself. If man would only cease to invoke the cruelty in Nature to excuse his own! He forgets how infinitely innocently even the most terrible happens in Nature; she does not watch it happen—she hasn't the perspective for that; she *is* wholly in the most dreadful, even her fruitfulness is in it, her generosity—it is, if one must put it that way, nothing other than an expression of her fullness. Her consciousness consists in her completeness; because she contains *everything*, she contains the cruel too;—but man, who will never be able to encompass everything, is never sure, where he chooses the terrible—let us say murder—of already containing the opposite of this abyss, and so his choice, in the very moment of making him an exception, condemns him to be an isolated, one-sided creature who is no longer connected with the whole. The good, the straightly determined, capable man would not be able to exclude evil, fatality, suffering, harm, death from those inter-relationships; but where one of them struck him or he became the cause of it, there would he stand exactly as one afflicted amid Nature, or, afflicting against his will, he would be like the devastating brook, swelled with those tumbling freshets whose influx into itself it is not able to shut out. . . .

But now you ask about me in connection with Switzerland. Indeed, it is not so easy to travel after five years of immobility! At first it looked as though I didn't know how any more. . . . I felt the need to take advantage of my "freedom" and see the country, which in other years, it is true, I always regarded as merely a country of transit, in a sort of mistrust of its too famous, too obvious, too pretentious "beauty." Mountains are just naturally difficult for me to grasp,—I was able to see the Pyrenees, the Atlas Mountains in North Africa belong to my grandest recollections, and when I read about the Caucasus in Tolstoy I had the indescribable fever of its immensity. But these Swiss mountains? They seem to me something of an obstacle anyhow, there are so appallingly many of them. Their shapes cancel each other; that somewhere a contour runs out clean against the sky, I can indeed establish with satisfaction,—but I lack, how shall I express it, the image, the inner sensible parallel to it which alone makes the impression into an experience. First I had a little to do with the cities: Geneva . . . then Bern: and that was very very lovely. An old, enduring city, still quite unspoiled in many parts, with all the characteristics of a dependable and active citizenry, even to quite a high self-assurance expressing itself in like-minded houses that toward the street bear themselves with a certain reserve above their arcades, but toward the Aar in their pretty garden fronts are of more communicative and open mind. Luckily I had Bernese friends there with fine old inherited houses of this sort, and that removed at one stroke the hotel atmosphere for me and helped me very much to experience the nature of the country, even where, as now once more displaced among strangers, I have to find myself to rights again from their level. About Zurich, that politically turbid city, there is hardly anything to say—, it made me very anxious to get out of the cities: country and, if possible, southern skies over it—that was in my mind's eye—, and that has now come to fulfillment for a while here, in a special manner. A map of Switzerland will easily show you the situation of Bergell, the haste of this valley to reach Italy; above the valley, halfway up the mountain, lies this little gneiss-tile-covered nest, on the declivity a church (unfortunately Protestant and therefore empty), quite narrow streets; I am living in the very midst of it, in the old ancestral house of the Salis (Soglio line), even among their old furniture, and into the bargain the palazzo has a French terrace-garden with the old stone balustrades, traditionally cut boxhedges and between them a profusion of the gayest summer flowers. But I must tell you another time of the chestnut woods that extend down the slopes, toward the Italian side, in grandiose beauty.

P.S. next morning: If only I had a certain book here: I would have liked to send it to you right away, in response to your inquiry about books; at the moment it is not to be had in Switzerland either, as the second edition was quickly sold out. I am now placing an order with the publisher to send it along to you in my name when it appears again, for the Austrian book business may be still slower now than it was anyway in the old days.—The book in question is Count Hermann Keyserling's *Travel Diary of a Philosopher*. A trip around the world by this excellent writer, which ended shortly before the war, is reflected in these everywhere fruitful notebooks, which, though they move in a wholly intellectual sphere, are still thoroughly effective for all they sense and see, the book of a man of the world in the rarest and most aristocratic sense, oriented in all directions, greatly assenting and approving, and at the same time mobile, accurate and of the most perfect tact of feeling and conviction. Some six hundred pages, grand for reading aloud to each other in the garden or before the fire! . . .

/ *Countess Aline (Alexandrine) Dietrichstein (born in 1894) had known Rilke in Munich in 1916; after leaving Munich around mid-June, Rilke had settled into this* Gasthaus *at Soglio, which had a fine library he could use in a quiet part of the house.*

TO ELISABETH VON SCHMIDT-PAULI

from Soglio (Bergell, Graubünden),
14 August 1919

That mountain of joys, Sister Elisabeth, from which you run breathlessly down into my expectation, always wide open for you—that mountain of joys is evidently higher than anything I have before me here,—its summit is suffused enduringly with the divine, and so I rejoice to know you full of blessings and full of inner tasks! May you succeed in much, and succeed *imperiously*, in the same spirit in which it has been laid upon you. All work in the present world is in vain that compromises with it; the absolutely-different must be presented to it, and even though this is at home in another sphere, one must move it down and into this world, implant it and naturalize it, even against the world's will. Now you know this just as well as I, only one should repeat over and over to oneself that compromising has no sense at this turning-point. Not between man and man, and not in general and absolutely not within one's own discussions with oneself.

. . . Switzerland [is] certainly no country for me; it strikes me like one of those painted or modeled nudes intended to make apparent all the "beauties" of many women in a single figure; that is, if I mistake not, the aesthetic of Switzerland—for us an abominable one; which is also why her artists so quickly turn pedagogical, for where examples of every type are present together, what remains but to point to them, to consider them picture-books and to educate through them. Bern, which is one of the most beautiful cities, first helped as a focal point to give me an idea of the old life-permeating force of these states; Swiss history, in which the forces of Nature (not the outward forms of these interior countries) have proceeded along a straight line, is unified and easy to survey, is beautiful; this variety, contradictory and running to intensest exaggerations, could only grow into an entity in man, and the Swiss, however differently the separate cantons may have developed him, carries the consciousness of all his federated landscapes in a singularly prepared and fruitful spot in an otherwise not easily penetrated mind. . . .

All through this letter I have avoided speaking of impressions. Even were this landscape less eclectic, I would be unable to take any in. Spain was the last "impression." Since then my nature has been worked from inside (*travail repoussé*), so strongly and steadily that it cannot be "impressed" any more. From all this you may understand what I am hoping from the winter. The beginning of that retirement granted somehow at last, for which I would now fully have the conscience, however much one ought on the other hand to be there for other people. Indeed I should then properly be there, infinitely more positive and able to hold out!

/ Elisabeth von Schmidt-Pauli later wrote a book about Rilke, published in Basel in 1940.

TO COUNTESS M.

from Begnins sur Gland (Vaud)
26 September 1919

Soglio is far behind me now. . . . I am writing you from Begnins, a village above Nyon, where there is a pension installed in a little château with which I had a cursory acquaintance, and where I am today to meet a young girl from Paris. I am curiously excited: Marthe, whom I found in the last stage of destitution when she was seventeen, was my protégée, a working girl, but of that spontaneous geniality of heart and mind that is probably to be found only among French girls. What surprises, what indescribable, yes, overflowing happiness she gave me in certain years through her wideawake understanding of the greatest and most perfect, which surpassed my own. I do not know if any human being has ever similarly shown me what a spirit can spontaneously unfold into if one gives it a little room to live in, a little quiet, a little bit of good climate. It will be almost a return to Paris for me, the meeting with this creature who knows about me with the deepest conviction; through her—even if it is only a few days I can spend with her—I shall soonest be able once more to heal on to the ruptured surface of my former life; Marthe's hands will hold the fractured end and the new beginning tenderly against each other.

. . . When I think it over, I would say you are entirely right, Munich had long since become only depressing for me, and when I think of the return to Germany—, it would be a relief to return elsewhere. . . .
I almost wish you would give up the city . . . , for the
winter will be in many ways more tolerable and more
natural in the country, from all they say and fear. . . .

Leaving Soglio was not easy. Many inner workings
were thereby interrupted. And what began as joy—
finding the little library so suitable and so made for
me—had to pass away in melancholy: some day to have
such a room for a long, long time, and all the solitude of
a house and garden with it—God provide it for me.
This only and nothing else. . . .

TO FRAU GUDI NÖLKE

from Locarno, Pension Villa Muralto,
on the second day of Christmas [Friday, 1919]

My dear Frau Nölke,

I'm almost afraid of having deprived the children
of something, when I realize that you spent all these
sheets of paper on me and so much thought for my
welfare, on Christmas Eve—yet I know that the spirit
of your little household is such that everything you use
is renewed and made up for again, so I take heart again
and thank you for your palpable assistance. I will just
say quickly what is in my thoughts: that I must never
again beg for hospitality, especially from strangers—I
made up my mind about that once for all after the
Ascona fiasco—so that now Hubert Landau's kind sug-
gestions are ruled out. *What* a lot of things would have

to be postulated for such a scheme to succeed, in which even intimate friends would find it difficult not to trespass. No, if anything of that sort is among the cards of providence, it will come out of itself one of these days, it doesn't do to stretch out one's hand and pull out the best card oneself. So much I've learned by now.

Going to Italy would still be very painful to me for the moment, I think; the area of Trieste especially, in which lies the war-ruined Duino that was my most wonderful sanctuary for work, would overwhelm me with memories that have assumed a tinge of melancholy in the meantime. The Rosenbergs: if I stay on here it might be pleasant to try and meet them and make contact with them (if only for the sake of the dogs), but seeking their hospitality would be a delicate venture—it's such a roundabout proceeding, after all—first getting to know people, and then when you're under their protection, having to avoid seeing them; and one can hardly introduce oneself to them with such a program.

Soglio ah, Soglio: How I gazed at the little new photographs with what recognition and longing! I shall send my publisher the two of the library, so that he can get an inkling of what it is I "require." It would be to his advantage, after all, if I could find it. He has just prepared me for the terrible disappointment that I can't have money sent me here except by the usual channels; a bookseller in Zurich had given me to understand that the new Booksellers' Agreement could be utilized for the purpose of remitting fees with the exchange compensation that has just been arranged for the book market. It can't be done—and I dare not incur the enormous loss of an ordinary remittance. So I may still be faced with immediate return. Countess Dobřčenský is in England—she's expected back, it's true, but suppose she's delayed? Or suppose her own resources won't allow her to continue the system of loans she arranged with me out of friendship for a fellow-countryman?—What then?

There is one possibility in the air, of which I will say nothing as yet, for fear of scaring it away (I'm so superstitious by now); an estate in the neighborhood of Basel, where there appears to be a little annexe, more or less the sort of thing I hoped for in San Materno—only, of course, not the south thrown in, which was one of the things that influenced me there. The proposal reached me on Christmas Eve, from people I'm fond of; it's anyhow worth considering. I should be on my own, as they only go out there in the summer.

I will tell you more about it as the plan grows clearer. Meanwhile, I must say, I should be glad to escape the fogs a little longer, which are peculiarly persistent in the north of Switzerland, as I became sufficiently convinced in November. Here we woke up on the 23rd to a thick snowfall, but by midday it had begun to thaw, and now, though the roads are a bit bottomless, it's true—unless they freeze over at night—only a hand's breadth above them you feel such cheerfulness in the air, such an unshakable southernness of existence, that as much of yourself as extends above your galoshes can't help being happy.

My last letter was so untidy, with its postscripts, and this one is no better, all my unrest and anxiety tugs at me while I write. If only enough money comes along for me to remain in this room for the present, I'll place it to fate's credit account.

My Christmas was a quiet one, a certain solemnity fell into it at the right moment, the bells in the church towers all began pealing in every direction. And as my little stove is heated with wood, even its crackling and hissing could easily be accounted Christmassy; so that there should be no doubt about it, I threw a little sprig of fir into it on purpose.

How splendid that Asa was able to get a parcel from home! One of the few signs of a healing world. Thank you for everything! And please say something nice to Hubert Landau for me on the telephone, before I write to him.

Yours
Rilke

I should like best to keep all the little photographs, the ones in the snow as well. The little picture of Renate and Raimund on the steps is delightful.

/ *Frau Auguste (Gudi) Nölke (1874–1947), who had spent ten years in the Orient, had gone to Switzerland at the end of the war to recover from a lung complaint; she was accompanied by her three children and their Japanese governess, Frau Asa, when Rilke met her at the pension in Soglio.*

TO LISA HEISE

from Locarno (Tessin), Switzerland
19 January 1920

. . . Where could you have found a place with your little son? I ask myself this question often, especially around Christmas time. I thought about it again and again. You write in your last letter about female students without indicating what the field of your instruction is. Have you been able to take it up again in your new place, with success? with joy—(perhaps?). What it must have cost you to leave the quiet old house, that I can really imagine, I who feel the lack of a country and the homelessness so intimately. How different would even the war years have been if I could have spent them under the protection of lasting and to-me-belonging things.

The "question" of your big letter—yes, my dear woman, where should one start? It is always again the "whole" with which one deals, but this whole, even if we can sometimes grasp it within ourselves in a moment of happiness or pure will, in the real world it is interrupted by all the misunderstandings, errors, insufficiencies, through the visciousness between man and man, through the helplessness and sorrow—yes, by nearly everything that happens to us every day.

It is a terrifying realization, that the moment of love which we feel as one, to us, so full and deeply unique and peculiar could be so completely determined, beyond one's control, by the future (the future child) and on the other hand by the past,—but even then: it still maintains forever its indescribable depth as escape into the self. To believe this comes completely naturally to me. It agrees with the experience that no matter how much the incommensurate existence of every one of our deepest delights frees itself from continuity and progress, they really stand directly in the direction of life, just as death stands also directly on them; they have more in common with him than with all the aims and movements of our vitality. Only through death (if one does not consider him as having passed away, but treats him as a transcendent intensity—), only through death, I believe, can love be justified. But even here the conventional concept of this great event stands in the way. Our traditions have become unable to guide us, dried-out branches that are no longer fed from the strength of the roots. And if one adds to that the absent-mindedness, unconcern, and impatience of the man, and that the woman is only deeply giving in the rare moments of good fortune, and that next to such broken and distraught people the child stands always as a fellow-creature, passing them up and yet equally unable to advise—yes, then one admits modestly that our lot is not an easy one.

Let everything between us continue in friendship from one time to the next.

RMR

TO LEOPOLD VON SCHLÖZER

from Pension Villa Muralto, Locarno (Tessin),
21 January 1920

. . . These linkings-up-again on all sides—Switzerland has granted me many, also some really remarkable connections with Capri and Rome days—are so far the only symptoms of the healing I so badly needed. For me, so far as myself is concerned, nothing remains but to hold myself so long and so closely to my sudden anguished ruptures of 1914 that I heal to them; in those days I began (from 1912 on) my big, perhaps biggest and most decisive works; the war reduced the sheltered place where I began them to a heap of ruins over countless soldiers' graves: the old castle of Duino (near Trieste) where I could do such grand days and nights of work. All that is gone, and with it Paris, to me so indispensable—and yet I do not want to, I *cannot* give it up, nothing, none of it. Within the last five years there has not been a single point I can hold on at, not one, the precipice has been so steep for me that I cannot root at its edge; also there is over it neither air nor

Nature nor sky, nothing but a dense mist of doom. . . .
During almost all the war years I was, *par hasard
plutôt*, waiting in Munich, always thinking it *must*
come to an end, not understanding, not understanding,
not understanding! *Not to understand:* yes, that was
my entire occupation in these years, I can assure you
it was not simple! For me the open world was the only
possible one, I knew no other: what did I not owe Russia—it made me what I am, from there the inner me
went forth, all my instinct's homeland, all my inner
origin is *there!* What do I not owe Paris, and will never
cease to be grateful to it for. And the other countries!
I can, I could take nothing back, not an instant, in no
direction reject or hate or despise. The exceptionalness
of the general situation has dictated to all an excep-
tionless attitude: no *one* nation may be particularly
considered to have gone beyond the bounds, for this
rashness has its basis in the helpless lostness of all.
Who is helping? On all sides only exploiters of the
turbid, nowhere a helper, nowhere a leader, nowhere
a great superior individual. There may indeed have
been such periods before, full of destructions, but were
they equally formless? With no figure to draw all this
around itself and expand it away from itself—*this* way
tensions and counter-tensions are set up without a
central point that first makes them into constellations,
into orders, at least orders of destruction. My part in
all this is only suffering. Suffering with and suffering
beforehand and suffering after. Soon I won't be able to
stand it any more. Please, do not believe the preacher
about the "bestiality" of the French in the Rhine-prov-
inces—we must stop making anyone out bad—it is the
confusion that now here, now there, creates excesses
and turbulences, it is no one's fault. *C'est le monde qui
est malade, et le reste c'est de la souffrance!* Since June

I have been in Switzerland now here, now there, without a place. Shall wait another two months on Swiss soil, then back—but whither? Even though I never made the most of being an Austrian subject, still I am now aware of the homelessness of the Austrian. I have done no work. My heart had stopped like a clock, the pendulum had somewhere bumped against the hand of misery and stood still. . . .

/ *Leopold von Schlözer (1859–1946), the German writer, was later (in 1931) to edit a book about Rilke on Capri, where the men had met in 1907.*

TO FRAU GUDI NÖLKE

from Palazzo Valmarana a San Vio, Venice
[Thursday], 24 June 1920

Dear Frau Nölke,

Did you suspect it? I've been in Venice for a fortnight—Seeing things again, grasping things again, occupies me so completely that I haven't been able to write to you. For this is really the first time I've been "outside," Switzerland is merely a waiting-room to me, all the more because I found no memories to renew there. Whereas here—how many, what inexhaustible ones! I couldn't—if you asked me—tell you how I'm reacting; the inner result accomplished each day is complex, bewildering; perhaps, unconsciously, I seek a way out by not always completing it. Finding everything unaltered here answers the wish I brought with me in secret, but I didn't think of the other side of this hope, the painful one, that I'm unaltered too! At least, so it seems to me—and that is wrong, after six years, which will anyway have to be counted as years of life and as years gone by. Holding my breath has certainly preserved me to some extent throughout those destructive calamities, and numbness and inertia of heart was what I most desired, but now that I can test my inward condition by what I once loved, it really frightens me to find it so fixed and unaltered, it's not natural. Living here opposite each other, this miracle of a city and I, we could still agree that it was the year 1914: there is something horribly lifeless about that. Fundamentally I have a great fear of mere repetition (except for moments in which repetition creates rhythm), and here a great deal is demanded of me once again, in a repetition the like of which I cannot ever remember, because at other times either the object or oneself had changed, or at any rate the dividing air between had become different, or the light, or the sensitivity of the eye. Now I'm being punished for the disasters—Venice doesn't stand still, it's true, but it survives backwards like a reflected image, only some obvious devastation could date it. What good reason it has to be proud of all its church saints! They show you maps with all the places marked where bombs fell; except for three or four they were all ineffective, in the Frari-Church, alongside the big *Madonna of the House of Pessaro*, a slender aerial bomb has been hung up, like a gigantic iron earring, which fell in the neighborhood without doing any further damage. This church has acquired new dimensions, its height has become more ascending, more aspiring, more celestial, simply because Titian's *Assumption* has been replaced in its frame above the high altar. In the Accademia, where we knew it, this *Assumption of Mary* had become a subject of artistic erudition, you could see anything and everything in it, apparently. Now, restored to its original destination, it unfolds once more the double miracle of the Marian consummation and the Titianic ecstasy—the pure figure against the background of the choir releases itself, filled with divine farewell, mounts, presses up, ascends to heaven and drags the whole church upwards into the immeasurable revealed bliss of the ultimate heaven. . . .

I saw this on my second day—otherwise I am far from looking at pictures in the way foreigners do, I hardly know how one could bring oneself to it nowadays. Once I'm seated in a church, I let it be round me as a whole, like some everyday thing, like nature—I couldn't do anything else now.

Prince Taxis was here until last Friday, the Princess till Monday. Then I moved into her (my former!) *mezzanino* in the Palazzo Valmarana, where I received the Duse in 1913, and lived with all my roses. (A few pictures and some silver were stolen, otherwise it's the same.) My Italian acquaintance picked up the old threads at once, the people are friendly and kindly disposed to foreigners, but the low rate of the lira is obvious from the frightful amount one has to spend.

My last days in Basel were so busy that Hans's little letter and such a kind note (or was it two?) from you have remained unanswered. My journey must be the excuse: it was no light matter for me. Much love to you all.

In truest remembrance,

Yours,

Rilke

/ Rilke was wrong about the time he "received the Duse" —it was not 1913 but 1912; his Italian acquaintances were the Valmaranas.

TO ANTON KIPPENBERG

from Palazzo Valmarana a San Vio, Venice,
1 July 1920

. . . Dear friend, I seem to be very much divided: I long so to be out in the world, among the images I was accustomed to receive from it, in foreign-speaking regions where no one knows me and where language, my own language, again flashes out in steady relief as the material of my work. On the other hand, the waiting-time quality of my Swiss sojourn has grown ever clearer to me, and I see that from this spring-board I shall for the present get no further into the open, but must go "back"—, if only the objective were more definite and more natural, I should not have let myself in for so many delays. Incidentally it has not even been possible to return to Munich—: news did not reach me until I got here that the energetic influence of a friend . . . has obtained a residence permit for me. But meanwhile I have sublet my apartment, so I can only use it as an accommodation; nor would I like anything better than to leave a place which for me will long remain part of the conditions of the war years, which was never really of use to me, and which at the end also provided plenty of other causes for dislike.

I do not quite see myself actually taking refuge at the Fürstenbergs'; the thought of being under obligation to new and entirely unknown people rather oppresses me, just as I shall always fear every expenditure of energy that must be wasted in adjusting myself to something not precisely suitable. But the place I

would need—in strict accord with my conscience, not
out of fastidiousness—is it to be found in the present
crowded Germany? . . .

/ *The friend with "energetic influence" was the Austrian
ambassador, Count Zech, who made it possible for Rilke,
now technically a citizen of Czechoslovakia, to return to
Munich; the Fürstenbergs' "refuge" was a house in the
Euganean hills, near Padua, offered to Rilke by Prince Egon
Fürstenberg.*

TO PRINCESS MARIE VON THURN
UND TAXIS-HOHENLOHE

from Schönenberg bei Pratteln, Basel-Land,
23 July 1920

. . . Oddly enough this time, my stay in Venice
began with a high point—our meeting again, which I
found so extraordinarily good and was so completely
grateful for from day to day,—but after your departure,
after I had to experience and to connect up with only
my own life there, every variation was lacking, not a
trace of more or less,—a complete uniformity, like the
warmth itself of all those weeks in which there was
scarcely a fluctuation; and no finish to it because all
proportion was lacking—like an always even ribbon
running through one's senses. . . . Only for this reason
was it so hard to go away, for this singular continuity
somnolent as it was, and yet not without invitation to
dreaming, could be given up at any point and still did
not have to be. It was one of those external conditions
that merge without delimitation into a state of mind
which they only attract rather than produce,—perhaps

I went too far in supposing this even flow must finally diminish or increase, and a moment must come that would introduce a before and after into something so undifferentiable. Nothing of the sort. Only later, when sometime it will be possible to take account of one's reflections, shall I be able to see *what* this time in Venice after your departure could really have been. As yet I only observe that life cannot be joined on to the broken surfaces of pre-war days in the way I had thought—, after all everything is changed, and the sort of traveling for "pleasure," to be taken simply and always rather leisurely—in short traveling of the "cultured" traveler will once and for all have run its course. It will "go empty" in future, which of course will not prevent many from continuing it without taking account of the desuetude of their undertaking. I believe that all aesthetic observation that is not immediate accomplishment will be impossible from now on,—basically impossible, for example, to "admire pictures" in a church, or not unless, open through sorrow or exaltation, one is again swept away before this one or frightened and blessed by that. You would not believe at all, Princess, how different, *how different* the world is become, the point is to understand that. Whoever thinks he can live from now on as he was "accustomed" to live, will find himself continually facing the sheerest repetition, the bare once-again and its whole desperate unfruitfulness.

The biography of Dostoevski, written by his daughter and translated into German from the French manuscript, was awaiting me here. I will have the book sent you tomorrow. . . . Even in the short introduction, Mlle. Dostoevskia, living on among her father's Slavophile associations, gives what would be the most wonderful and forward-looking interpretation of conditions in Russia today:—The Russian muzhik, the inexhaustibly surviving and constructive element of Russia, is, in her belief, already at work, is creating big and deep contacts toward the East and is using Bolshevism only "as a scarecrow" to keep off the Westerners and their dogmatic and disturbing interference. Even if it does not yet look so today, I am sure Liubov Dostoevskia is only telling ahead of time, through her father's eyes, what is bound sooner or later to have its turn, else the whole world must stand still. Among its next movements, however, this will be the grandest and the most just. . . .

TO PRINCESS MARIE VON THURN UND TAXIS-HOHENLOHE

from Geneva,
19 August 1920

I am enormously reckless—in Geneva a fortnight and cannot tear myself away. Four—four days I had allowed myself for leave-taking, but there is always an excuse for yielding, and always a tendency on my part to give in. It is not Geneva alone, it is everything here that recalls Paris and almost makes it real: the playing grey light in which bright clothes and the planes of a face take on the same sweet haziness that makes many a time of year in Paris so fatally attractive. This must actually be true, Geneva was so lovely, the open lake with the lateen sails, the quays and along the shores the great Genevan *campagnes* with their magnificent trees. I don't quite know why, I feel I ought to be so indescribably open to it all, as though it were to be the last for a long time; for the return seems to me, God

help me, a somber picture, much as I try to save out
the little house and Lautschin in general from the rest
of the dismal background. . . . It is a tour de force for
God to keep his hand so long over my little house,—
surely he has already let it go and some worthy man is
living in it with whom I cannot stand comparison. I am
prepared to have trifled away this lovely prospect, and,
j'en conviens, I deserve nothing else. What does Kassner say to my not coming? . . .

I see Pitoëff almost every day. You know, the Russian who has set up the wonderful theater here, whose
experiment and success I am so keen about. For the
first time I recognize the "work" of the actor as exactly
as central, independent and big as, in another realm
of art, Rodin's work was in its magnificence and utter
independence; and one always experiences the same
happiness in seeing how an ability thoroughly realized
at one point takes the whole world in an unexpected
manner into its possession and from that center out
renders it inexhaustible. Yesterday we went through a
very fine play, and one ought to see Pitoëff—with what
vision he penetrates an author's scenery and words: he
emphasizes something, and suddenly the imaginary
bench from which he has just risen, the wall from
which he moves away, simply leap from his eyes. *That
is theater,* I have never known anything like it. If I
could arrange it I would work near Pitoëff for a year,
attend all his rehearsals—, genius is after all the only
thing that really grips us and matters to us; how much
one is ready to forgive the world if only at some one
spot a single unswerving determination of this sort is
happily at work. By and large, in the outside world the
bungling of recent years continues—, I hope you are
not too much aware of it. The children will have come
home meanwhile . . . and everything will surely go

well according to program—only my numbers have had to be canceled until further notice. All the more do I want news, Princess, *please* news, so that at least in spirit and endeavor I can count myself included. . . .

/ *"The little house" was in the park at the Princess's residence at Lautschin, in Bohemia; Georges Pitoëff (1880–1939) was a Russian-French actor and producer.*

TO MERLINE

from the Bellevue Palace, Berne,
24 August 1920

I have been reading and re-reading your letter to try and understand your state of mind, which no imagination could have foreseen. Dear, the capacity of your heart has infinitely increased, and I think you were not mistaken in your first impulse to use it generously for all those over there who approach you and are worthy of being dear to you. Try again, and do not be discouraged by somewhat disappointing acoustics —remember that we lived for an instant (or a long time, who can say?) in a space quite different from that of reality (properly so called); I assure you, it's not that your words at present do not ring true—say them all the same—it is that your ear is still clinging to other dimensions.

It is difficult, I know, my Friend, to reconcile "an almost unknown happiness" with known circumstances, but since in the depths of our being we only live by intensity, how can a memory that preserves for you, so to speak, the discovery of a new degree of intense existence, not serve to enrich all your actions and make them more beneficent than they have ever been before? Try, try again, have confidence, a rich heart cannot belie itself; be that heart ingenuously and you will convince the whole world of it. In my opinion, with a little effort of self-examination you could use your tortured powers to achieve a degree of clear-sightedness which would help others in the problems that now beset them.

My friend, I don't know whether I am expressing myself clearly, but I do feel that I can give you some consolation. One must look from the Whole to the Whole (*vom Ganzen zum Ganzen*), one must start from the center, and since yours, as you told me lately when you were writing from B . . . , has become a lit-tle sun, you wouldn't have much difficulty in orientat-ing yourself towards it. Recapture all the calm you felt on the Holy Mountain—or do you mean me to fear that we have destroyed that calm, instead of strengthening it?

As for me: for some time lately you have been mak-ing me experience towns, first with you and then with-out you;—an exercise that is not without a certain se-verity. . . .

Now listen: you must keep me thoroughly posted as to your plans and dates. I may be staying on in Berne a few days longer, because Mme. de W. has just lost her mother very suddenly, and I think I may be of some help to her by remaining here, even if I do not see much of her.

If you are still thinking of returning on the 26th or 27th (which would be next Friday) I could arrange to wait for you at the Bellevue, instead of risking Zurich and all the hindrances that might fritter away and en-cumber what moments we could spend together there.

Let me know in time, so far as you are sure of your arrangements.

I love your room as though I knew it, and I wish that it may do you good. . . .

And your two hands . . . I hold them gently, and I *support* them. . . .

René

/ Merline, to whom Rilke wrote some of his most intimate letters, was Elisabeth Dorothee Klossowska, who painted under the name of Baladine (Mouky) Klossowska.

TO MERLINE

Tuesday, 28 September 1920

My most dear, tell me, do I sustain you so badly that in spite of all my loving help you let yourself fall into such a terrible misbelief in life? I am not reproaching you for it, I suffer with you, that's all, and rather than make a useless attempt at false consolation, tell you that I understand you.

I understand—no one could do so better—your oppression, your distress, and how at times you feel forsaken by all the strength that grew from the contact of our fiery lives. My Friend, if our separation was so great a wrong, do you think it would have been forced upon us? What makes it so painful is that we are both unable to enrich it with all the true consequences of our prodigious happiness. If you were alone now (as you wrote yourself the other day) you could have created a quite different consciousness for yourself, valiant and consenting. I too am bewildered for want of solitude and concentration,—I am obliged to see people and talk all day; at dusk in the evening I take refuge in the garden of the hotel; there I stay for hours, and at times I rush towards you with such rashness of heart that I don't know whether I am doing you good or harm by my too merciless approach. These irresistible appeals, Friend, when shall we learn to quell their violence? Let us implore each other, mutually, for a little kindness from the hands we stretch out, at times, too fiercely.

You question me again about my long stay here: It is entirely taken up in making plans for remaining in Switzerland, if only for a few weeks. Some friends of mine are prepared to establish me all by myself in a little old château a few hours from Zurich, which would be quite habitable even in winter; but as I can't have money sent either from Austria or Germany, I see no chance of providing myself with the means of subsistence. Discussions are still going on about various arrangements—I feel rather torn between all these things. My responsibility towards my life, interrupted and distorted as it has been by these last years,—towards my work, which no longer belongs to me for lack of continuity and equilibrium,—has become so pressing that I realize I must not shrink from the harshest decisions. I must choose a place for what it promises with regard to my work, so long neglected,—and I have a horrible struggle to fend off the most legitimate influences that might sway my clear and resolute purpose. I emerge quite torn to pieces at times, but I remind myself that one of the fundamental promises of our love was never to force anything, and to bow to the necessities of the moment. For if we were to lay hold, so to speak, of this happiness in the making, we might be the first to destroy it; it must be left on the anvil of its creator, under the blows of his laborious hammer.

Let us put our whole trust in this admirable craftsman: it is true we shall always feel the shock of his tool, wielded pitilessly by him according to the rules of a perfected art; but then as a reward we shall be called upon from time to time to admire his favorite work, which he will bring to final perfection. How we admired it even at first sight! We shall scarcely be so much as collaborators in our love, and for that very reason it will remain superior to commonplace dangers. Let us seek to know its laws, its seasons, its rhythm, and the march of its constellations across its starry sky. Let us be still, my Friend, let us be still, let us admire!

I know very well that all I am saying here imposes a very unequal burden upon us two: you are too much of a woman not to suffer infinitely under that postponement of love which this task seems to imply. Moreover, in gathering my whole self together around my work, I am assuring myself of the means to my most abiding happiness; while you,—at the present moment at least, —when you turn towards your life, you find it encumbered with half-petrified duties. Don't let this discourage you, Dearest; you may be sure that all this will change. The transfiguration of your heart will itself enable you to influence, little by little, the obstinate facts of reality; all that seems impenetrable to you now will be rendered transparent by your burning heart. Don't think about it too much at the moment, and forbid yourself to judge of life during these hours of fog which prevent you from seeing its expanse.

Dearest, tell me about these plans, all the same,— God knows whether they are as unrealizable as you think. Tell me about them all the more because mine are at present in a pretty bad way, in a dark dead-end from which I should not like to return without having stirred up at least a few new ideas, if only fanciful ones.

The "little bunch of roses" didn't arrive till yesterday, Monday: it was mine in its entire significance. . . .

René

/ The "old château" near Zurich was probably Schloss Berg am Irchel, where Rilke lived from 12 November 1920, to the middle of May 1921.

TO COUNTESS M.

from Hotel Foyot, rue de Tournon, Paris,
27 October 1920

You will not, I believe, be nearly astonished enough, my dear Countess, when you read this address—? You have always believed me capable of progress of this sort, the most extensive! But just look, just look!: what shall I say, everything is absolutely, absolutely all right; for the first time since the dreadful years I am feeling the continuity of my existence again, which I had been ready to renounce; for even Switzerland only prolonged the interruptions (more mildly, more pleasantly, under cover, if you will—), but here, here: *la même plénitude de vie, le même intensité, la même justesse même dans le mal*—: by and large everything has remained independent of political stewings and doings and is pressing, stirring, glowing, shimmering: October days: you know them.

I fit at all the broken spots, yes, and now I hardly feel it any more. If I could remain here, I should have my life tomorrow, all its dangers, all its blessings: my entire life: *ma vie, depuis toujours mienne*— —But, the exchange prevents that: it will have been only four or five days,—but even so it is right with me and I like it:

I now *know* again, my consciousness has given over its constraints, the standing-still-in-one-spot has stopped, I am again revolving in my consciousness. *One* hour here, the first, would have sufficed for that. And after all I have had hundreds, days, nights—and every step was an arrival. . . .

In haste: for outside is the Luxembourg, shimmering: so how can I hold out any longer at my desk? . . .

/ *Rilke made a brief visit to Paris before settling in at Schloss Berg am Irchel.*

TO MERLINE

from Schloss Berg am Irchel,
Thursday, 18 November 1920

No, Merline, I am not at all surprised to find you so strong, what makes you valiant now is that same freedom that allowed you to penetrate into the sanctuary of our love and kneel down there, not as a mere adorer, but as a priestess-elect holding up to the god the final sacrifice, with arms straining under the delicious weight. And you would be wrong, Dearest, not to make me admire your whole heart; alone with it you will discover so many hitherto unknown talents in it—only now will you take possession of it, it will be quite new and at the same time more recognizable, it will no longer be a heart's phase but the whole heart, rounded, the star—which will light you with your beams of childhood and first youth.

Reap the harvest, Merline, the first harvest of Love; labor to store in the Granaries of the Soul the innumerable crop that we have ripened by our constant warmth. A "hunter of images," I go up into my mountains, unsociable, taciturn; I lose myself. But you, my delicious valley, you, flute of my heart, you, vase of clay to which I, a humble artificer of love, have given the inspired curve that marks you for divine uses forever,—may you have the innate imperturbable patience of the landscape and the flute and the sacred vase! May you succeed, my Love, in following the rhythms of the seasons and of the mouth and the hand. Let us not be satisfied with telling each other a story of the heart, let us make its legend. Love, is it not, together with art, the only license we have for transcending human conditions, for being greater, more generous, more sorrowful, if need be, than the majority of mankind? Let us be all these things, heroically, my loving friend,—do not let us renounce any of the advantages belonging to our quickened condition!

Since this solitude closed around me (and it was quite complete from the first day) I have been experiencing yet again the terrible, the inconceivable polarity of life and supreme work. How distant is work, Merline, how distant are the Angels!

I shall pursue my way, slowly, I shall advance each day by a step only, and I shall often fall back. And I shall always seem to be going further away from you, for where I am going no name can count, no memory dare persist, one must arrive there as one arrives among the dead, surrendering all one's strength into the hands of the Angel that is leading one. I am going away from you, Merline, but as I am going all the way round, I shall come nearer again at every step. The bow is bent for shooting the arrow at the celestial bird; but if the arrow drops down again it will have passed through the bird without killing it, and from on high it will fall into your heart.

Do not expect me to talk about my interior effort,—
I must be silent on that score; it would be unwise to
render account, even to myself, of all the changes of
fortune I shall have to undergo in my struggle towards
concentration. This reversal of all one's forces, this
changed direction of soul can never be accomplished
without a number of crises; most artists avoid it by
means of diversions, but that is just why they never
again succeed in touching their center of production,
from which they started at the moment of their purest
impulse. Always when you begin to work you must recreate this first innocence, you must return to the ingenuous place where the Angel discovered you when
he brought you the first binding message; you must
find once more the couch behind the briars where you
were then asleep: this time you will not sleep there:
you will have to pray and groan,—no matter: if the
Angel deigns to appear, it will be because you have
convinced him, not by tears but by your humble resolve to be always beginning—to be a Beginner!

Oh, Dear, how many times in my life—and never so
much as now—have I told myself that Art, as I conceive it, is a movement contrary to nature. No doubt
God never foresaw that any one of us would turn in-
wards upon himself in this way, which can only be permitted to the Saint because he seeks to besiege his God
by attacking him from this unexpected and badly de-
fended quarter. But for the rest of us, whom do we approach when we turn our back on events, on our future even, in order to throw ourselves into the abyss of
our being, which would engulf us were it not for the
sort of trustfulness that we bring to it, and which seems
stronger even than the gravitation of our nature? If the
meaning of sacrifice is that the moment of greatest danger coincides with that when one is saved, then cer-

tainly nothing resembles sacrifice more than this terrible will to Art. How tenacious it is, how insensate! All that the rest forget in order to make their life possible, we are always bent on discovering, on magnifying even; it is we who are the real awakeners of our monsters, to which we are not hostile enough to become their conquerors; for in a certain sense we are at one with them; it is they, the monsters, that hold the surplus strength which is indispensable to those that must surpass themselves. Unless one assigns to the act of victory a mysterious and far deeper meaning, it is not for us to consider ourselves the tamers of our internal lions. But suddenly we feel ourselves walking beside them, as in a Triumph, without being able to remember the exact moment when this inconceivable reconciliation took place (bridge barely curved that connects the terrible with the tender . . .).

Dear, I shall never talk to you about all this any more,—I take a vow of silence, and if sometimes, rarely, I give a little sign of life, I shall talk to you rather of my surroundings, of the visible, of the "frame" of my present existence. As for this, it is perfect, and nothing is wanting to my comfort, nor to the silence of this solitary retreat. It is absolutely all I could have wished. The château is simple, calm, full of the sense of security afforded by these ancient abodes that have had time to develop a house consciousness. There was very little alteration needed in the rooms. A vast writing-table has taken the place of the little arrangement that used to be in front of the windows. The table for my meals is in the middle of the room against the big leather sofa facing the fireplace, where I settle myself for reading. Everything is simpler than it looks on the postcards, more serious and more evocative. Even the park, seen from the window, has a more rustic air, especially as it is entirely open at the end, and gives way, beyond the final avenue, to the meadows that ascend by a gentle gradient towards the "Irchel." This wooded, modestly proportioned hill softly closes the horizon without too much encumbering it. The principal role is allotted to the fountain which rises with an almost statuesque gesture from the middle of its unbordered pool. It talks to me day and night, even through the closed windows one's ear catches its vital sound limiting the silence. In the night, from my bed, I can even hear through the open window all the gradations of its cadence, modulated by every slight change in its falling waters. And imagine this persevering fountain, which seems placed, not in a closed park but in the very bosom of nature, borne in upon me like a vision from the *Metamorphoses*. Merline, can it be your heart endlessly mounting before me and falling back in its assured happiness? . . . The moment this idea occurred to me, I asked if the water was not turned off in the winter. No, the fountain will always be there! it will always support the vault of my vision with its moving double column, and its murmur will forever enter my ear and form the constant warp of the tissue of my dreams. . . .

But before ending, I must go back to some earlier details. The little basket I sent you will have told you I had found one for myself, for your pretty embroidery. This was much admired by the saleswoman, who picked it up several times to look closely at it, expressing the joy its tender workmanship gave her. The basket I bought is quite simple, the little piece of needlework just covers the bottom of it: it is always on my table with "zwiebacks" in it, bread would be too heavy for your leaves and your little flowered name.

Dearest, embrace B. for me (without telling him so). I am sorry not to have done it, it was one of those stupid restraints that one always reproaches oneself for; when I return I shall do it with all the tenderness I feel for him. I have had a talk over the telephone with his publisher; we are going to draw up the contract in a few days' time, but I shall be the only one to sign it, for B. . . . not being of age, cannot enter into any agreement.

How you showed me Geneva under this mild and still generous sky! Here too there is an unspeakable softness which seems at times more like spring than the pensive meditation of autumn. The red hues of the hornbeams dominate the landscape and even the atmosphere, which here inclines more to gold than to the silvery limpidity that we love so much. I go out very little for fear of disturbing my efforts at concentration, to which the house is more favorable than any other surroundings. In any case most of the roads are barred on account of foot and mouth disease, so that I am a prisoner of the park and my château.

Dear, I am slow,—I have been writing to you ever since this morning and my clock has just struck four. I think of you, my Dearest,—you have closed behind you that door of expectancy beside which I was always watching for some one who was to come. It was that anxiety that interrupted me at every moment. I feel it no longer. I feel your advent, Merline, and my heart overflows with it.

René

/ *"B." refers to Mme. Baladine Klossowska's small son Balthusz, for whose book* Mitsou *(pictures he drew of his cat) Rilke had promised to write a preface, which he did later.*

TO R. S., who in sending in manuscripts, called special attention to his having gone blind.

from Schloss Berg am Irchel,
Canton Zurich, Switzerland,
22 November 1920

Your letter of October 16th went a long way round to reach me; so my delay is not quite so great as it might seem.

Now as to my answer, it is more concerned with your letter than with the work you enclosed. My conscience does not allow me to express "judgment," since I know how much I lack the movable yardsticks for appraising the more or less in artistic endeavors; I have no link with the manifestations of art other than that of admiration, and so I am in every way made, while I live, to be pupil to the greatest and their acknowledger, rather than finding myself able to act as adviser to those who have not yet truly found their way into the essential nature of their tasks. For these I may only wish that they hold joyfully to the road of longest learning, until there comes to them that deep and hidden self-assuredness which—without their having to ask anyone about it—pure necessity, that is, irrepressibility and thoroughness of their work secures to them. To hold our innermost conscience alert, which with every fully formed experience tells us whether it is thus, as it now stands, altogether to be answered for in its truthfulness and integrity: that is the foundation of every artistic production, which ought to be laid even there where an inspiration kept in suspense can, so to speak, do without the ground.

Great decisive misfortune, such as has been your lot, is singularly enticing to those winged inspirations that like to settle down wherever a privation has become greater than any possession we can imagine. You could not help simply setting this consummate misfortune, when you noticed how attractive it is to the invisible and spiritual, in the center of your rearranged consciousness; it remains, rightly, the unshiftable point from which all distances and movements of your experience and your mind are to be measured. But now that this arrangement has once been hit upon, your quiet practice should be directed toward enduring this central misfortune more and more without any special name, and this would manifest itself in your artistic efforts somewhat in this way: that nowhere any more would it be possible to recognize in them what limitless restriction is the occasion for your laying claim in the earnest entreaty of your work to limitless compensation. Art can proceed only from a purely anonymous center. But for your life too (whatever else it may be destined to bring forth) this endeavor seems to me decisive; it would be the real kernel of your resignation. While you bore your misfortune as a nameless and then at last unnamable suffering, you would be preparing for it the freedom of being at certain moments not misfortune alone but: dispensation (—who can see that far—): privilege. Unequivocal destinies of that sort have their god and are thereby forever distinguished from those variously complicative fates whose privations are not deep enough and not closely enough joined to serve as negative mold for the casting of such a greatly responsible form.

TO COUNTESS M.

from Schloss Berg am Irchel,
Canton Zurich, Switzerland,
25 November 1920

. . . How has this come about? It has come about
by a miracle.—There's no other way of accounting for
it. How shall I hasten to impart to you the incomprehensible thing that has befallen me? Imagine, the same
privilege that allowed me to go to Paris has, so to speak,
had a second act in that, at the moment of my return,
the remote little old Schlösschen Berg was offered me
(to me, all alone!) as an abode for the winter. You can
see it fairly well on the enclosed card: a solid old house
of hewn stone, dating back in its last form to the seventeenth century, with a set-back gable roof seen from
the side,—in the front a somewhat neglected park, in
which high trimmed beech alleys mark out right and
left the unbordered *pièce d'eau*, in the center of which,
day and night, like a playing tree (*un arbre de luxe*)
the fountain figure stands slim. (And this, with its continually modulated cascade, is indeed the measure of
all sounds, seldom can anything be heard above it!)
Looking in the direction opposite from that given by
the card, out of one of the windows (mine are those
on the ground floor) into the garden, one sees it in the
background, beyond the wide-set alley of old chestnuts, running on into the landscape, into meadows
which, in gentlest ascent, reach up to the foot of the
Irchel, that wooded hill which gives way, as it were,
closing the picture without perceptibly shutting it in.—
My rooms are fine, large, full of sympathetic old things

—big tile stoves, in addition to the fireplace, provide the heating—and whenever the sun is out it shines radiantly in at all my windows. A quiet sensible housekeeper looks after me, exactly as I need to be looked after, and doesn't seem to show any particular surprise at my being silent and reserved (for so I must be in order to get at work!)—I've been telling a fairy tale, have I not? Well, what do you say to my being the center of that tale, unexpectedly? Am I really happy? No, my heart beats with worry over whether I shall be able to wrest from these conditions, to the last degree favorable and congenial, that which they now at last really allow and which I (after all the distractions and disturbances of the last years) must urgently, unrelentingly expect of myself. Now there's no excuse! Shall I be able to do it? Shall I be strong, clean, fruitful, productive?: the having seen Paris again, which was so healing, obliges me to be, and here this obligation is now really so clearly and unambiguously set up round about me—, if I fail this time, here, at Schloss Berg—then there is no help for me. The first thing a stranger walking in here would say is: How one must be able to work here! Shall I be able to do it? My fear (my cowardice, if you want to call it that) is just as great as my joy,—but that joy is really immense.

From a place like this . . . I can measure doubly well how sad it must be for you to give up your Carinthian estate: it is true, an indescribable amount of life goes into a piece of permanent property one has built up, and this cannot be pulled out when one gets into the position of giving the place away. Here the Escher portraits, such as have remained in the château, still predominate over everything that the Zieglers, despite four children grown up here, have been able to impose upon the surroundings!

The mourning border on your letter I explained to myself at once, even before I read it—, in the sense of that great near loss that had unfortunately lain not outside the realm of a certain expectation. It is true, one must, particularly under the present bottomless conditions, muster a sort of reconciliation with the going of those who would not have been able to endure such great changes without continual amazement and suffering. I myself could scarcely get possession of myself or get at my work if I had to notice too much of the helplessnesses that everywhere don't want to admit they are that, but in the form of false certainties, would like to overpower the world.

Had I wanted and been able to "profit" by the exchange in Switzerland I would perhaps have become strong enough to acquire your Carinthian estate—I say that jokingly, of course—but still with the thought in the back of my mind that perhaps the original home of the family, which I have never learned to know, would be the country where a comparatively homelike striking of roots (should I ever get to it) would come to me not unnaturally.

For the spring I am thinking of Paris anyway—to continue the life there would seem to me the most perfectly straightforward thing that could happen to me. But, in any case, as I remain dependent on Insel-Verlag as concerns my income, it is not exactly to be foreseen how the disastrous German exchange is to serve me in the realization of this plan.

No—I was not longer in Paris, six days. It was so perfect that duration played no rôle. My heart, my mind, my passionate remembrance of what had there been achieved and fought for were so magnificently and surely satisfied in the very first hour, that when that was over I might have left without any real deprivation. I long ago accustomed myself to take given things according to their intensity, without, so far as that is humanly achievable, worrying about duration; that is perhaps the best and discreetest way of expecting everything from them—even duration. If one begins with that demand, one spoils and falsifies every experience, indeed, one hinders it in its own inmost inventiveness and fruitfulness. Something that is really not to be got by entreaty, can never be but an extra gift,—and I was just thinking that often in life things seem to depend only on the longest patience! . . . That I ever should have grumbled!

TO MAJOR-GENERAL VON SEDLAKOWITZ

from Schloss Berg am Irchel, Switzerland,
9 December 1920

Your letter and its duplicate were forwarded to me by the Insel-Verlag as soon as I was again to be reached at a more permanent address, after several months on the move.

Had I acted on the feeling aroused by your remote recollection, I must have thanked you at once—, and you thought it a little strange too, as the repetition of your letter shows, not to get any answer from me.

Meanwhile the emotion that agitated me was so complex that I had to let a few weeks pass, comprehending it, as it were, if my thanks were not to be superficial and, in a certain sense, embarrassed,—which would in no way have satisfied your sincere wish to renew acquaintance.

A voice that appeals to those most distant years (it is the only such voice that ever sought to find me!) was bound at first—you will pardon the directness of my expression—to be incredible. I would not, I believe, have been able to realize my life—that which I may now, without taking it in the whole, go ahead and call so—had I not, for decades, denied and suppressed all recollection of those five years of my military training, what, indeed, have I not done for the sake of that suppression! There were times when the slightest influence out of that rejected past would have disintegrated that new and fruitful consciousness of my own that I was struggling for—, and when sometimes it inwardly obtruded itself, I had to lift myself out over it, as over something belonging to a most alien, a quite unrecognizable life.—But later too, when I found myself more surrounded and protected in a life increasingly my own, that affliction of my childhood, long and violent and far beyond my age at the time, seemed incomprehensible to as little as the miracle that finally—perhaps at the last moment—came to free me from the abyss of undeserved misery.

If you, Sir, find exaggerated the embitterment without which even today still I cannot so much as enumerate those facts of my early life,—I beg you to consider for a moment that when I left the military college, I stood as one exhausted, physically and spiritually misused, retarded, at sixteen, before my life's enormous tasks, defrauded of the most spontaneous part of my energy and at the same time of that preparation, never again retrievable, which would have built me clean steps for an ascent that, weakened and damaged, I had now to begin before the steepest walls of my future.

You hear me state all this and you will ask, how then was it conceivable to retrieve these indescribable things I had missed and head into the paths along which my original instincts could still drive me ahead, weary as I was: this question it probably was which made you doubt for so long my identity with the "pupil René Rilke." I cannot tell how such a thing could have happened either. Life is very singularly made to surprise us (where it does not utterly appall us). Of course I looked around for help in those years of dismay; much as I remained apart—for my contemporaries were in a normal and incomparably clearer position and did not come into consideration as companions for me—I was not spared the drawing of comparisons and the realizing ever anew what entirely different preliminaries I might have expected for my talent. That did not help me. But it is present to me even now, how, in my moroseness, I found a kind of help in those five evil and anxious years of my childhood having been so utterly cruel, without a single mitigation.

Dear Sir, do not think me unjust: I imagine I have achieved a certain degree of fairness and I wish for nothing more than some day to be allowed to recognize even in the boundless suffering of those years those brighter spots in which—because there was no longer any other way—some kindness befell me as if by chance. For the workings of Nature penetrate far into the unnatural, and an attempt at striking a balance might occasionally take place even there.—But how slight that was measured against the daily despair of a ten-, a twelve-, a fourteen-year-old boy.

So—for individual later moments of my youth—I had to be granted the support of including that which happened so long ago in the feeling of one single terrible damnation, out of which I was cast up merely as out of a sea that is stirred to its depths with destructive intent and is not even concerned whether it leaves here and there upon its devastated shore a live thing or a dead.

When in more reflective years (for how late I arrived at a state where I could read calmly, not just to make up for lost time, but purely receptively!) Dostoevski's *Memoirs of a Death-House* first came into my hands, it seemed to me that since my tenth year I had been admitted into all the terrors and despairs of the convict prison! Please take all the pathos out of this statement. It means to express nothing but a simple recognition of an inner state the external causes of which— I will admit at once—were different enough from the surroundings of Siberian convicts. But Dostoevski, when he endured the unendurable, was a young man, a grown man; to the mind of a child the prison walls of St. Pölten could, if he used the measure of his helplessly abandoned heart, take on pretty much the same dimensions.

Twenty years ago it was, I spent some time in Russia. An insight, prepared only in a very general way by the reading of Dostoevski's works, developed, in that country where I felt so at home, into a most penetrating clarity; it is hard to formulate. Something like this, perhaps: The Russian showed me in so many examples how even a servitude and affliction continually overpowering all forces of resistance need not necessarily bring about the destruction of the soul. There is here, at least for the Slavic soul, a degree of subjection that deserves to be called so consummate that, even under the most ponderous and burdensome oppression, it provides the soul with something like a secret playroom, a fourth dimension of its existence, in which, however crushing conditions become, a new, endless and truly independent freedom begins for it.

Was it presumptuous of me to imagine that I had,

instinctively, achieved a similar complete submission
and resignation in those earliest years, when that block
of an impenetrable misery had been rolled over the
tenderest first shoots of my nature? I had, it seems to
me, some right (with an altered standard naturally) to
assume something of the sort, since indeed of any other
endurance of disproportionate, over-lifesize wrong
there is nowhere any indication.

So I hope you realize that even a long time ago I
undertook to enter upon a certain reconciliation with
my older destinies. As they had not destroyed me they
must at some time have been laid upon the scales of
my life as additional weights—, and the counterweights
that were destined to bring the other side into balance
could be made up only of the purest performance, to
which, too, I found myself determined after those days
of mine in Russia.

If thus I no longer suppressed altogether the old
days in military school, I still could admit them only
in the large and in general, somewhere behind me. For
an examination or even a reconstruction of details my
energies, otherwise busy in any case and working toward the future, would never have sufficed.

So that when you speak to me of some particular
recollection, as happens in your letter, I should have
difficulty in unexpectedly describing such memories,
never having cultivated them.

The irony you manifested for my writings must have
been a highly justified and educational one,—even that
fragment from the later letter of 1892 (!) shows indeed
how very right one would have been even then in
strictly and severely trimming the ragged and crinkled
edges of my expression!

That you incidentally kept that letter among your
papers and were even able to find it again, fills me,

my dear teacher, with a peculiar emotion, which I may hide the less as nowhere in these brusque remarks have I yet thanked you for your new sympathetic communication. It is done at this point, believe me, without any reservation.

Must I, in conclusion, reproach myself for having gone into so much detail and above all to such a length? Should I have taken the renewal of acquaintance in your kind letter more "unconcernedly"?—No; I believe that for me there was only the choice, either to remain silent or really to let you take part in the emotion which the only voice that has ever come across to me from thence was bound to arouse in me.

If you, Sir, can take this unusual answer in a sense as just as it is forbearing, then you will also feel that I cannot close in any other way than with the expression of sincere wishes for your welfare. How should I not see a special privilege in your remembrance ever having afforded me the pleasure of expressing them!

/ *Major-General von Sedlakowitz had been one of Rilke's teachers at St. Pölten (1886–90).*

TO A FRIEND

[from Schloss Berg am Irchel?
mid-December 1920?]

. . . You know that I am not one of those who neglect the body in order to make of it a sacrificial offering for the soul, since my soul would thoroughly dislike being served in such a fashion. All the soarings of my mind begin in my blood, for which reason I precede my work, through a pure and simple way of life that is free from irritants and stimulants, as with an introductory prelude, so that I cannot be deceived over the true spiritual joy that consists in a concord, happy and as if transfigured, with the whole of Nature.

. . . A little time yet, and perhaps I shall no longer grasp all the conditions out of which these songs (the *Duino Elegies*), begun some time ago, arose. If you know some of these works some day you will understand me better; it is so difficult to say what one means.

If I look into my conscience I see but one law, relentlessly commanding: to lock myself into myself and in one stretch to end this task that was dictated to me at the very center of my heart. I am obeying.—For you know that being here I have wanted only that, and I have no right whatever to change the direction of my will before I have ended the act of my sacrifice and my obedience.

I have now done almost all the preparatory work, that is, I have redressed the uncomfortable delays of my correspondence. Think, I have written—I counted them this morning—115 letters, and not one was less than four pages, and many ran to eight, even twelve in close writing. (Naturally I do not count what has gone off to you. That is not writing, that is breathing through the pen.) How many letters! There are so many people who expect of me—I hardly know what: help, advice —from me, who find myself so helpless before the most imperative urgencies of life. And although I know they deceive themselves, are mistaken, still I feel tempted— and I don't believe it is vanity—to tell them something out of my experiences, some of the fruits of my long hours of loneliness. There are young women as well as young girls terribly deserted even in the bosom of their family. Young married women appalled at what has happened to them. And then all these young working people, mostly revolutionaries, who come out of the state prisons without any orientation whatever, take refuge in literature and write drunken, malicious poetry. What shall I say to them? How raise their despairing hearts, how shape their formless will, which under the violence of events has taken on a borrowed, quite provisional character, and which they now carry in themselves like an alien strength, the use of which they scarcely know.

Malte's experiences oblige me from time to time to answer these writings from people I do not know. He, *he* would have done it, if ever a voice had reached him. . . .

Furthermore it is *he* who obliges me to continue this sacrifice, exhorts me to love with all my love's capacities all things to which I want to give form. That is the irresistible force the usufruct of which he left to me. Imagine to yourself a Malte who should have had a lover or even a friend in that Paris that was so terrible for him. Would he then ever have entered so deep into the confidence of things? For these things (he often told me in our few intimate conversations), whose essential life you want to reproduce, first ask you: Are you free? Are you ready to dedicate your whole love to me? To lie with me, as Saint Julian the Hospitaller lay with the leper, in that ultimate embrace that can never be fulfilled in an ordinary and fleeting love of one's neighbor, but has for its impetus *love*, the whole of *love*, all love to be found on earth? And if a thing like that sees (so Malte told me), if it sees you busy with even a single line of your own interest, it will close itself to you. It will perhaps bestow a rule upon you with a word, make you some slight sign of friendship, but it will forgo giving you its heart, entrusting you with its patient nature and its starlike steadfastness, which makes it so much resemble the constellations of the sky.

You must, in order that it shall speak to you, take a thing during a certain time as the only one that exists, as the only phenomenon which through your diligent and exclusive love finds itself set down in the center of the universe and which in this incomparable place on that day the angels serve. What you read here, my friend, is a chapter of those lectures I received from Malte, my only friend during so many years full of suffering and temptations, and I see that you mean the same, absolutely, when you speak of your drawings and paintings, which seem to you valid only because of that infatuation with which *brush or pencil carry out the embrace, the tender taking of possession.* Don't be frightened at the expression "fate," which I used in my last letter. I call fate all external events (illnesses, for example, included) which can inevitably step in to interrupt and annihilate a disposition of mind and training that is by nature solitary. Cézanne must have understood this when during the last years of his life he removed himself from everything that, as he expressed it, might "hook him tight," and when, religious and given to traditions as he was, he yet gave up going to his mother's funeral in order not to lose a working day. That went through me like an arrow, when I learned it, but like a flaming arrow that, while it pierced my heart through, left it in a conflagration of clear sight. There are few artists in our day who grasp this stubbornness, this vehement obstinacy. But I believe that without it one remains always at the periphery of art, which is rich enough as it is to allow us pleasant discoveries, but at which, nevertheless, we halt only as a player at the green table who, while he now and again succeeds with a "coup," remains none the less at the mercy of chance, which is nothing but the docile and dexterous ape of the law.

I have often had to take away Malte's writings from young people, forbidding them to read them. For this book, which seems to emerge in the proof that life is impossible, must so to speak be read against its current. If it contains bitter reproaches, these are absolutely not directed against life. On the contrary, they are the evidences that, for lack of strength, through distraction and inherited errors we lose almost completely the countless earthly riches that were intended for us.

Try, my dearest friend, to run through the overabundance of those pages in this spirit. This will not spare you tears, but will contribute to giving all your tears a meaning clearer and, so to speak, more transparent.

/ *This letter, written in French, was first published in the* Nouvelle Revue Française (1 February 1927), *addressed as "A une amie"; it is one of the most difficult Rilke letters to date and place, and is possibly two separate letters (with a possible break between "dexterous ape of the law," and "I have often had to take away"); evidence points to these sections having been written about mid-December, 1920; a postscript (not reproduced here), containing a poem in French, points to the addressee as Baladine Klossowska (Merline). Obviously, parts of this letter are identical with parts of the following one, also to Merline, and it is not known whether the two were, in fact, two different letters or whether the former is a published version of sections of the latter, with material added from another source.*

TO MERLINE

from Schloss Berg am Irchel,
Thursday, 16 December 1920

Oh, my Friend, I knew all along that these preparations for the "Escalade" would give you too much to do, and now you're going to work for Christmas. Dearest, *I beseech you* (still the same tune), give yourself a little rest first, *a respite*, I beg you seriously, keep very quiet for a few days around this Sunday, do, my Friend, *—it is of the utmost importance that you should be well for Christmas.*

As for myself, I promise to behave properly and pay more attention to the food that the tongue-tied peasant girl brings me; you know I'm not one of those that neglect the body to make a sacrifice of it to the soul; my soul would not care to be served in that way, for every impetus of my mind begins in my blood,—that is why I prepare for my work by living simply, purely, without excitant or stimulant, so as not to be mistaken in the true joy of the mind, which consists in a joyous, so to speak glorified, harmony of one's whole nature. Only I find myself now in such an extraordinary internal situation because of the long, forced interruption, and because I have to return to emotions, still very valid, but bearing the date 1912. In a little while, perhaps, I should no longer understand all the conditions from which these hymns, begun long ago, arose. If you come to know some of this work one day, you will understand better, it is so difficult to explain.

If I lean over my conscience I can see only one law within, and that a pitilessly imperative one: to shut my-

self up in myself and complete at a single stroke the
task that was dictated to me at the center of my heart.
I obey,—for as you know, that was what I came here to
do, and I have no right to change the direction of my
will until I have accomplished my act of devotion and
obedience!

Oh, no, it was not "too egoistic" of you to summon
me, as you said in your last letter but one,—it was, I
assure you, "altruistic" too, and in the highest degree.
I have only to imagine that I am going to Geneva
(without even entering the rue du P. J.), merely to go
with you to your grocer in the rue de Carouge, and
then, after getting in everybody's way, being obliged
to return to the station and come back here,—*happiness, such felicity,* even if we did not speak, even if
you were too busy with your shopping, even if you
scolded me about I don't know what . . . Dearest: take
this feeling as a measure, and realize, judge by this
if it would not be very "altruistic" to wish me to return. . . .

But oh, Dear, how grateful I am to you for encour-
aging me, bravely and valiantly, in your letter of yesterday, to *stay on.* With those few words, which did not
sound too sad, you lifted my heart from the depths
where it was still lying, and put it back on the altar
where it must burn for a few months more. Oh, as
though my feeling for you *could* still increase, I experienced such a fullness of it at that moment that I
was obliged to shut my eyes and clasp myself in my
own arms (as I did that night I told you about) to contain myself. Yes, Dearest, help me in this heroic fashion, join forces with this calm landscape, with these
peaceful walls that protect me,—protect me with them,
—be, oh be that fountain that has been repeating to me
all this time: stay, stay—I am here, I am setting you

the example of the movement that you must accomplish within yourself. And if, delving again into the deepest depths of my work, a dim miner disappearing from the light, I send you nothing but laconic tidings now and then, little signals from the stalker who dare not speak lest the precious game that is approaching should take fright,—don't be grieved, my tender loved one, don't feel yourself deserted, forsaken, forgotten. Think that there, where I lie buried, I am drawing near, as it were, to the other side of your heart, silently,—for how near our heights were to that sublime center where my laborious ardor bursts into flame!

I shall work, and take no heed of the Festivals. Perhaps on Christmas Eve I shall kneel down for a moment, I shall bury my face in my hands, on the little handkerchief, now growing old, on which your tears lie transfigured,—and we shall adore the Child Jesus together.

My most dear, I have such a longing to fold my arms round you, they keep opening even without my knowing it, and if your tenderness becomes personified beside you (oh, I saw it, I saw it!), mine, I swear to you, fills the whole of the space between us; everything that surrounds you as far as you can see, everything you breathe, *is my tenderness*, be sure of it.

I've nearly finished all the "preliminary work"; that's to say I have wiped out the appalling arrears of my correspondence,—just think (I counted them this morning), I've written 115 letters, not all of them as long as the one to General S[edlakowitz], but none less than four pages, and many running into eight and even twelve, pretty closely written. (Of course I'm not counting all that has gone to you, that's not writing, it's breathing with the pen.) What a lot of letters! Oh, Dearest, there are so many people expecting I know not what of me—help, advice (from me, who am always so *rathlos* in face of the sternest emergencies of life!). And although I know quite well that they are mistaken, that they are deluding themselves,—all the same I feel myself lured (and I don't think it's out of vanity) into handing on to them some of my own experience, some of the fruits of my prolonged solitudes, in the way I did for that blind man. I see that you were touched by that letter, so I can't have done wrong to write it. . . . And women and girls terribly forsaken even in the bosom of their families,—and young married women frightened by what has happened to them, —and then all the young men, workmen, mostly revolutionaries, who come out of the State Prisons all bewildered, and run astray into "literature," composing poems in the vein of a spiteful drunkard. . . . What can one say to them? How can one raise their despondent hearts, how can one mold their formless will, which by the force of events has assumed a borrowed and purely temporary character, and which they now bear within them like an alien force that they hardly know how to use!

Malte's experience obliges me at times to reply to these cries from the unknown; he would have done so if ever such voices had reached him,—and he has left me a sort of legacy of action which I am not free to divert from a charitable purpose. It is he too that obliges me to continue in the infinite devotion which requires me to love all the things I want to give shape to, with all my faculties of loving; that was his own irresistible force, of which he has left me the life-interest. Imagine Malte, in that Paris that was so terrible to him, having a lover, or even a friend! Would he ever have penetrated so far into the confidence of things? For (as he repeatedly told me in our few inti-

mate conversations) the things whose essential life you
wish to express, begin by asking you: "Are you free?
Are you prepared to devote *all* your love to me, to lie
with me as St. Julian the Hospitaller lay beside the
leper, giving him the supreme embrace that no simple,
passing charity could accomplish, because its motive is
love, the whole of love, all the love that exists on earth?"
And if the thing sees (said Malte), if the thing sees
that you are preoccupied, with even a mere particle of
your interest, it shuts itself up again; it may perhaps
give you a countersign, it may make a little, faintly
friendly sign (and even that is a good deal for a human
being imprisoned among others obstinately pursuing a
meaningless eloquence) but it refuses to give you its
heart, to disclose to you its patient being, its sweet
sidereal constancy that makes it so like the constellations! If a thing is to speak to you, you must regard it
for a certain time *as the only one that exists,* as the
one and only phenomenon, which, thanks to your laborious and exclusive love, is now placed at the center
of the Universe, and there, in that incomparable place,
is this day attended by the Angels.

What you have just read, my loving Friend, is a
chapter from the lessons I received from Malte (my
only friend for so many years of suffering and temptation)—and I see that you say the same thing, absolutely, when you speak of your drawings and paintings
as seeming valid to you only because of the amorous
entanglement, of which the brush or pencil executes
the embrace, the caressing and voluptuous act of possession. The *dormeuse,* and certain parts of the *jeune
fille au balcon rouge du printemps,* as well as the vision
of the other girl in the tragic embrasure of the eternal
window—gave me palpitations, not merely sensuous
but *infinite* ones; you know, the sort of palpitations that

could come from running fast, and from the advent of the lover, and from the terror of happiness that the influences of spring sometimes assail us with: it was like an emotion *caused by all that at the same time*—and I leave you to imagine how powerful it was. This was what I meant, actually, when I wrote that, in every one of the pastels, what astonishes me most is the unity of consciousness with which the object is always apprehended; a single violent gasp of feeling, a single gesture of passion has dragged it in, close to the heart, as a single whole; there is never any sense of one thing having been grasped after another. It is Merline again —oh, in love with earth and heaven—that I sing! Again the power of your arms, and their ineffable glory in rendering such obedience to your sovereign heart, your heart old and new, your spring and summer heart, your heart which, if it had not blossomed out in this dazzling fashion, would long ago have been a star, not as terribly great as Venus, but of the same fire, the same celestial conflagration!

Dear, listen, I am glad not to be going away. Everything is beginning to enclose me again, and I must come back to my earlier feeling that this enclosedness is good and kindly and the accomplishment of all my desires. If I were to leave on the 22nd, the time up to then would be merely a waiting-time, do what I would, and the time between my return from Geneva and the arrival of the Z.s [Zieglers], likewise a wort of waiting, —so that right up to the middle of January it would be all after-effect and interruption! And my forces that are now marching towards the interior centers would have to retrace their steps and bend them unceasingly towards the exterior, towards the *visible*. It's true that I have time—*months* of it, for in all probability the Z.s [Zieglers] will not come back to Berg till May,—but can

275

one ever be sure? These luckless years have left me with a sort of apprehensiveness (*Schreckhaftigkeit*), a constant dread of all the things that might come in order to destroy. Don't be afraid of the expression "fate" that I used in my last letter, I call "fate" all the outward events (including illnesses for instance) which, inevitably, may come and interrupt and overwhelm one whose disposition is by nature solitary. Cézanne was well aware of this, when for the last thirty years of his life he steered clear of everything that might "come and grab hold of you," as he put it, and when, believer though he was, and devoted to tradition, he nevertheless refused to go to his mother's funeral, so as not to lose a day's work. It went through me like an arrow when I learned all this, but like a flaming arrow which after piercing my heart left it in a blaze of clearsightedness. Few artists of our day have any conception of this obstinacy, this violent persistency, but I believe that without it you remain forever on the outskirts of art, which are rich enough in themselves to afford you agreeable discoveries, but where you merely play the part of a gambler at the green table who, though he may now and then bring off a "stroke of luck," remains subject to chance, which is no more than the docile and dexterous ape of law.

It was time for lunch, I remembered your orders, I ate slowly, with the attention of a schoolboy thinking out a problem, of which the solution is in his mouth: noodle soup, rice, carrots, and a sweet, after that my coffee—and now I'm going on again. A fine snow is falling, and right in the middle of the sky, above the fountain which is only distinguishable at the very top, by its falling motion, from the whiteness of the background, stands a vaguely rounded sun, without rays and without strength, that in another moment will be swallowed up by the misty atmosphere, which is opposed to this attempt at illumination. Even now, looking up again, I can only see a faint glimmer, like a spot on a piece of greyish paper where someone has scratched with a penknife to remove an inkstain, destroying some of the thickness of the sheet.

Dearest, don't misunderstand, all that I have just written to you *is not said to defend myself from your appeal*—you have reduced it yourself to its perpetual and internal state, which does not demand any real accomplishment for the moment; it is against the appeal that I feel in myself, constantly drawing me towards you, that I am defending myself. Let me explain: I am talking to myself in front of you: understand that, Friend.

Oh most Dear, reading the letter that tells of the tortures of my childhood, you were reminded of "that afternoon" when I talked to you for the first time about that deadly period that beset me when I was very young and filled my soul with painful astonishment and a terror really beyond nature. "That afternoon" . . . I often think of it, doing sentry-go in the park; only the other day I saw it all, with that tender yet forceful recollection which perhaps overwhelmed the Angel, thinking of the moment when, trembling himself, he brought the piercing Annunciation to the Virgin Mary. Oh, if ever I could tell you, with that voice that is in you before it has even left my mouth, the History of our love, you would be transported with an astonishment of felicity; for it is so much more beautiful than we imagine; our memory, expanded though it is by the multiple crop of this year of benediction, would still not suffice to contain all the harvest: three-quarters of it, you may be sure, have been left outside in the open.

That moment when you looked at me "like a girl." Your face all at once lost all expression, *every kind*, it abdicated, it rid itself of everything, of all complaisance, all amiability, all its habitual charm, it became quite dark, quite empty for the thousandth part of a second—and in that new space, which was a moment of creation, there was born, there arose that new light, oh, a light that neither man nor Angel will ever be allowed to describe, that only a child could conceive in the morning air of its most innocent summer day. . . . *I saw that*. From that moment, as far as life is concerned, I can die. Seeing your face transfigured by love, and all filled with that youthfulness, that virginity that had been preserved in you for the sake of dazzling me one day,—I realized that the sum of splendors exceeds by far the number of all the horrors and all the sufferings I have ever undergone. Do you understand? Meditating on this the other day, a line recurred to me that I wrote long ago to Night, apostrophizing it:

You Darkness made of Light—

That is what your adorable face was like, surprised by a new radiation in the midst of its obscure transition: in the midst of its inmost seriousness, which was Youth, the splendor of all lives arose,—*of all lives*. . . .

As for that instant (and many others, even some that were so to speak inconspicuous—(*unscheinbar*), I do not understand how it contrived to pass! More than once after that event there was no time around us, only a duration free of all movement, all decay, a constancy of life, a pure existence. . . .

I don't know, Merline, if such words have ever been written between lovers, but I carve them on this paper as though it were granite, and I tremble as I trace them.

Dearest, if you are ever seized by distress, by an

anguish of body or soul, call up within you your own face, your face of a holy virgin, of a chosen adolescent —for you felt, I know, the transfiguration that radiated from you, just as Saint Theresa felt the divine penetration in the flash of stigmatization. . . .

I believe that the "Black Virgins," at the moment when they yield to the believer kneeling before the altar, his heart heavy with vows and offerings, I believe that at the moment of the expected miracle, they have the golden smile of a youth that comes back to them from the earliest age of the world, that dark luminosity that casts no shadow. . . .

Oh Friend,—almost the whole day has been spent in writing to you, in an hour's time they will be coming for the post. I must end.

Au revoir, Friend, au revoir,

Take care of yourself, take care of yourself,

Love yourself for

René

Thursday about 4 o'clock.

Forgive me if I have this registered, and they come and disturb you,—but there are so many things of importance in these pages of heart. . . . My Love . . .

TO PHIA RILKE

from Schloss Berg am Irchel,
17 December 1920

My dear Mama,

Once more at our blessed hour, most loving remembrance of Christmas days of longest ago, and the wish that now, after such bad times, there may be granted you celebrations each year more quiet, more peaceful, and finally too in a little home of your very own again!

Now that this has been expressed, really everything has been expressed, for now it is a matter not of reading, but of going-into-oneself and, in one's own heart, for the year's holiest hour of celebration, preparing the manger, so that therein, this hour, and in it the Savior, may with all fervor be born into the world again!

What I wish for you, dear Mama, is that on this evening of consecration, the remembrance of all distress, even the consciousness of the immediate worry and insecurity of existence may be quite checked and in a sense dissolved in the innermost knowledge of that grace, for which indeed no time is too dense with calamity and no anxiety so sealed that in its own time —which is not ours!—it could not enter and penetrate what seems insurmountable with its mild victory. There is no moment in the long year when one would be able to call so vividly into one's soul its ever possible appearance and then omnipresence, as this winter night, autonomous through the centuries, which, through the incomparable coming of that child who transformed all creatures, all at once outweighed and surpassed in value the sum of all other earthly rights. Though the easy summer, when existence seems considerably more bearable and more effortless, when we do not have to guard ourselves against such direct antagonism from the air and from serenely absorbed Nature—, though the happier summer may pamper us with consolations,—what are they all beside the immeasurable comfort-treasures of this outwardly unassuming, even poor night that suddenly stands open toward the inside, like an all-embracing and warming heart, and which with beats of its own bell-toned center really does reply to our hearkening into the inner-most cell.

All annunciations of previous times did not suffice to herald this night, all hymns that have been sung in its praise did not come near the stillness and eagerness in which shepherds and kings knelt down—, just as we too, none of us, has ever been able, while this mira-cle-night was befalling him, to indicate the measure of his experience.

It is so truly the mystery of the kneeling, of the deeply kneeling man: his being greater, by his spiritual nature, than he who stands! which is celebrated in this night. He who kneels, who gives himself wholly to kneeling, loses indeed the measure of his surroundings, even looking up he would no longer be able to say what is great and what is small. But although in his bent posture he has scarcely the height of a child, yet he, this kneeling man, is not to be called small. With him the scale is shifted, for in following the peculiar weight and strength in his knees and assuming the position that corresponds to them, he already belongs to that world in which height is—depth,—and if even height remains unmeasurable to our gaze and our in-struments: who could measure the depth? . . .

But this is the night of radiant depth unfolded—: for you, dear Mama, may it be hallowed and blessed. Amen.—René.

/ "Our blessed hour" recalls the custom of Rilke's father of ringing bells at six o'clock on Christmas morning.

TO MERLINE

Tuesday, 22 February 1921

My Love, trembling with emotion as you yourself were when you wrote it, I read your letter last night on returning from Zurich, by my good fire, about nine in the evening. The table was covered with letters, some urgent,—I tried to read a few, but couldn't understand any but yours, Friend,—I came back to it again and again, at midnight it was still before me. . . .

No, I have never dared to "push on as far as Geneva" even in thought, in spite of all impatience for you, in spite of all longing! I see and know only too well—and feel every day—what is at stake for me now. This rushing out over such wide spaces, towards you, who are to me like the most open places in the blue of the sky, through which one can go further than it is possible to feel,—this rushing out, Beloved, is right in itself, but at this moment, at this time, it is "temptation,"—the very kind that one dare not succumb to once one has got so far as to be saving oneself up for the greatest fulfillments and achievements. You see, I can't be deceived (even if I would!), my inward eye is indescribably sharp,—even when my feeling sets everything vibrating, it sees beyond that a pure, oh so pure outline: I know, now that I am back here once more, I've got to begin all over again with my innermost organization and resumption, just as I did that time in November. . . . You must never forget what years I have behind me, and what their assaults have made of me;—the "deliberation" that has become essential to me is not the simple transition from receptiveness to productivity, from dispersedness to concentration; it is the process of healing a wound, which needs endless immobility and seclusion and patience: only after I am healed, and that is a long way off yet, shall I be able to begin producing, walking again, advancing, flying.

Beloved, have patience with me.

Life is not the power that, as you say, "has given me everything,"—that is not true in my case,—I guessed at, I knew, many things beforehand, which it never gave me, and its "giving," as it is called, was too much for me from my childhood upwards: where others were aware of the gift, I felt only the weight: just because I had understood the spirit of such coarse presents beforehand. Love often seemed to be demanding of me that I should force a fruit I had admired into the eye it had entranced, as though it were a mouth,—yes, I can say with truth that it (love) has given me everything only when it was able to remain on the wing, without even setting its foot on my heart!

My Friend, I am not asserting anything of which you need be afraid, for how many moments of sublime lightness of heart have there been between us from the first, and what an inexhaustible discovery did we make only the other day, on that unforgettable Sunday morning, here, in front of my fire. . . .

After all I have undergone . . . I can only hope that fate has no designs upon us (we are no stuff for that), —but that outside its sphere we may continue to achieve—what has always been the essence of our enchantment—an almost godlike rapture, somewhere on islands of space on which the ordinary laws of gravity do not prevail: oh Beloved, we will never spy on *what* it is that transports us to each other and to that exaltation in our common god. The secret that we experience in him must always belong to *him* and not to us, so that we suddenly stand forth with it in the "real" world, as if with stolen treasure that draws the eyes of men upon itself.

Let me now, Love, in the next few months, for as long as this refuge is granted me, arrange and clarify my life. (I can't go on forever in this state of confusion!) I am not concerned with the *Elegies* or any other productiveness,—I am not an "author," who "makes books." Even the *Elegies* (or whatever may one day be vouchsafed me) will merely be the result of an internal organization, an internal progress, a purer, more comprehensive development of my whole interrupted, shattered being. That was why I was so terrified when you spoke of the *Elegies* the other day as a piece of "work"—and (oh, forgive me!) almost reprimanded you.

Understand me: much as I belong to, and am the servant of, my work, I cannot evoke it,—that is why I was so struck by that saying of Bonsels', that no one has ever got further than "readiness"—it is for "readiness" that I am struggling now, and now nobody must touch me or shake me, for like the formation of a crystal it depends on the most distant influences, which can only reach us when we are standing in the constellation, undisturbed by chance, caprice, greed or resistance! Oh, my Love, believe me, I do know the "world"; I don't want to do otherwise than "remain within the law": how can that do you any harm? Are we then asking our love to give us any other proofs or benefits than those that rest upon that same law: woe to the caress that is against the stars!

I am weak now, like one that has allowed himself to be degraded by the daily influence of disasters; the war years seemed to put me in the wrong, my whole existence was false in their twilight,—I must come into my own again within myself.

At certain hours your love has had an infinite share in fortifying me,—for days on end I feel I owe my future to its breadth and splendor. But decisions can only be arrived at in solitude, and I must be allowed to seize and fill up my solitude again, and enlist it in the great relationships that I longed for even as a child, more, oh so infinitely more than any happiness.

Everything is glorious between us: surely you know that? Have two lovers ever stood so towards each other, with such expectancy in their open arms, as though up to now there had been only *anticipation* between them, as though they had never yet seen each other, as though all demonstrations were only a foreshadowing in their hearts of what they had already felt?! Doesn't it speak well for us, Dearest, that we can keep it like this, and let it go and take it back again?

. . . You are right: let us promise each other the summer—as far as possible—in some quiet spot. So that we may at last have time to look at each other and imbue ourselves with each other. . . .

I'm writing all this in haste, it may be full of mistakes —I have no time to read it through again. Three important business letters still have to be posted.

But I will write to you again this week, Dearest, and give you my news, before embarking for the Isle of Work. . . .

Oh understand, feel and feel, even if you suffer, that it is bliss you are suffering.

René

TO BALTHUSZ KLOSSOWSKI

from Château de Berg am Irchel,
Canton de Zurich,
at the end of February 1921

My dear friend B.,

A number of years ago in Cairo, I met an English writer, Mr. Blackwood, who in one of his stories expresses a rather neat hypothesis; in it he claims that, always at midnight, a tiny split appears between the day ending and the one beginning, and that a very clever person who could succeed in gliding into it would escape from time and would find himself in a kingdom independent of all the changes we undergo; in that place all the things we have lost are heaped up (Mitsou, for example) . . . the dolls broken by children, etc., etc.

It is there, my dear B., that you ought to sneak off on the night of 28 February, in order to take possession of your birthday, which hides there, by returning to light only every four years! (I imagine how, in an anniversary exposition, the anniversaries of the others would be shabby compared with the one which is well looked after, and which one takes out, at long intervals, all resplendent from its storehouse.)

Mr. Blackwood, if I am not mistaken, called this secret and nocturnal split the "crack"; now I advise you, for the satisfaction of your dear mother and Pierre, not to disappear into it, but to look at it only in your sleep. Your birthday, I am sure, is there joined with others; you will see it at once, and perhaps you will have the luck to glimpse there other splendors too. In waking on the first of March, you will be filled with astonishing and mysterious remembrances and, instead of your own birthday, you will give it to others, generously, by telling them your stirring impressions and by describing to them the magnificent state of your unusual anniversary—absent, but intact and of the highest quality!

This discreet anniversary, which most of the time lives in a species of the beyond, will certainly give you the right over many unknown things here (it seems to me more important and more exotic than the Brazilian uncle). I hope, my dear B., that you will be capable of convincing a few people on our earth to grow on, in spite of the difficulties of our uncertain seasons. . . . A bit as M. de Jussieu had done with that cedar of Lebanon which has become the main attraction of the Jardin des Plantes!

As for "our book," I am going to finish my manuscript someday soon, profiting from those little changes that M. Vildrac proposes, and I hope to send it off, with my definitive text, on the first of March: in honor of your birthday. May this be a good omen for our mutual and fraternal success.

The other day, in Zurich, I ordered sent to you a small (but very small) package, for the day that finds itself substituted for your invisible birthday; I hope that they will be punctual; me, I shall be so, unfailingly, with my sincere vows and with all this friendship which I put at your disposal.

René

(*From the French*)

/ *Balthusz Klossowski, born in 1908, is the son of Baladine Klossowska (Merline) and is now a painter in Paris; "Mr. Blackwood" was Algernon Blackwood (1869–1951), the English novelist; "your birthday" refers to Balthusz Klos-*

sowski's having been born on 29 February (1908); M. de Jussieu was a French botanist and onetime director of the Jardin des Plantes; "M. Vildrac" refers to Charles Vildrac, the French poet, (born in 1882).

TO MERLINE

from Schloss Berg am Irchel,
Monday, 7 March 1921

Dear, this little letter is instead of one I wrote you for Sunday and didn't send; I brought it back from Flaach, it is before me now. It contains the tender reproaches that you know by heart, and repeats things that I have expressed better before, so that I felt it was useless.

It worries me when, as in your last two letters, you talk of an "abyss of suffering" and of your "sadness,"— and after looking at them for a long while, I should have liked to be a powerful sun to dry . . . many future tears you are preparing in some valley of your heart where it's always raining.

I'm so selfish at the moment that I could wish, not of course to read that you are happy, but at least to receive some proof of your tranquillity, your courage. Is it too much for me to ask that of the strength of your love? Is it impossible for you to use it a little in my favor, to be calm, to become a part, and so to speak the rampart, of the tranquillity, the equilibrium I have so long desired for myself, and which is (as you know) the fundamental condition of my existence here? But here I am again, repeating things that you have heard before, and if you write to me in a different strain, it must be because you lack the strength to master your heart, and so I must resign myself to it: for you have used so much of it—of your strength—these last months. . . . All the same, with what joy do I greet the least gleam of light in your letters,—alas, you have scarcely shown it before you extinguish it with your own hands. Why? Why? You say: "The other day I almost had an impulse to create something for myself," and you hasten to add: "but it has gone again." Dearest, tell me about this, I beseech you,—let us discuss all the possibilities that seem open to you. . . . It is heartbreaking to see you giving way to the idleness of a harmful sadness which does not even furnish you with dreams. I should be easy in my mind if I knew you were taking responsibility for your own life, as you did all the time at G. with such admirable energy; do you wish to crush me under the weight of the suspicion that it is I who have destroyed in you that youthful impulse, joyous in spite of everything? . . .

Oh how I should bless the day that brought me better news of you, of the kind you sent me some ten days ago, after getting my letter, which you said you had understood and which seemed to have restored you to yourself.

Make me suffer less for a time, Friend, support yourself,—let happy memories sustain you if your strength fails you; they are always there, and their current does not run backwards, even across foggy country it floats towards the future! My God, if only I could show you the smile you wore that Monday when we were saying goodbye in the train,—it was rich enough to live on for three years!

I have again begun reading Keyserling's important *Travel Diary*, it holds one's attention and one's most intense interest from the first page. In one of the first chapters, during the voyage in the Indian Ocean, he notes: "If I am to accomplish what I am here for, my nervous system must be absolutely in tune, my attention unhindered, my temper serene . . ." That is just how it is with me; you see, I can give myself everything else, but this serenity of temper must come to me now from you, Beloved. Is it wilfulness on my part to persist in imagining that you could be the guardian angel of those conditions which your love is so inexhaustibly capable of producing so long as it has a share in the result? Is it so very different, doing the same for the absent one, silent and preoccupied with himself?

It is not for this reason, however, but for many others more important to yourself, that I wish you would read Keyserling's *Diary*—you were not in the mood for it when you were here. It is the most educational book of our time, not in the sense of being instructive, but because of the way it works on one and influences one; dissolving dependences in order to replace them, almost always, by relationships. He adopts authoritatively the freest and most receptive attitude that a European mind can achieve today,—and if Hausenstein's book could affect you so much, as a restoration of things lost to us by their apparent absence, you would welcome as a gift Keyserling's idea of the survival of the actualities of this world. I have just been given the complete work again, so that the first (borrowed) volume, which I brought up to your room that time, is at your disposal. Will you try it? (I won't send it unless you tell me to, because I've just smothered you with a lot of other books)—I wonder whether there might not be something in it that would be useful not only to you but for your evenings in common?

Today I had to make an act of renunciation that I found very hard: Hermann Keyserling is to speak tonight in the Reading Circle at Rollingen, and the peo-

ple he is living with had specially invited me to spend
the rest of the evening at their house, with their famous
guest: it really cost me an effort to say no,—but there
was no help for it, since Berg is now to claim me without the slightest interruption. Graf Keyserling will not
have his lectures printed, because he considers that the
spoken word is only intended to be spoken,—so that
even the positive loss cannot be made good, to say
nothing of the personal meeting at the Martinis'. . . . .

As for my friend B[althusz], I was not so wrong after
all in advising him not to disappear in the "crack,"
since as far as school was concerned, he was there already. Fortunately it was discovered in time! I remain
convinced that "B[althusz] exists," only it will always
be extremely difficult to agree as to the place where he
exists!

I have some splendid wallflowers (*Goldlack*) on the
chest of drawers, everything else is as you remember
it; that is to say, the desk has been here some time
(I'm writing upon it), leaning against the cupboards
on the left, without seriously disturbing the corner that
you like. (Since you don't see the *Journal de Genève*,
I enclose the article on the Pitoëffs in Paris,—please
let me have it back next time.)

And tell me about that "impulse": *you must*.

Rene

TO MERLINE

from Schloss Berg am Irchel,
Friday, 8 April 1921

I'm quite surprised to be writing to you for a
Saturday again; yesterday for a while I thought you

were on your way, but now it seems you are leaving
on Sunday, and I see that the route via Basel is much
shorter and more direct. I'm glad, Dear, that you've
come to this calm and tranquil decision, beyond the
reach of circumstance, and I admire your inventive
activity: that you should have been able to finish the
portrait of the little boy. . . .

As for me, I'm forcing myself not to think of the future and its vague worries; it would deprive me of the
remainder of my "present" at Berg—which has anyhow
suffered a nasty shock owing to a quite unexpected
disturbance, which has irritated and exasperated me
for the last two days: just think, they have set up an
"electric sawmill" exactly opposite the right-hand entrance to the park, which has been working since Tuesday and makes a continual, atrocious noise of singing
steel, attacking with the cruelty of a dentist the poor,
beautiful wood brought in from the Irchel forest. My
nerves are not very strong at the moment, and I suffer
terribly from this penetrating obstacle, which will have
to be fought every day with part of the strength I
wanted so much to concentrate on a single purpose. I
find that my sensitiveness in the matter is not at all
exaggerated, for Leni, in spite of her peasant constitu-
tion, complains of it too and understands my despair.
If one keeps the windows *completely* closed, and the
wind is not blowing from that direction, one hears it
relatively little, but all my walks in the park have become impossible from now on. My beautiful silence!
Where are the days when I wrote that the lovely fountain set the measure of all the noises here? This disturbance of one's pure hearing is so frightful to me,
because for any thought to become real, I must first
be able to state it in sound equivalents, projecting it
on to the purest possible auditory surface; to find my

hearing crammed with such alien matter is just like having to write on paper that has been blotted and scribbled all over. . . . Forgive me for writing so much about this, but it has rather upset me: my lovely silence,—only last Saturday and Sunday I kept thinking I should at least have that for a few quiet months, the wonderful silence of which the fountain formed so to speak the texture, embroidered now by the little bird voices and the melancholy of the frogs. . . .

But not only for *my* purpose (a very special one, if you like), for every other purpose Berg has lost its principal charm owing to this unfortunate mechanical installation; for even if one is not contemplating any intensive work, even a person wishing merely to wander about the park and read there in the summer—will be deprived of all pleasure by this continual probing noise, which distracts one's attention and must set on edge, I feel sure, nerves far less sensitive than mine. In a word, it's a disaster! The railway has never come this far, but thanks to this industry "time," our time, has crept into Berg to rob the little manor of the consciousness of its tradition, heretofore intact. Really it's enough to make one weep. And the frightful machine is always "ready for action"; this morning it woke me at five o'clock,—they're like children who've been given a trumpet, these madmen, they blow and blow from five in the morning till 7.45 in the evening, they hardly leave themselves time to eat, the devils. Yes, it's the Devil that has played me this trick,—or is it the good God's Providence trying to make it easier for me to leave Berg? Well, in his omniscience he could employ no better means,—only, inaccurate and universal as he is, he has set it in motion too soon (what are one or two months in his reckoning! From his viewpoint the two things coincided more or less, the beginning of this infernal sawing and my decamping! Oh accuracy, where art thou?)

As it happens, the die was cast yesterday: Berg is let! The Colonel came with the lessees, and now I have actually met my "successors." *When* they intend to move in was not expressly mentioned,—it looks as though I should have about eight weeks left. But I shall ask Z[iegler] to let me know as soon as a date is settled. Well, well, everything is drawing to a close. What, in the last resort, what will Berg, kind protective, agreeable Berg—Leni included—have meant to me? What can I still wrest from it? I shall do my utmost in spite of all obstacles!

Your letter of yesterday has just come, my loving Friend,—so our rooms were inspected *almost at the same time.* Z. was here yesterday at two o'clock, before the new tenants. The sawmill was not working just then, so they will be considerably let down, the future Herr Schmidt, etc.—I think that is the name—when they become aware of this "illustrated" silence. Thank you, Dear, for your calm, firm letter, overflowing with love, considering everything patiently and judiciously, in spite of what you call your "volcanic temperament." I can imagine your farewells to Geneva, I am with you everywhere you go, and it is I myself working in your heart at every "shock of memory."

How beautiful it was to us, that city, how bright, how generous,—and your room, there all my thoughts come to a stop,—I can never say all that it was to us. . . . I believe that the moment you leave your room, the gods will transplant it among the stars, Beloved, and we shall look up at it now and again,—it will be a fine new star revolving round Venus.

René

TO MERLINE

from Le Prieuré d'Etoy, Canton de Vaud,
19 May 1921

It is hardly likely that I shall succeed in writing to you,—you too in your many letters, three of which came this morning, you *talk* to me, your pen hardly plays any part in it,—you talk to me, Dearest, and if you ask me whether I hear your voice, I can affirm that I do, *yes,* I hear it—it is both sweet and painful to me.

My poor Friend, what it means to me to know you are suffering so much in your whole beloved body and the greater part of your heart,—do you know what it means to me? And if like J . . . I admire you, like G . . . I fear for you, if you are taking morphia to make yourself sleep. My loving Friend, instead of that, put this letter on your eyes to serve them as eyelids. . . .

You have not shared my suffering, my Dearest, you have done far more by being day and night (for how long?) under the atrocious tyranny of this illness; I myself have suffered a great deal, and still suffer, but what I am suffering from is an ache of the conscience that I can share with nobody and must endure all alone! For having to leave Berg was not the worst (I'm used to leaving places I'm fond of, and this exercise of dying to surroundings that have sustained me for a time will forever be a part of my heart's apprenticeship), my deepest torments arise from the fact that I was not able to give last winter the shape I intended it to have. . . .

The last few days, my God, sloped so steeply and rapidly towards the end, and I had to pull up so many little roots from that hospitable soil, that I hardly had time to think about the future. A few days before leaving I noticed a very modest advertisement in the *Journal de Genève*,—I just had time to write for a few further particulars,—they were fairly reassuring, so I only spent one night at the Baur au Lac. . . . Things here are just as the little advertisement described them; everything is comfortable, calm,—I have a light room looking towards the lake in the distance, a flat view, cut in two by a solitary poplar; my bed is in a recess at the back, and what is charming—a rose-bush in full bloom climbs up towards my window: *Gloire de Dijon* roses, wide open already and filling with their scent this little den that I stay shut up in most of the time, having all my meals here. The garden is not a big one, —a wide terrace, wandering off to the right into a rather shabby little orchard; I don't go there much for fear of meeting the other boarders, whom I keep away from entirely, having no wish (as you may imagine) to make acquaintances.

But at the end of the orchard, guess, Dear, guess what I see: the tower of the Château d'Aubonne,—it's only an hour and a half from here. . . . If we had continued our walk that led us to the village you no doubt remember, a little more than half-an-hour would have brought us to Etoy!

Oh my Dearest, what a lot of memories!

Of course I thought of Sierre to begin with,—but it would have been too dear (I must manage on very little for the rest of my stay in Switzerland) and then I dared not go there without you. . . . (Two whole months ago I bought a few lottery tickets; . . . there have been two draws since then: fortune, inattentive as usual, seems to be occupied elsewhere!) No, you can understand that I couldn't bear to go to Geneva;—in

a day or two, if I'm feeling a bit rested, I shall let the
Salises know where I am; I should so much like to see
them before I leave,—perhaps they will be enterprising
enough to come and see me here . . . and then I'm
expecting the Princess Thurn und Taxis, whom I
should so much have liked to receive in Berg; she is
supposed to be coming to Rolle towards the end of the
month, to see her charming grandchildren, who are at
school there.

I have long wanted to see this revered friend, who
for many years advised me in all my plans,—I should
like to talk to her about the place in Bohemia that was
thought of for me a long while ago; it is so difficult to
explain all the details by letter. The little house opposite the château of Lautschin, which the Prince wanted
to keep for me, has had to be given up under pressure
from the municipality, but perhaps if I present myself
in person they may be able to get the authorities to
change their mind. . . . I should like to discuss all this
with the Princess before making any real plans. . . .
At any rate, by the autumn I must have some sort of
"Berg," not so much to begin the coming winter in, as
to re-commence, with a stronger will, the one that was
spent between fears and felicities, far from the foundation of laborious serenity on which I had hoped to base
it. I'm telling you all this with absolute frankness (how
could I do otherwise?) and I feel strong enough to dis-
miss from my feelings, often full of bitterness, the least
shadow of reproach that might fall on your bright and
beautiful figure. I must account to myself alone for my
lack of firmness, and I would rather give up my life
as I conceive it than allow my ingratitude to rise up
against your heart, admirable as a rose and generous
as a whole happy garden.

But where, where my loving Friend, are the great

trees of *our* summer that I undoubtedly saw in a moment of sublime clairvoyance? You talk of going to take a cure at Tolz. . . . I'm sure, my Dearest, what you need is a good treatment, a cure carefully applied. How I should love to be near you, my Friend, during your convalescence; I feel that at no time could my tenderness do you more good, and that it alone can efface in you the memory (beyond human endurance) of so much suffering in body and heart.

I drink deep of the pleasure of being once more in a French country, and I still have no very precise idea of the date when I shall have to cross the shunned frontier.

My relations with Gide continue; this morning I had a very kind letter from him, he had just shown Paul Valéry the few lines in my last letter that might interest him. On my arrival here I found a book, also published by the *Editions de la Nouvelle Revue Française*, in which Jean Schlumberger had written a dedication to me; I became quite absorbed in these moving pages, which at times attain the happy precision of a masterpiece. This present helped me to get through the first moments in these fresh surroundings, which I hated to begin with, on account of the inevitable drawbacks of boarding-house life, which I had almost forgotten.

So I am ending my stay in Switzerland very near where I began it, two years ago; the view from my window reminds me very much of the one I had from the "Farm" at Nyon where Comtesse D. used to put her guests when her little chalet wouldn't hold them all. Unfortunately she is still in England, whence she will go direct to Czechoslovakia.

Dearest, I must end! Ah, make no mistake, if this letter affects a certain calm,—I'm keeping myself under control; but I'm just as impatient as you, my poor

Friend, to see you, to take your face, grown thinner from so much pain, into my two tender hands, and never leave off looking at it.

What can I do, what can I do to make you feel a little, a little of my tenderness? Read what is between the lines, my dearest, my Friend, my tender child, rest, sleep, and smile a little at every attempt at happiness that awakes in you.

René

TO MERLINE

from Le Prieuré d'Etoy, Canton de Vaud,
6 June 1921 (Monday)

The temptation is too strong, my dearest Friend, I must try the lovely paper you've given me, at once, —in exchange I've sent you the June *Vogue*, from Lausanne, where I spent a few hours. . . .

The Princess has not yet announced herself—"my honorable protectress," as you call her—a little maliciously, for that is something she has never been; haven't you noticed, Friend, that you always speak with a certain irony, or even an incomprehensible harshness, of people who are dear to me on account of our long, friendly intercourse? It grieves me for the simple reason that it makes it almost impossible to talk to you about them, openly and innocently, as the fancy takes me. Of course I know it's your suffering expressing itself in this way,—it's not your own voice: but don't you think we have much to gain by forcing our pain to sing nothing but what we are? . . .

I too, my loving Friend, might commit many injustices if I allowed my heart to avenge itself for all it has had to suffer these last months; but with no wish to boast, I can assure you that, on the contrary, when you speak of your friends, even those I don't know, I love them in proportion as I feel that you are loved by them. I had often meant to ask you if you had not made any attempt to trace your Russian friends of 1914, but I refrained for fear of reviving the memory of them to no purpose; and now you tell me you have just spent hours of tender intimacy with these *êtres d'élite*. I'm delighted to hear it. How I should enjoy meeting them some day with you; not long ago I myself was steeped afresh in the Russian atmosphere by the receipt of a touching letter from a young friend who was thought to have been lost in the war. And fancy, he writes that in Russia, for some time, I too was said to be dead.

I will show you his beautiful letter. Have you read Schickele's prose essay on his journey through Alsace and his stay in Paris (with Barbusse)? It's very fine. I possess this number of the *Rundschau*, because Regina Ullmann sent it me with another little contribution of her own, very curious in parts, but not as good as the *Wirtshausschild*. I'm amused to hear that the little story I came across in Bonsels' *Autobiography* is connected with Mme. S.'s sister. *Eros und die Evangelien* is not a good book, though very attractive and even fascinating here and there. It suffers a great deal by comparison with *Menschenwege*, in which, actually, both subjects have been treated already with far more delicacy and restraint. In *Eros und die Evangelien* everything is carried to extremes and becomes insupportable from sheer deliberateness and obviousness. To produce his contrasts, he piles up exaggerations on both sides, and unfortunately the two "cases" he exhibits have, so to speak, no need of words. The strength of the poor little dying girl, once her god is out of danger, lies in her silence,—and the other personage, a most active one, is beyond words for the opposite reason, and has little use for them. So long as he's writing about the cobbler, it's wonderful; if only he'd stopped at that! (Lou Andreas-Salomé said this when she was giving an account of the book)—and I know I felt exactly the same when I read it. Nevertheless the admirable side of Bonsels' obviously dual make-up appears in certain passages with all the charm of his best moments. How fine, how palpitatingly fine, is the one in which the stranger, in the garden, talks up to the open window.

Oh my friend, "in the garden": that reminds me: the little photographs in my letter of the other day don't give you any idea of ours at the Prieuré; you can't see how wide it is, two broad terraces before the vineyard begins behind the little mannikin. If you could see, if you could see the roses! Such prodigality everywhere, —and believe me, Beloved, it means nothing to me. My eyes absorb nothing of it, everything remains *in front of them*,—only conjointly with yours can they take possession of it. I am aware of this every day, and never trespass into joy, however near it all lies and however ready it is to give itself. A few days of rain, many thunderstorms, and immediately afterwards the penetrating heat,—everything burst into irrepressible bloom, the jasmine stood covered with its stars just when the Salises were here, now it's dark again, with only its last little blossoms left; I've seen a laburnum somewhere, and the acacias . . . are dropping; is it conceivable that the limes will flower and we shall not inhale their scent together! Merline, I've had a lot of confidential talks with my fate, day and night,—and Muzzano doesn't look anything like so clear and credible (perhaps because I don't know the place), but Sierre: Sierre,—I kept seeing us at Sierre: I feel that fate owes us that, it ought to waft us over there, on to our terrace, with our books. . . . Dear, if one wishes, if one *believes*, everything is possible; as soon as my visitor has gone, won't you come there? I've written to the Hotel Bellevue already, and had a very nice reply,—I don't think there will be many people there just now. The Prieuré might be lovely too; so long as I'm alone, keeping aloof, I'm not so much aware of the boarding-house, nor of the smallness of the place,—but *à deux* one might be affected by it, and one would anyhow be rather under observation in such narrow quarters. . . . I'm writing this, my dear Friend, because the idea keeps overwhelming me with its immense promise. . . .

René

TO FRAU GUDI NÖLKE

from Château de Muzot sur Sierre, Valais
[Saturday], 24 December 1921

Don't be taken aback, please, at my writing this in haste, on the spur of the moment (and in strictest confidence). The idea, as such, is altogether so precarious and fantastic—but haven't I always found, throughout these two years in Switzerland, that it's just the fantastic that stands the best chance of becoming reality. What I want you to think over is briefly this:

The crippled Prince Alexander Hohenlohe, in Zurich, is now faced with the very thing which, thanks to continual miracles, I have so far always been spared: having to leave Switzerland. This sick and aging man is most painfully affected by his harsh necessity, which could only be avoided now if his sequestration in Paris were lifted, and he fears that even *if* this were done, it would come too late. Germany, as it is today, would be a really terrible place for the Prince—we keep trying to think of a *whither* that would be kindlier, more suitable, less inimical, less opposed to his opinions and to the creed he has clung to and professed so purely and repeatedly all these years. He is today a completely *un*-political man, and is writing his personal, also completely unpolitical, memoirs—but in Germany he would be obliged to adopt a combative attitude that would be absolutely repugnant to him, besides being unnecessary, and which, moreover, would be the ruin of his health, severely affected as it is already. In a letter I had from Hohenlohe today I found the following: ". . . I should have liked the (Italian) Tyrol best, but even that won't do (on account of the exchange)." This leads me to my absolutely mad idea, which I beg leave to put before you all the same, just as it occurred to me. Whether the "Praderhof" (I'm not acquainted with it, as you know), might be able to offer the Prince a temporary asylum, in which he could be, *to a certain degree,* a guest!—He would need *one* or two rooms and a little room for his valet. The Prince's crippled state is not such as to entail any troublesome or disagreeable consequences—his life, as I have witnessed it at the Baur au Lac for two years now, is the most regular, the quietest possible—he could hardly prove a tiring or oppressive housemate. A refuge of this kind (I don't know of course whether, or to what extent, such a thing could be arranged in the Praderhof at all) with relatively little expense, in a favorable climate and sympathetic surroundings, in which he could find shelter, might at least form a transition to the next stage, so difficult to decide upon for the moment. Now that I've written all this down, I can see for myself that there's no hope of such an arrangement being made—I can see from here the utter impossibility of it. Must I reproach myself for having written to you about it?

I'll risk it, for I feel so concerned about this respected man's fate, that even telling you about it does me good —and perhaps, dear Frau Nölke, you who have had the same sort of thing to think out and struggle with, might have some quite unexpected solution to suggest?!—Forgive this haste, for one thing the letter must go *before* Christmas, for another, if it doesn't go at once, I'm afraid I shan't send it—even now, writing more slowly, I feel it won't get addressed: it's so absurd, on the least reflection. (So be it, all the same!)

In sincerest friendship,

Yours

Rilke

P.S. (Herr Ompteda, at Schloss Winkl, has sent me his novel *Es Ist Zeit* [*It* (*There*) *Is Time*]—now the question is, *ach*, whether I *have* any for these 415 pages!)

/ *Prince Alexander Hohenlohe* (1862–1924) *was a German exile living in Switzerland; "Praderhof" was the pension at which Frau Nölke was living in Obermais-Meran.*

TO ILSE BLUMENTHAL-WEISS

from Château de Muzot sur Sierre,
28 December 1921

. . . So far as the influence of my books is concerned, surely you greatly overestimate its power and effect on you; no book, any more than a helpful word, can do anything decisive if the person concerned is not already prepared through quite invisible influences for a deeper receptivity and absorption, if his hour of self-communion has not come anyway. To move this hour into the center of one's consciousness some one thing suffices: sometimes a book or art-object, sometimes the glancing up of a child, the voice of a person or a bird, even, in certain circumstances, the sound of the wind, a cracking in the floor,—or, when we still used to sit before open fires (which from time to time I have done in my life), a gazing into the changing flames. All this and many slighter things, apparently accidental, can cause and confirm a finding of oneself or a finding-of-oneself-again (such as you are celebrating!). The poets —yes, now and again even they too may be among these good inducements. . . . Not out of modesty, not at all, but because his indescribably penetrating art has meant so much to me through the years and has so often led me to collect my own inner faculties, I am inclined to believe that *Jacobsen* deserves much, much more credit for your delightful, happy experiences and progress. Give *him* the honor; and your dear child . . . and, if you absolutely insist, me too, but as one nameless among a hundred unnamable influences. Belief!— there is no such thing, I almost said. There is only— love. The forcing of the heart to hold this and that for true, which we commonly call belief, has no sense. First one has to find God somewhere, experience him as so infinitely, so utterly, so enormously present; then *whatever* one feels toward him—be it fear, be it astonishment, be it breathlessness, be it after all *love*—it hardly matters any more. But for belief, that compulsion to God, there is no room where one has begun with the discovery of God, in which there is then no stopping any more, at whatever point one may have begun.— And you, as a Jewess, with so much most spontaneous experience of God, with such ancient fear of God in

your blood, should not have to bother about a "belief."
But simply *feel* his presence in yours: and where He,
Jehovah, wanted to be *feared*—it was after all only because in many instances there was no other means of
contact between man and God except just fear. And
fear before God is only, so to speak, the *rind* of a condition, the inside of which does *not* taste of fear, but
can ripen to the most ineffable namelessness and
sweetness for him who loses himself within it.—You
have, do not forget, one of the greatest gods of the universe in your descent, a God to whom one cannot just
be converted at any time as to that Christian God, but
a God to whom one *belongs,* through one's people, because from time immemorial He made one and formed
one in one's forefathers, so that every Jew has been established in Him (and in the one whom none may dare
to name), ineradicably planted in Him, with the root of
his tongue!

I have an indescribable confidence in those peoples
that have *not* come to God through belief but have experienced God through their own race, in their own
stock. Like the Jews, the Arabs, to a certain degree the
orthodox Russians—and then, in another way, the
peoples of the East and of ancient Mexico. To them
God is origin, and therefore future as well. To the
others he is something deduced, something away from
which and toward which they strive as really strangers
or as people who have grown estranged—and so they
are always needing the intercessor, the mediator, him
who translates their blood, the idiom of their blood into
the language of the godhead. What *these* people
achieve then is indeed "belief"; they must conquer and
train themselves to hold for true that which *is* a true
thing for the God-descended, and for this reason their
religions slip easily into the ethical,—whereas a God

originally experienced does not separate and distinguish good and evil in relation to men but for his own sake, passionately concerned over their being-near-to-him, over their holding- and belonging-to-him and over nothing else! Religion is something infinitely simple, ingenuous. It is not knowledge, not content of feeling (for all content is admitted from the start, where a man comes to terms with life), it is not duty and not renunciation, it is not restriction: but in the infinite extent of the universe it is a direction of the heart. However a man may proceed, wandering to right or to left, and stumble and fall and get up, and do wrong here and suffer wrong there, and here be mistreated and over there himself miswish and mistreat and misunderstand: all this passes into the great religions and upholds and enriches in them the God that is their center. Even the man who lives on the last periphery of such a circle *belongs* to this mighty center, though he may but once, perhaps in dying, have turned his face to it. The Arab's turning to the East at certain hours and casting himself down, that *is* religion. It is hardly "belief." It has no opposite. It is a natural being-set-in-motion inside an existence through which God's wind sweeps three times daily, since this at least we are: pliant.

I think *you* must understand and feel *how* I mean this,—and so may it somehow enter into the calm and open frame of mind you call your convalescence, and there work on to your security and joy!

TO LOU ANDREAS-SALOMÉ

from Château de Muzot sur Sierre,
Valais, Switzerland,
29 December 1921

. . . Well, it has just been possible to arrange that
I am to sit in my strong little tower until further notice; I am really only just beginning to turn its protection, its silence to account, and wish for nothing but a
good spell of seclusion and that it may be long and uninterrupted.

Though one cannot escape a certain sense of immobility, still one feels the wholesomeness of neutral terri-
tory very much here and added to that this magnificent
landscape (reminding me of Spain and Provence). I
have done everything to hold myself in it; and in re-
inforcing this effort the old masonry walls within which
I sit have been not unessential. . . .

But above all the quiet winter must first have come
and gone. If I am allowed a long and uninterrupted
one, I hope to get a little further than last year in Berg,
—if not to catch up with myself altogether, still *so* far
that I can see myself walking on ahead of myself with
space enough between to fetch longer breaths. The interruptions of the war years have left me with an incredible difficulty in concentrating, so that I cannot
manage to get through without the support of this most
literal being alone. More than ever, every communication becomes for me a rival to my work, which probably comes to be the case with everyone who more and
more has in mind only *one thing* and thus in giving,
whether to himself or to the world, gives out *this* same

one thing. A few days ago I was offered a dog; you can imagine what a temptation that was, especially as the lonely situation of the house makes the presence of a watchdog quite advisable. But I felt at once that even this would result in much too much relationship, through my interest in such a housemate; everything alive, that makes *demands,* hits upon an infinite desire in me to fall in with it, from the consequences of which I must then painfully disengage myself again when I realize that they are using me up completely.

Are you in Vienna, dear Lou? then greetings to Freud—: I see with pleasure how his work is now beginning to have an important effect in France which has so long turned a deaf ear. Not much reaches me thence, save now and then a word from Gide; only the poetry of Paul Valéry really astonishes me, whose *Le Cimetière marin* I managed to translate with an equivalence I scarcely thought could be achieved between the two languages. When I am a little more certain in my own work, I hope to have a try at his prose too; there is a glorious dialogue, *Eupalinos*—, like all Valéry's few works of a serenity, a calm and equanimity of language that you too would entirely appreciate. Paul Valéry stems from Mallarmé; about twenty-five years ago a remarkable article appeared (*L'Introduction à la methode de Léonard de Vinci*), which he has now—1919—published with an extraordinarily beautiful introduction; but starting from Mallarmé meant with the next half step landing in silence, *dans un silence d'Art très pur,* and so it was too: Valéry kept silent and worked at mathematics. Only recently, during the war, 1915, or 1916, did the need for artistic expression arise again, so much the purer, in the man of fifty: and what has since come from him is of the greatest distinction and significance. . . .

I think of you a great deal, it is the time between the two Christmases, the first and the Russian . . . That you *could* get news from there: it almost seems incredible that the one over there is still alive and can still communicate itself to us here. . . .

P.S. A brood of little ladybugs is wintering with me (which might somehow have happened in Schmargendorf too); one, a particularly successful one—they don't all turn out equally well in this parlor-winter—has just wandered across the paper: take it for a good omen!

TO XAVER VON MOOS

from Château de Muzot sur Sierre, Valais,
30 December 1921

. . . No, I am not in the least disappointed that you "extremely seldom" write down any poetry and do not give yourself over to hopes of achieving something final and perfect in this field. On the contrary, I am glad to see this restraint in you at a time when the barriers against the realm of artistic achievement have almost all been torn and trodden down by those who want to have everything in common. The taking up of some other definite particular profession (to which will you want to belong?) will surely not prevent you (in whom the tools of constructive language seem already assured and prepared) from confidently producing, when the hour has come, something responsible and necessary. I would like to emphasize that my confidence in you in this respect is extraordinarily sure. And of course you have examples enough, if you needed any, of there being no harm in performing, in a subsidiary office, this, the most glorious high mass of the soul:

think of Mallarmé—, or, what lies much closer, of your great Spitteler, whose most enduring poems, if I am not mistaken, were written at a time when he was still far from putting all his energy into this powerful service. And Paul Valéry, who was altogether silent for something like twenty years and, I believe, worked at mathematics, besides carrying on some civil-service job as well,—does he perhaps not owe the repose and finality of his poetic word to this long-suffering abstention?

When my father in his day expected me to carry on as an avocation (alongside the profession of officer or of lawyer) the art to which I felt myself destined, I did indeed rebel most violently and persistently, but that was entirely because of our Austrian conditions and the rather narrow milieu in which I grew up; to put through, with divided energy, anything artistically true and distinctive in such a milieu, with its furthermore so close proximity to the artistic dilutions of the eighties of the last century, would have been entirely unthinkable—, indeed, I had, in order to begin at all, to free myself completely from the conditions of family and home; belonging to those who, only later, in homes of their own choosing, could test the strength and bearing capacity of their blood. Since then so much has changed. Much pioneer work has been done, art has been freed, there was air and room enough (at least before the war) for everyone who inwardly needed them . . . And as I myself have time and again regretted not being in a daily profession which, independent of the currents of grace, can always be carried on, simply, every day, so I would also advise every young person at least to live his way far into tasks of that sort before wholly identifying his existence with the relentless demands of being an artist. . . .

TO FRAU GERTRUD OUCKAMA KNOOP

[? January 1922]

What shall I say?—Little as you were able recently, after copying those notes, to write me anything besides, so little am I myself now able to communicate myself to you as long as I am still the reader of those pages, bent over them, always, despite all looking up. I had had no idea of all that, I scarcely knew any particulars of the beginnings of that sickness—, and now all at once it was the introduction into something so manifoldly moving, affecting, overwhelming to me. If one were to read this, and it concerned any young girl one hadn't known, it would already be close enough. And now it is Vera, whose dark, strangely concentrated charm is so inexpressibly unforgettable and so fabulously evocable that, at the moment of writing this, I would fear to shut my eyes lest I suddenly feel it quite surpass me, in my hereness and presence.

How much, how much, how much she *was* all that, *that* to which these memories of her suffering bear so deep and irrevocable a witness,—and isn't it true? how wonderful, how unique, how incomparable a human being is! Here there came into being, now that everything was allowed to consume itself, suddenly, which otherwise might have lasted for a long being-here (where?), here there came into being this excess of light in the heart of the girl, and in it became visible, so infinitely illumined, the two extreme limits of her pure intuition: *this*, that suffering is an error, an obscure misunderstanding arising from the physical that drives its wedge, its stony wedge, into the unity be-

312

tween heaven and the earth—, and on the other hand this united oneness of her heart, open to everything, *with* this unity of the existing and enduring world, this assent to life, this—joyous, deeply moved, capable of the ultimate—belonging in the here-and-now—ah, in the here-and-now only? No (which she could not know in these first attacks of break-off and parting!)—into the *whole*, into a much more than here-and-now. Oh how, how she loved, how she reached out with the antennae of her heart beyond all that is graspable and encompassable here—, in those sweet hovering pauses in pain which, full of the dream of recovery, were still vouchsafed her . . .

It seems, dear friend, that fate has set store upon leading you out beyond the common bourn, each time as it were on an overhanging crag of life, to the ravine of death and with heart laid ever barer. Now you are living and looking on and feeling out of infinite experience—.

But for me . . . it has been like an enormous obligation to what in me is innermost and most earnest and (though I attain it only from afar) most blissful, that on the first evening of a new year I was permitted to take these pages into my possession.

/ Frau Knoop's daughter Vera had died a little more than two years before, at nineteen; her mother wrote an account of her death, which she sent to Rilke; this was partially (along with an engraving of Orpheus he saw in a shop window in Sierre) the inspiration for the fifty-nine Sonnets to Orpheus, which Rilke wrote between the 2nd and 17th of February.

TO GERTRUD OUCKAMA KNOOP

from Château de Muzot sur Sierre,
Valais, Switzerland,
7 February 1922

In a few days of spontaneous emotion, when I actually intended to take up some other work, these sonnets were given to me.

You will understand at first glance why it is that you must be the first to possess them. For, undefined as the relation is (only a single sonnet, the next to last, XXIVth, calls Vera's own figure in to this excitation dedicated to her), it dominates and moves the course of the whole and penetrated more and more—this irresistible creation that so staggered me.

Take them kindly into your hallowed memories.

Were one to let the *Sonnets to Orpheus* reach the public, probably two or three, which, as I now already see, presumably just served the current as conduits (as for example the XXIst) and remained empty after its passage, would be replaced by others. Then we should also discuss in what form you want the name to stand (in the subtitle). In my first draft here too, until your closer agreement, I have just: V.O.K.

/ *This refers to the first of the two parts of the* Sonnets (*some of them were rearranged later*).

TO MERLINE

Thursday evening, 9 February 1922

Merline, I'm saved!

The thing that weighed upon me and frightened me the most is done, and gloriously, I believe. It only took a few days, but I have never gone through such a hurricane of the heart and mind. I am still trembling from it—last night I thought I was going under; but there it is, I've conquered. . . . And I went out to caress the old Muzot, just now, in the moonlight.

From now on work will be smooth, stable, day-to-day, sure,—which will seem like a dead calm after this divine tempest, too great for any one, whomsoever. . . .

I can't write. But you will think it enough to have this good news. Give me your own, Dearest, dear, dear Friend. . . .

René

P.S. I'm sending you the Valéry—copied a fortnight ago, but I had no time to dispatch it. You'll see how beautiful it is—sublime at times—though perhaps not so "remote" as *Eupalinos*,—in fact the Dialogue appears to be carried on on the earth. This fact alone prevents it from attaining the final independence of the other. . . . Your hyacinth has broken through its little islet of earth; fancy, only four days ago!

TO PRINCESS MARIE VON THURN UND TAXIS-HOHENLOHE

> from Château de Muzot sur Sierre
> (Valais), Switzerland,
> 11 February [1922], evening

At last,
      Princess,
at last, the blessed, how blessed day when—as far as I can see—I can announce to you

the end
of the Elegies:
Ten!

From the last, the big one (to the opening, begun once upon a time in Duino: "Someday, emerging at last from this terrifying vision/may I burst into jubilant praise to assenting angels . . .") from this last one, which was also meant, even then, to be the last,—from this—my hand is still trembling! Just now, Saturday, the eleventh, at six o'clock in the evening, it is finished!—

All in a few days, it was a nameless storm, a hurricane in the spirit (like that time at Duino), all that was fiber in me and fabric cracked—eating was not to be thought of, God knows who fed me.

But now it is. Is. Is,
Amen.

So I have survived up to this, right through everything. Through everything. And just this was what was needed. Only this.

One, I have dedicated to Kassner. The whole is yours, Princess, how could it help being! Will be called:
the *Duino Elegies*

In the book (for I cannot give you what has belonged to you from the beginning) there will be no dedication, I think, but rather:

The property of . . .

And now, thanks for your letter and all its communications; I was anxiously awaiting it.

Of me, only this today, don't you think? . . . It is indeed, at last, "something!"

Farewell, dearest Princess.—

Your
D. S.

Just now, a kind letter from Princess Öttingen. Please, commend me to her. I shall write soon.—All my best to the Prince, Kassner,—etc.

P.S. Please, dear Princess, do not consider it a subterfuge of my laziness when I tell you why I am not copying down and sending you the new elegies now: I would be jealous of your reading them. I feel as if it should be I, absolutely, who first reads them to you. When? Well, let us hope, soon.—

D. S.

/ *Besides writing the* Sonnets to Orpheus *in this "great February," Rilke completed the* Elegies *he had begun at the Princess's castle of Duino in 1912; Princess Öttingen (1857–1941), born Princess von Metternich-Winneburg, was the widow of Prince Franz Albrecht; on receiving Rilke's letter, Princess Marie von Thurn und Taxis sent him a telegram ("letter received am happy") from Vienna and a letter, also enthusiastic, accepting the dedication.*

TO LOU ANDREAS-SALOMÉ

from Château de Muzot sur Sierre
(Valais), Switzerland,
11 February [1922] (evening)

Lou dear Lou, so now:

at this moment, this, Saturday, the eleventh of February, at six, I am laying aside my pen after the last completed *Elegy,* the tenth. The one (even then it was destined to become the last) to the beginning already written in Duino: "Someday, emerging at last from this terrifying vision/may I burst into jubilant praise to assenting angels . . ." As much as there was of it I read to you, but only just the first twelve lines have remained, all the rest is new and: yes, very, very, very glorious!—Think! I have been allowed to survive up to this. Through everything. Miracle. Grace.—All in a few days. It was a hurricane, as at Duino that time: all that was fiber, fabric in me, framework, cracked and bent. Eating was not to be thought of.

And imagine, something more, in another context, just previously (in the *Sonnets to Orpheus,* twenty-five sonnets, written, suddenly, in the fore-storm, as a memorial for Vera Knoop) I wrote, made, the horse, you know, the free happy white horse with the hobble on its foot that once, at the approach of evening, came galloping toward us on a Volga meadow—:

how

I made him as an "ex voto" for Orpheus!—What is time?—When is present? Across so many years he sprang, with his utter happiness, into my wide-open feeling.

318

So it was, one after the other.

Now I know myself again. It really had been like a mutilation of my heart that the *Elegies* were not—here. They are, they are.

I went out and stroked, as if it were a great old beast, the little Muzot that had sheltered all this for me, that had, at last, vouchsafed it to me.

That is why I did not write in answer to your letter, because all the time in these weeks, without knowing toward what, I was keeping silent toward this, with heart taken farther and farther inward. And now, to-day, dear Lou, only this. You had to learn of it at once. And your husband too. And baba, and the whole house even down into the good old sandals!

Your old Rainer

P.S. Dear Lou, my little pages, these two, breathlessly written last night couldn't go off, registered, today (Sunday), so I took advantage of the time to copy off for you three of the completed *Elegies* (the sixth, eighth and tenth). The other three I shall then write in the course of days, and send them soon. To me it will be so good when you have them. And besides it puts my mind at ease if they exist somewhere else too, outside, in accurate copies, safely preserved.

But now I must for a moment into the air, as long as there is still Sunday sun in it.

Прощай

/ *"Baba": grandmother; "Прощай"* (Proshchai: *goodbye*); *the sandals he mentions were his own, kept at Lou's house for him.*

TO LOU ANDREAS-SALOMÉ

from Château de Muzot sur Sierre
(Valais), Switzerland,
Sunday [19 February 1922]

That you are there, dear, dear Lou! to confirm
it so joyously into my innermost heart!—In reading
your good, knowing letter: how it came over me once
again, this certainty from all sides, that now it is here,
HERE, that which had arisen so long ago, as if it had
always been!

I had in mind to copy off the other three elegies for
you today since it has already got round to Sunday
again! But now, just think, in a radiant after-storm, another elegy has been added, that of the *Saltimbanques*.
It rounds out the whole most wonderfully, only now
does the cycle of *Elegies* seem to me really closed. It
is not added on as the eleventh, but will be inserted
(as fifth) before the *Hero-Elegy*. Besides, the piece
that has hitherto stood there seemed to me, through
its different sort of structure, to be unjustified at that
place, though as a poem beautiful. This will replace it
(and how!), and the supplanted poem will come under the heading of *Fragmentary Pieces* which, as a
second part of the book of *Elegies*, will contain all that
is contemporaneous with them, what time, so to speak,
demolished before it was brought forth or has so cut
off in its development that it displays broken surfaces.
—And so now the *Saltimbanques* too are here which
actually, even from the very first Paris time, concerned
me so absolutely and have ever since been a task to me.

But not enough with that, scarcely was this elegy

on paper before the *Sonnets to Orpheus* continued too; today I am arranging this new group (as their second part)—and have also quickly copied off (kept!) for you a few that seem to me the most beautiful. All out of these days and still quite warm. Only our Russian white horse (how he greets you, Lou!) is from the earlier first part, from the beginning of this month.

And with that, finis, for today. I must catch up on letters several of which have accumulated for answering.

I well know that there can be a "reaction"—, after being thrown like this, the falling somewhere; but I am after all falling into the spring which is already nearer here, and then: since I was permitted the patience, the long patience, for what has now been reached—, why shouldn't I be able to manage a little side-patience through baddish days; and finally, gratitude (of which I never had so much) should outweigh in them too everything depressing and confusing!

Thanks for having written me at once in spite of all your work!

Your old Rainer

Elegies 5, 7, 9—: soon!

/ *The* Saltimbanques Elegy *was inspired by Picasso's painting; the material intended for* Fragmentary Pieces *was scattered through several posthumously published volumes.*

TO COUNTESS MARGOT
SIZZO-NORIS-CROUY

from Château de Muzot sur Sierre,
Valais (Switzerland)
17 March 1922

My Most Esteemed Gracious Countess, the seven-teenth is too beautiful a date not to feel tempted to put it quickly at the top of a few pages in which I beg to be allowed to reply to your kind letter (received yesterday). I feel the more free to do so, since my work, intensely and long interrupted, seems to be saved—, it not only lies completed, but in addition, as a bonus, a small volume of *Sonnets* (the *Sonnets to Orpheus*) has emerged out of the unpredictable de-velopments of my tempestuous toil. Those major poems, of which I spoke—, yes, indeed, I am referring to that work, begun in the winter of 1912 in Duino and continued in Spain and Paris, the completion and shaping of which I often feared thwarted by war and its aftermath. That would have been painful, for these poems contain the most important and essential things I had been able to establish at the time of my middle life—, and it would have been the most bitter destiny to remain unexpressed at the moment of greatest inner maturity and not to be allowed to create that for which so many foundations of sorrow and so many dreams of bliss had been the precursors. These *Elegies* (such was the name of the poems from the beginning—there will now be ten) will now be retained under the title the *Duino Elegies,* all the more since the course of war has destroyed almost to the last trace the sheltering walls of that wonderful Adriatic castle (in whose hospitable solitude the two first Elegies were created and several fragments now appearing in the later poems). ("*Le buste survit à la cité*," wrote Théophile Gautier, if I cite correctly, in one of his completed sonnets.)

Here too, here too, alas, here too—, life and art somehow stand in conflict. Since you are thinking of Dehmel, this conflict might be treated in a peculiar way, especially with reference to and concerning Dehmel: Dehmel's wish to put the poet in the midst of life (letters he wrote me also show how much he returned to this theme again and again) probably sprang at first from a reserve toward, in fact an abhorrence of, the desk literatus, in which aversion he found himself so heartily in accord with his friend Detlev von Liliencron, for instance (in fact with everybody!), but in the end there was an error there somewhere, a lack of having thought and observed deeply. Do we, perhaps, no longer find life at this desk, to which one may withdraw, so to speak? Do fate, existence, non-existence, all that is distressing, dangerous and powerful not perhaps extend as far as the fugitive (as we may call him) at the desk? What makes his creation weak, untrue, redundant or ridiculous is not the location he maintains but the fact that at this spot (which could well represent as vital a center as any other spot in the world) he learns to look away from life, which here too crowds and surges around him,—that he no longer is aware of life at all, but only of the paper and the blot of ink on his index finger: this renders this type —so eminently German—so hopeless and repugnant. But why fight him—is it not sufficient to ignore him? —So many things deserving of downfall come to their end, if one lets them be; they are constantly busy playing themselves out anyway.—But Dehmel had a fight-

ing nature, pugnacious to the point of complete lack
of good taste (in this respect the manners of the eighties of the previous century clung to him fatally—this
age of manners might have been the most lacking in
taste in all history). His pugnacity at any price had,
within his own work and relationships, good and bad
consequences, as the case may have been. This determination in him not to erect barriers against "Life"
(one really should put it in the quotation marks), is
probably not innocent of what you sense as something
abruptly unpleasant, even repulsive, in his books. In
order to have life present at any cost, he was capable
of rolling "the raw material of life," unworked, into an
otherwise strong and transformed verse—, of commit-
ting one of those crudities through which people from
time to time pretend to prove the immediate presence
of their strength. Nevertheless, in my youth my admiration for Dehmel's art was very great—, but even
then I understood very well when someone once admitted to me that in the midst of a beautiful Dehmel
poem he was afraid to turn the page, because on the
next page some brusqueness might be found which
would have been all the more painful to someone who
had just entered into the true splendor of some verse
lines with feeling and empathy.

On the other hand, Dehmel's example and influence
in having lyrics spring from life have certainly awakened poets: that whole, at first anonymously appearing, Nyland Group developed, as far as I know, in the
factories or with other hard-working young people:
they were, from 1912 or even before, attached to Dehmel with enthusiastic joy and might well have found
in him a powerful and very genuine reinforcement.
Joseph Winckler and particularly Gerritt Engelke, who
died prematurely (or, if I am not mistaken, as a war

casualty) without a doubt owe the courage to use their
giftedness imperturbably, from their particular station
in life, to Dehmel's encouragement, and even to his
strong emotional enthusiasm, which he always generated for any erstwhile nameless activity with a com-
radeship and readiness that was the eternally youthful
in him and perhaps his most beautiful feature.—That
someone should begin to sing at his herditary occupation, be it even behind a machine or at the plow
(which would even be a very privileged position!), is
of course quite in order; on the other hand, however,
it would be wrong always to take into consideration
the individual's "métier" in order to displace the creative writer (I avoid the distasteful "author") from his
own. No one would think of thrusting a ropemaker,
cabinetmaker or shoemaker away from his craft "into
life," in order that he may be a better ropemaker,
cabinetmaker or shoemaker; also the musician, the
painter, the sculptor one would rather let carry on
theirs. Only, with regard to him who writes, the craft
seems to be so lowly, so naturally accomplished
(everyone can write), that some (and among them at
times also Dehmel) were of the opinion that the person
occupied with writing would immediately fall into
empty play if he were left alone too much with his
craft! But what a fallacy! To be able to write is, God
knows, no less "difficult a craft," all the more since the
material of the other arts is removed as a matter of
course from daily use, while the poet's task is increased
by the strange obligation to set apart his word from the
words of everyday life and communication thoroughly
and fundamentally. No word in the poem (I mean
here every "and" or "the") is identical with the same-
sounding word in common use and conversation; the
purer conformity with the law, the great relationship,

the constellation it occupies in verse or artistic prose, changes it to the core of its nature, renders it useless, unserviceable for mere everyday use, untouchable and permanent: a transformation as it takes place, incredibly, splendidly, sometimes in Goethe (*Harz Journey in Winter*), often in George. How different Dehmel's interpretation might also have been in this regard was shown surprisingly clearly in a small controversy that arose between us on the occasion of a meeting many years ago. Dehmel (who always had a kind of expectant apprehension for me, as I could notice later) point-blank took me to task about my constant living abroad. It was impossible for me to enumerate for him all my reasons for this (his attitude later on, during the war, proved to me more than ever how little he would have understood most of them), and so I limited myself to saying, among other things—not by any means boasting of it, but, if you will, admitting it as a weakness—that while working I could not stand hearing German (mostly spoken so disgustingly badly and corruptedly!) around me, but preferred to be surrounded at such a time by some other language with which I was familiar as means of communication, and which was congenial: German then, I told him, through such isolation (which he might have perceived as enormously unpatriotic), took on a peculiar composure and clarity in me; removed from all daily use, I could feel it, for me, as the suitable splendid material (how splendid: only if one were to have a command of the Russian language could one find a gem of expression with greater facets of contrast!)—. Dehmel was so perplexedly amazed at my statement that I added, jokingly, that it would be extremely distressing for a sculptor, to give an example, if the clay he used for modeling were to be at the same time smeared about (as a form of communication and for other practical uses), in all cases most inaccurately and carelessly. . . . We both laughed, and the conversation was never continued in this direction.

—Now, however, Esteemed Countess, concerning the kindness and indulgence with which you assess *The Life of the Virgin Mary*, I would (almost, almost) be inclined to take a Dehmel point of view; namely, that of life, from which alone must come art. One can naturally not exclude completely [the fact] that the arts too merge into and affect one another; but where any artistic creation consciously gives rise to another form of art, the artist responsible for it must contribute heavily from his living experiences in order that, nevertheless, something completely honest may be wrested second-hand from such stimulus. This has occurred sometimes in the poems of the small *Life of the Virgin Mary*; not always. Moreover, it is not so much the existence of these verses I debate as, rather, their time of origin; were these by-products set perhaps ten years earlier, then I would have all tolerance for them. But, as I described to you already, they reached far back in tone: that you will have to grant me later, in any case, when you will know the first *Elegies* (those of 1912); you will hardly want to believe that it concerns "contemporaries" of *The Life of the Virgin Mary*.

And now, however, one more thing, Gracious Countess. . . . Were I vain . . . (and no one knows really to what degree he is, insofar as it is important to everyone to be allowed to represent a certain identity between his inner and his outer self)—well, then, were I so vain, as I in all probability am somewhere, then I should be truly unconsolable if the Zwintscher picture should come before your eyes. As painting, it is very inferior; considered as a portrait, it is simply an un-

truth, a frivolous, repulsive dishonesty. Never has a
"likeness" been made in a more irresponsible way; its
history is the following: In the year 1901, O. Zwintscher
came to us for a few weeks because of another portrait
I had asked him to undertake. At the end of his sojourn (the intended picture was about completed), he
asked me, too, to sit for him a few times, which I finally did reluctantly (for nothing has been ever for me
more understandable than the gesture I once saw an
Arab woman in Kairouan [Tunis] make, clapping both
hands before her face when she perceived with horror
that a camera was aiming at her; this, exactly this horror comes to me always, quite involuntarily, when it is
the case of being "taken" by paint or painting or pho-
tography)—in short, Mr. Zwintscher succeeded in pre-
vailing over me, and I sat for him four or five times;
during the last sitting, at the end, dismayed with his
result, he scraped his work off to the bottom of the
canvas—, and thus, *la toile vide*, he departed (to my
relief) for Meissen! A year or two later I found out
that there was, nevertheless, a picture of me painted
by Zwintscher—he even sent it to exhibitions—and my
dismayed inquiry revealed the fact that Z. had recon-
structed my portrait again "from memory"—, and alas,
again a few years later, I was by chance able to ascer-
tain, at an exposition in the Bremen Art Gallery, with
grief, how very abominable and also how arbitrary a
Zwintscher memory is constituted. Therefore, Most
Gracious Countess, do me the one favor—forget it. (It
really touches me that you wrote on account of this,—in
spite of this, I should say—that the beautiful Adamocz
would be pleased to open its portals to me sometime:
please not to him, this completely strange Zwintscher
creation that has never existed; please: not to him!)

Since I avoid reading writings dealing with my

work, I do not therefore know Soergel's book; only recently Insel, which has long been instructed to suppress the Zwintscher picture wherever it comes up (also all the others, by the way, except for the bust by Fritz Huf from the Museum in Winterthur, which I authorize, perhaps too easily, where absolutely necessary), began a fight against this reproduction. I think it will disappear on the occasion of the next edition, to be replaced, if they insist on presenting an illustration, only by that bronze of Huf's. *Que des ennuis inutiles!*—Enough, at the end of the seventh sheet: forgive this want of moderation!—But the book with the scenery of your childhood: may I really expect it sometime?! (When the mail is safe enough?!) With what joy will it be received and viewed!

Your gratefully devoted
R. M. Rilke

P.S. The newspaper clipping is enclosed. Thanks. It is of course an *étourderie* and malevolence not to mention Stifters, for instance!

/ *Countess Margot Sizzo-Noris-Crouy (born in 1889), the Countess Crouy-Chanel, was the wife of Christoph Peter Joseph, Count Sizzo von Noris; "the Adriatic castle" was, of course, Duino; the quotation from Théophile Gautier (1811–1872) is from his* Emaux et Camées; *Richard Dehmel (1863–1920) was a German poet and dramatist; Detlev von Liliencron (1844–1909) was a poet who dealt mainly with war themes; the "Nyland Group" was the Westphalian Workers' Association of Nyland House, which attempted to be both Romantic and modern; Joseph Winckler (born in 1881), the author of the* Iron Sonnets, *joined this group; Gerritt Engelke (1892–1918) was a laborer-turned-poet who was killed toward the end of the First World War; two of the poems of* The Life of the

*Virgin Mary (published in 1913) were written by Rilke in
1900, and the others were "presented to him" at Duino in
1912; Oscar Zwintscher (1870–1916) was a painter and
professor at the Dresden Academy; Albert Soergel had
written a book on modern poets; Fritz Huf (born in 1888)
is the Swiss sculptor.*

TO MERLINE

from Hôtel Bellevue,
Château de Muzot sur Sierre, Valais,
21 June 1922

My dear Friend, so you are coming to Switzerland! It's only right you should, for nowadays, ever
since the archway of roses began to bloom,—and you
know how fast these things happen here!—I can never
go up to Muzot without the garden reproaching me
for your absence; it has no thoughts but for Merline,—
as for myself, it just tolerates me.

You, Dearest, are a born guest at Muzot; I should
tell you to come here directly you have crossed the
frontier, were it not for your wish to be alone for a
time during your stay with Francine, which might certainly be pleasant for a few weeks. But if it's not such
a success as you hope, for one reason or another,—
Muzot is always there, waiting for you *always,* and
God knows whether you might not find the wished-for
solitude there too; for sometimes I feel very tired of
this part of the world, and perhaps I shall need a far
greater change than Bellevue to steep myself afresh in
reality, which is blunted here (in spite of its magnificence) because I have suffered too much in it, and
dwelt too much on its qualities and on the intimate
succor afforded by these generous surroundings. But

as I told you in my last letter, I know very little about myself, and I may be mistaken as to the reasons for my quasi-indifference towards this young summer, which will enchant your grateful eyes; perhaps I shall be able to see it as you do, if your joy is strong enough to raise mine to its starting-point (which will be exactly that of your arrival).

Ever since my friends went back to Montreux, I have been almost alone at the hotel, it's delicious,—I have all the terrace to myself . . . the apricot trees, alas, will not be able, this year, to bestow on us their morning generosity; they were the ones to be sacrificed to the last frost of this late spring,—but the other trees in the orchard are very promising, and the vineyard now in blossom is busy sunning its grapes to come.

Don't think from what I said earlier that I'm ungrateful to this beautiful country, with which so many memories are forever connected; but I don't see it as well as I did, either because of a passing fatigue, or because of that involuntary laziness that benumbs us when we think we "know" a place, forgetting that our admiration might at any moment give a turn to things that would make their appearance new and inexhaustible to us. This time, my dear Merline, Muzot must pay you back the strength you lent it when you worked with such warm and imperturbable conviction at its installation, at its living existence. . . . Rest will be the order of the day, or if it's work, it will be yours! Don't forget to bring all you need for your painting, you must create the whole art of the Valais,—you know there is nobody else to do it. Only yesterday, towards evening, going along a path you don't know (I discovered it later) I called you several times, and I should have liked to set you down at that moment in front of the *motif* . . . which loved you. . . .

How splendid is the softness of the shadows, the purity of the "features" of this landscape,—really, at certain times it seems to possess everything that constitutes the charm and the spirit of a face one loves.

As though you didn't know it!

Do you remember the date of the day we went up to Muzot for the first time with Mlle. Raunier? I didn't make a note of it, and I'm not even sure of remembering the date when we first went into Muzot. . . . Will you be there for one of these anniversaries? No, we ought rather to celebrate that of the adorable Sunday morning when we camped on the bank opposite Muzot, and couldn't yet get in. . . . You were quietly occupied in doing the first "portrait" of Muzot, and I, meanwhile, went to kneel in the little white chapel. . . . Do you remember how long and sweet and light and all permeated with tender benediction that morning was? Do try and find that date again, if you possibly can. . . .

René

TO FRAU GUDI NÖLKE

from Château de Muzot s/Sierre
(Valais), Switzerland,
the last day of October 1922 [Tuesday]

My dear Frau Nölke,

We have been such a long while without news of each other that I don't know whether to address this to the Praderhof or Schloss Winkl: I understand from a letter of Landau's at the beginning of the summer that you had thoughts of renting the latter from the Schlozers; he said you would be sending me news. The longer you delayed, the more I felt inclined to stir you up and challenge you with some news of my own; but the summer went by—partly owing to the weather, partly to the unrest to which the whole world still seems condemned, and which even the stout walls of Muzot are not sufficient to keep out—without affording me any quieter, more lucid moments. Now that it's over, and the autumn daylight often takes on a wintry hue, though the grape harvest isn't yet finished everywhere, I must reckon it a bad, wasted summer and be satisfied with having been able to make good and enduringly profitable use of the first part of the year 1922. You will see (on the inside of the jacket, at the end of the book sent herewith), that the events of March and February 1922 are already being transmuted into durable and palpable form! The *Duino Elegies*, as well as the *Sonnets to Orpheus*, are now in print: a few extracts from the latter have been included in this number of the *Insel-Schiff*. But even if the inner realizations are still secure on the foundations inexpressible and often undemonstrable, that one has *tant bien que mal* built up for oneself: what current today carries (and whither?) a printed book and whatever else one may succeed in realizing? Only winged things now, that can hover above so much abyss (opening wider and wider), are capable of existing, are saved, and may perhaps save this or that man if he is strong enough to lift himself up to them.

Mme. Klossowska came to me here for a few months, as she did last year: although her presence is of the greatest comfort to me, this time she made me more sensible than ever of the indescribable insecurity and misery, not only of our generation, but of the next. You will have heard a good deal about her from Landau.

Ever since, with her two talented boys, she has had to leave Geneva (where she lived so bravely) these children's lives, like her own, have been broken off, and as we all know—nowhere do pain and care gnaw their way in more greedily than into a fractured surface of life. I'm really extraordinarily worried about her and the boys, Balthusz and Pierre. The former (the artist of *Mitsou*) is in Switzerland too—not with me, as a guest of other friends in Beatenberg; his elder brother Pierre is remaining in Berlin for the moment, where, however, his situation—obtained with great difficulty and sacrifice—will be of little profit either to him or to his mother. I have done all I can to help this gifted boy of seventeen to find his way—it seems that something may be **matur**ing, with the help of Swiss friends (although even they are now in difficulties enough).

But I am no less anxious about Balthusz and his mother: conditions in Berlin have become so much worse, almost impossible, and to the K. family (used like myself to life in Paris) the place is like a prison, the air is poisoned.

Supposing Mme. Klossowska and my little friend Balthusz *can't* or don't go back to Berlin for the time being . . . what is to be done? Muzot is too cramped to house them, and after all I'm only a *sham* master here, I'm a guest myself, and can't put extra weights into the scales of hospitality without authorization, however big the scales may be. If you didn't know as much as I feel you do, about the children and their youthful mother, I should not have the courage to ask you the same question with regard to Balthusz and Mouky K. that you considered so kindly before in the case of Hohenlohe.

Would you think it at all possible to take Mme. K.

and the fourteen-year-old younger Klossowski into your house? For a few months? Mme. K. could do a lot in the way of housework (she wanted to look for a job of that sort here!) and it might be very nice for the children to have dear little Balthusz as school- and playmate. When we went to see him at Beatenberg in September, he was just painting Chinese lanterns, with a flair for the oriental world of form that is amazing. Then we read the little *Book of Tea:* one can't imagine where he gets all his assured knowledge of Chinese Imperial and artistic dynasties. . . . I can't help thinking *what* it would mean to this boy, so strangely oriented towards the East, to talk to Asa!

Of course I haven't said anything to anybody about the possibility (it may be anything but this), which I am suggesting so frankly. It may be that now, as at the time of the French Revolution, out of such combinations of *émigrés,* who would otherwise not have met one another, a *Future* is most likely to arise. . . . Who can tell?—Something urges me to pass on this inspiration to you: no matter *what* you may think of it, I know you will not feel it to be an impertinent demand. And you, on the other hand, know that no "No" can estrange or offend me.

I'm writing in the greatest haste, and with many mental reservations of unrest and disorder; without a housekeeper for three weeks, I made a bad choice, and an outraged Vaudoise, who had taken too much upon herself, is at this moment leaving the house with her numerous luggage. . . . Will the next one be any better?—I am longing to begin my peaceful winter (towards the interior, with my domestic problem more or less solved)!

With how many good wishes, dear Frau Nölke, dear

friend, do I think of you and the children, and greet
you all! Including Asa!

Ever most sincerely
Yours
Rilke

with an *Insel-Schiff*.

/ Insel-Schiff, *Part 6, August 1922, contained eight of the*
Sonnets to Orpheus *and advertisements for the book of the*
Sonnets *as well as that of the* Duino Elegies.

TO PRINCE HOHENLOHE

from Château de Muzot sur Sierre, Valais,
23 December 1922

. . . Proust,—you mention Proust: It pleases me
immensely that you have found relish and interest in
his work. By a chance, of which I shall tell you sometime, I was one of the first (1913!) to read *Du côté
de chez Swann,* and hence also one of the first to admire Marcel Proust, which was the natural, immediate
consequence of that reading. On the occasion of his
death recently, André Gide reminded me of the fact
that I have my place among the earliest admirers of
this great writer,—and now you can imagine how I had
gone along with him in the same state of mind from
volume to volume and how strongly the death of this
significant man affected me. It is simply not yet possible to foresee all that has been opened to us and those
to come with these books, they are crammed so full of
a wealth of discovery, and the strangest thing is the
use, already so natural and in its way quiet, of the bold-
est and often most unheard-of; anyone else would have

336

been able to risk such lines of connection from event to event only as auxiliary lines,—but in Proust they also at once acquire the beauty of the ornamental, and they retain, even as design, validity and permanence. While by some intuitive stroke he dares the most remarkable connection, it seems again as though he were merely following the existing veins in a polished piece of marble, and then one is surprised all over again at the perfect tact of his interpretation, clinging nowhere, which, playing, lets go again what it just seemed to be holding to and which, with scarcely surpassable nicety, everywhere admits and leaves free that which is sheerly incalculable.—In his cork-slab lined (almost bare) room which he left only now and then at night, this strange soothsayer must have seen life continually open before him like a gigantic hand whose lines he so essentially understood that they could not give him any more surprises—, only, day by day, endless tasks!—How one must love work, once one has got that far! . . .

/ *Prince Hohenlohe was the brother of Princess Marie von Thurn und Taxis-Hohenlohe.*

TO COUNTESS MARGOT SIZZO-NORIS-CROUY

from Château de Muzot sur Sierre, Valais,
Epiphany [6 January] 1923

My Esteemed, Most Gracious Countess, only a few days ago I reread your happy letter of the summer and was unable to comprehend the negligence of my pen, which could leave these kind, in so many ways communicative lines without a reply for so long. And yet

I did not write immediately! It is as if my pen—unfortunately one has the same for all written matters, work and correspondence—wanted to force for itself a rest after the great efforts of the previous year. . . . And I myself, too: Such a work-expenditure is followed every time by helplessness; not that one is actually empty, but certain reserves of one's own being are changed, expended and, as it were, withdrawn forever from one's own personal use. One does not wish to look around immediately for another inner possession—one is not really certain what one likes; it is a condition of hesitation, of a slow turning of one's self—and one finds that at such a time one is reluctant to say "I," for what could be stated about such an "I" without exertion and coercion? Formerly in such moments, a change of scene was often useful to me. It was advantageous for resting as well as for a new beginning (—one part of my restlessness may even be explained by the fact that every time after such an intensive period, I welcomed any change that offered itself); this time, too, it would perhaps have happened in such a way—I had decided to leave Muzot, be it to move again to Paris (which was long necessary for certain studies I plan), be it in order to search out our original home—still unknown to myself—Kärnten, and see if it would be possible to settle there. . . . The family coat of arms, inscribed, I believe, with a date somewhere in the fourteenth century, is said to be still in the House of Assembly in Klagenfurt, regularly restored—and I, not only because I am the last male member of my clan, feel it is appropriate for me to close such a wide circle by a kind of homecoming there, if this is possible without violence, in order to settle down for some time there where, as legend and tradition assert, we began! ("Csakathurm," as it is called, one of the oldest feudal estates of the Kärntner Rilkes, is now, if I am not mistaken, a hereditary estate and title of the Count Festetics family, your relatives!)—Then, however, the slightest attempt to become mobile immediately involved so many difficulties that I gave in more and more and shut myself up in Muzot for another winter, with the best intention of making the present seclusion as fruitful as possible. I undertook immediately several works of translation, which will keep me well occupied through the quiet months, and I would have gone further with them if health disturbances had not occurred with each increased exertion and excitement, obviously also a consequence of the somewhat forced performance of the previous work period.

This all about me, dear Most Gracious Countess! while your latest letter really brought such direct and unexpectedly painful cause to speak about you and to you. But especially because this is so very necessary, I wished to bring myself to your attention again, after such long silence, so that the warm words of sympathy I feel naturally pressed to address to you might not come across to you from too vague an origin. So that you will feel all the better who says them and from what position. Words . . . can they be words of consolation?—I am not certain of it, I also do not truly believe that one can or should console oneself for a loss of the suddenness and magnitude you have suffered. . . .

"Woe to those who are consoled," or something to that effect, the courageous Marie Lenéru notes in her remarkable *Journal*. In such a situation, consolation would be one of the many distractions, it would be a diversion, therefore in the deepest sense something frivolous and fruitless.—Even time does not "console," as the trite saying goes, at most it clears away and es-

tablishes order,—and it is only because we later take
this quietly established order so very much for granted
that, instead of admiring it and giving it the credit for
adjustment, solace, and reconciliation in general, we regard these things, because they no longer hurt us so
much, as stemming from our own forgetfulness and
weakness of heart. Alas, how little does the heart forget
—and how strong would it be, if we did not withdraw
its tasks from it before they are fully and duly completed!—Not to want to console ourselves for such a
loss should be our instinct, it should rather become
our deep, most painful curiosity to explore it completely, to experience the special nature, the uniqueness of this loss, its effect within our life; we even
should muster the noble avarice to want to enrich with
it, with its meaning and gravity, our inner world. . . .
The deeper it affects us, and the more violently it
touches us, such a loss is all the more a task of repos-
sessing in a new way, and finally, that which by its loss
became inconsolably pressing: this, then, is an infinite
accomplishment, which immediately overcomes all the
negative aspects clinging to sorrow, all lassitude and
indulgence, which are always a part of sorrow, this is
active sorrow influencing the inner self, the only kind
of sorrow that has meaning and is worthy of us. I do
not like the Christian concepts of an afterlife, I am re-
moving myself from them more and more without, of
course, thinking of attacking them . . . they may have
their rightful place among so many other hypotheses
concerning the supernatural periphery of life—but for
me they contain principally the danger that we not
only make those who vanished more nebulous and for
the moment more intangible—; but we ourselves, too,
in our yearning are pulled away from this life and so
become vaguer and more ethereal. Whereas during the

time that we are allied to tree, flower and earth, it behooves us to remain of them and eventually to become a part of them always. For myself, those things that have died have, in dying, entered my own heart. When I searched for the vanished one, it was so moving for me to feel that his only existence now was within me, in a way so strangely and surprisingly concentrated that my enthusiasm to serve his existence there, to deepen and glorify it, won out almost at the same point where sorrow would otherwise have invaded the whole scenery of the mind and destroyed it. When I remember how I—often with great difficulty of understanding and accepting one another—loved my father! Often in childhood my thoughts went straying and my heart froze with the mere notion that at some time he would cease to be—; my being seemed to me so completely conditioned by him (this being of mine, which was yet so fundamentally differently bent!) that his parting was to my innermost soul the equivalent of my own destruction . . . but so deeply does death lie within the nature of love that death contradicts love at no point (if we were only able to recognize it for what it is and not be misled by the uglinesses and suspicions that surround it): where else, finally, but into the heart itself may death thrust the unutterable things we bear in our hearts, where would the "image" of the loved one, indeed even his abiding influence (made abiding by the fact that during his sojourn with us it grew increasingly independent of presence) . . . where else but in ourselves would this mysterious effect be more secure?! Where can we come closer to it, where celebrate it more purely, when obey it better, than when it appears united with our own voice, as if our heart had learned a new language, a new song, a new strength! I reproach all modern religions for having presented to their faithful the consolations and extenuations of death, instead of giving their souls the means of getting along with death and coming to an understanding of death, with its complete and unmasked cruelty: so enormous as entirely to close the circle: this cruelty approaches again an extreme mildness, so great, so pure, so completely clear (all consolation is murky) as we have never, not even on the sweetest spring day, imagined mildness to be. If some of us could sense such profound mildness with conviction, it would perhaps gradually pervade all aspects of life and make them lucid. However, humanity has not even taken the first steps toward the experiencing of this richest and most absolute mildness,—unless perhaps it was in the earliest and simplest ages of time, the secret of which is now almost lost to us. I am certain that the sole purpose of the [ancient ceremonies of] "initiation" was the transmission of a "key" to the understanding of "death" that had no negative aspect. Like the moon, life surely has a side constantly averted from us, which is not the opposite of the side we see but, rather, the complement of it, rendering it complete, full—the true whole and complete sphere and globe of existence.

One should not fear that our strength might be insufficient to endure any experience of death, be it just any or be it the most terrible; death is not beyond our strength, it is the measuring line at the brim of the vessel: we are full whenever we reach this line—and being full means (for us) being heavy . . . that is all.—I do not want to say that one must love death; but one should love life so generously, so without calculation and selection, that one constantly involuntarily includes death (life's averted half) and loves it too—this is always true in the great turmoils of love, which are irrepressible and limitless. Only because we exclude death, when it breaks suddenly into our thoughts, has it become increasingly a stranger, and because we have kept it an alien, it has become an enemy.

It is conceivable that it is infinitely closer to us than life itself. . . . What do we know of it?! It has become more and more clear to me over the years, and my work has perhaps still only that one meaning and message, to bear witness to this insight (which so often overtakes me unexpectedly) more and more impartially and independently . . . prophetically perhaps, if that does not sound too presumptuous . . . namely, that our effort can only be directed toward presuming the unity of life and death, so that it may gradually prove itself to us. Prejudiced as we are against death, we do not achieve its freedom from distortions. . . . Believe, dear Most Gracious Countess, that death is a friend, our most intimate and only friend, who is never, never confused by our attitudes and vacillations . . . and this, of course, not in the sentimental-romantic meaning of life-renunciation and negation, but our friend especially at a time when we most passionately and profoundly embrace earthly existence, activity, Nature and Love. Life always says at the same time: Yes and No. He, death (I implore you to believe it!), is the actual yes-sayer. He only says yes. In the face of eternity.

Think of the "sleeping tree." Yes, how good that it occurs to me. Think of all the small pictures and the captions under them—how there, in youthful, unsuspecting confidence, you have always recognized and affirmed both in the world: The sleeping and the waking, the light and the dark, the voice and the silence . . . the presence and the absence. All these seeming contradictions that come together somewhere, in one

343

spot, that sing in one place the hymn of their marriage
—and this place is—for the time being—our heart!

As ever your constantly devoted

Rilke

/ *Part of this letter, the section following the reference to*
Marie Lenéru, was published in the Norton two-volume
edition of 1948; Marie Lenéru (1875–1918) was a French
dramatist who at the age of eleven began keeping a diary,
which was published in 1922 as the Journal de Marie L.
The identity of the person whose death Rilke writes of in
this letter and the letter of 12 April 1923 is not known.

TO LOU ANDREAS-SALOMÉ

from Château de Muzot
sur Sierre (Valais), Suisse,
13 January 1923

. . . today must be the Russian New Year! But
even the other day, on the western New Year's morning, and between Christmas Eve and it, I was often
with you in thought: at that time I still thought, if I
put off writing a little, I could lay the *Elegies* and the
Sonnets right in with the next letter: I was far off in
my calculations: on the last day of the year there appeared, instead of the first copies, one more *Elegy*-
revision, still fairly faulty, which I could then spread
out for myself exactly over the threshold of the year. In
the dying note of midnight and in the first stillness of
1923, I was just in the midst of correcting and reading
the fifth *Elegy!* I rejoice that I was allowed to begin
thus (if a division is to be granted at all). And you?
I am often *greatly concerned,* dear Lou, about *you,*

about all of you, when I hear and picture how everything in Germany has become more and more absurd and living and living costs practically impossible. It seems—and that was my impression in 1919—, that the only right moment, when everything could have paved the way for understanding, has been missed on all sides, now the divergences are increasing, the sums of the mistakes can no longer be read off, so many-digited have they become; perplexity, despair, insincerity and the opportune wish to draw some profit at any cost out of even these calamities, even yet out of them: these false forces are shoving the world ahead of them . . .

But perhaps the world isn't going along, perhaps *nothing* is going on in politics, scarcely does one get, no matter where, into some layer beneath them, when already everything looks different, and one thinks a most secret growth and its sheer will are using those confusions only in order to keep themselves unharmed beneath and hidden from otherwise occupied curiosity. (In France particularly, among people not politically minded, in those who are inwardly active: *how* many turnings, renewals, wide vistas—, what new orientating of a spirit suddenly, almost against its will, increasingly reflected . . . I don't know whether you have followed Proust, his influence is tremendous—, but not only *his* influence is transforming, but what emanated from him is emanating now from other and younger men . . .) I have the advantage here of being able to follow all this without much difficulty; I translated Paul Valéry and felt my resources so corresponded with his great, glorious poems that I have never translated with such sureness and insight as in this, in itself often very difficult case. (You know that he, P. V., a friend of Gide's, descending from Mallarmé, after a few early publications kept silence through nearly twenty-five years, occupied with mathematics, only since 1919 has he been living into poetry again, and now every line has, added to the pace of it, that deep repose which none of us is able to command. A glory.) And Valéry, although he is completely excluded from Germany by ignorance of the language, wrote me, when he was traveling through Switzerland in the fall on account of lectures: *"Vous étiez l'un des objets principaux de mon voyage."* How full of premonition and how unrestrainable all real connections are. And for all that, I was unfortunately not able to see him for the silliest of reasons; the impossibility of having Austrian or German money sent out is making me more and more of a prisoner in the old walls of my Muzot, *in* them I have everything for a while yet, but every step outwards, though it be only to Lausanne, is becoming more and more impossible! But how could I help taking this inconvenience comparatively lightly when I think of the distresses that would beset and hem me in at a less out-of-the-way and sheltered spot. One may not now attach much value to freedom of movement; it would only bring one into touch with calamities. In the summer I had all sorts of plans; but so many warnings at once stood at the border of the slightest realization that, quite the reverse, I left no stone unturned in order to be able to go on keeping myself in Muzot. Were the world less awry, a change, at the moment of this for me significant conclusion, would certainly have had sense, and it probably would also have taken place. But as it is, the best thing was to hold fast to the given and tried and to be loyal and grateful to it. Especially as my health is going through singular upheavals: again and again every excitement, even that of work (which often for weeks has not allowed me to eat *quietly*), casts itself upon that center in the pit of my stomach, the sympathetic nerve, the "solar plexus," there I am so truly annihilable, and I am going through remarkable experiences of the rivalries and unisons of the two centers, the cerebral and that more focal one which after all is supposedly our *middle:* as regards the visible as well as the invisible!

Meanwhile: I am not worrying too much about these fluctuations attacking the central organs; at most that I should use my energy to "turn off" for the meal hour the intensive vibrations emanating from mind or mood just as I mostly succeed in doing with regard to sleep. That great god: Sleep; I sacrifice to him without any time-avarice—what does time matter to *him!*—ten hours, eleven, even twelve, if he wants to accept them in his lofty, mildly-silent way! Only unfortunately I seldom manage now to go to bed early; evening is my reading time. The presence of enticing books, the stillness of the old house intensified to the point of improbability, keep me awake for the most part past midnight. The little caring-for-itself of a mouse in the many never-discovered interstices of the deep walls further contributes then to increasing the mystery out of which the tremendous night of the countryside, eternally *without* care, nourishes itself.

Strangely dulled I am, was so, to my astonishment, even in the summer—, toward the countryside itself, the so deeply experienced magnificence of which I must keep before me with an effort and deliberately, in order to participate in it still. Does the leveling of our senses really go *that* far under the continually renewed presence of the surroundings in contact with them? How manifoldly then must habit put us in the wrong toward people and things: one should console oneself with the fact that the curve of delight continues on in one's inner realm: but how follow it there where it will surely be refracted in the density of the medium, perhaps become unrecognizable and display emphasis only *there* where other curves, of just as lost an origin, cross it in the curious vortex of the intersection points. . . .

TO LISA HEISE

from Château de Muzot sur Sierre,
Valais, Switzerland,
2 February 1923

The same fears and unspeakable apprehensions that cause you so much suffering make me grow increasingly speechless; how often had I intended to answer your moving letter, the one before the last, dear friend, and postponed it for a better and happier hour: so that you can really know how it (with its large four pages) was received in my heart. But the summer and especially the fall were full of uncertainties, and when I now try, lonesome, in my old tower, to make my winter somewhat similar to that good last one, then this is also an effort, partly because my health is less even, partly because of those intruding disturbances that the again degenerating general conditions import to everything (just as it was during the war!). As far as this is concerned, I could call many a sentence you write my own; the one: "Already during the day half of my thoughts are no longer my own, and the nights are full of feverish visions." This and others . . . because I feel the same way.—What happens? And what is our role in these events? It is, still just as it was during the war, obtrusive and at the same time hardly of concern to us, a foreign misfortune in which one becomes involved. Does it not often feel as though one could rise above this with one breath? Often also, just as when one brushes against a small blossom on a walk through a summer meadow and it answers with a liberating scent, one finds some insignificant comfort in the soul that is immediately communicated, as if it came out of a restrained abundance. . . . Your letter is full of such surprises, full of those pure sweet scents of the heart that only he, who has experienced complete poverty, knows.

For me, as I see and experience everything according to my attitude and personality, there is no doubt that it is Germany which holds back the world, because it does not understand itself. The complex composition and extensive education of my soul give me a certain distance to perceive this. Germany, in 1918, in the moment of the collapse, could have put the entire world to shame and shaken it by one act of deep truth and inversion. Through one clear, decisive renunciation of its false prosperity—in a word: through that humility which would have been so much a part of its being and an element of its pride, and which would have taken precedent over everything that could have been imposed on it as foreign humiliation. At that time—as I had hoped for a moment—that lost trait humility, which in the drawings of Dürer is so constructively indicated, should have been reintroduced, added into the peculiarly one-sided and consenting German face! Maybe there were a few people who felt that way, whose desires and hopes were directed toward such a correction—now it is becoming apparent and taking revenge for not having happened—something which could have put everything right did not happen. Germany has missed its opportunity to offer its purest and best, its old-established moderation—, it has not basically changed and reconsidered, it has not achieved that dignity which is based on humility, it only thought of salvation in a superficial, quick, distrusting, and greedy way, it wanted to function and rise up and escape instead of, in accordance with its innermost nature, bearing, overcoming, and getting ready for its miracle. It wanted to remain as it was rather than change. And therefore one feels now: . . . something is missing. A foundation to hold on to is missing. A step is missing in the ladder, therefore "the indescribable worry, the fear, the anticipation of a sudden and momentous fall." What to do? Each of us holds on to his quiet, still-reliable little island of life, the self resting on it, the self suffering and feeling. My [island] is for me no firmer and safer than yours is for you—I am guest, where you are tenant; but should your contract now really be cancelled in the fall, after you have awakened and developed his land for him, the owner, during the past three years? Is there no chance to make him reconsider? I can imagine how very difficult it must be now to find a similar position—; to go to the Argentine would not fit your attitudes and needs, to have some relations with a more trustworthy, somewhat understanding soil—, moreover the conditions there are no longer, as they once were, favorable for one's spirit and strength. . . .

But nevertheless, what experiences, what fulfilling and great reward, when you look back on the years at Weimar! So certain is the gain that even if you had not thought on the third page to draw the line and to form the tentative conclusion, I would still have extracted from your—though fearful—lines, as from espaliers, the good and healthy fullness.

This lets me continue to hope that you will find the GOOD, which I wish for you and which you have become able to love so deeply.

RMR

TO COUNTESS MARGOT SIZZO-NORIS-CROUY

from Château de Muzot sur Sierre, Valais,
12 April 1923

My Esteemed Most Gracious Countess, it is time that I now follow up the two small packages of last week with something verbal and communicative; the main thing is to state my thanks for the kindness and friendship of your letter of March 10th. Believe me, I have read it again and again, to be near to you and to understand and comprehend completely the present condition of your grieving. How deep must it be, since you could reach in it the point of ultimate stillness (few people, only because they distrust grief, reach it)—, and how genuine it is, since you follow it into the physical realm and can experience it in both its extremes: entirely in the spiritual way, in which it overshadows us so infinitely that we sense it only as calm, as pause, as an interval of our nature, and also again, suddenly, in its other aspect, where it is like a physical pain, the awkward incurable pain of a child, which makes us moan. But is it not wonderful (and is it not somehow an act of motherliness) to be so guided through the contrasts of one's own soul? And you actually feel it often as an initiation, an introduction into the whole and as if nothing evil, nothing deadly in the evil sense could happen to one, once this elementary sorrow has

351

been suffered purely and truly.—I have often told my-self that this was the impulse or (if one may say so) the sacred strategy of the martyrs, that they desired to [experience and] be done with grief, the most terrible grief, the excess of all grief—that which otherwise, unpredictably, measures itself out in small or larger doses of physical and spiritual suffering over one's life and mingles with its moments—to call up, to conjure all at once this whole potential of suffering, so that after it, after such suffering has been endured, there might remain only the bliss, the everlasting bliss of gazing upon God, which nothing can disturb at the hour of victory. . . . Thus this loss whose shadow lies over you is also a task of endurance, even the using up of all the grief that can befall us—(for with a mother's leaving, all protection goes); a tremendous toughening has to be endured—but the exchange (and that, too, you already began to feel) . . . in exchange the power to protect is passed over to you, and all the mildness, which it has been up to now yours to receive, will bloom more and more deeply within yourself; and it will now be your new faculty (immense, inherited and acquired at the highest price) to impart it on your own as your own.

I have already more than once hinted to you how more and more in my life and in my work I am motivated by the endeavor to correct our old repressions everywhere, which have removed and slowly estranged from us the mysteries by which we might live infinitely out of the fullness. The terribleness has frightened and terrified the people: but where is there something sweet and splendid, which would not ever wear this mask, this mask of the terrible? Life itself—and beside it we know nothing—is it not terrible? But as soon as we admit to its terribleness (not as an adversary, for how could we be equal to it?), but somehow with a confidence that this very terribleness may be something completely ours, only for the moment something still too big, too wide, too incomprehensible for our learning hearts. . . . I believe that as soon as we assert its most terrible terribleness, at the danger of perishing from it (i.e., from its excessiveness for us!)—then a presentiment of the most blissful, ours at this price, opens itself to us. He who does not at some time, with definite determination, consent to the terribleness of life, or even exult in it, never takes possession of the inexpressible fullness of the power of our existence, but walks on the edge and will, sometime when the decision is made, have been neither alive nor dead. To prove the identity of terribleness and bliss, these two faces on the same divine head, indeed even of this one single face, which presents itself only this way or that way, according to the distance from it and the disposition in which we perceive it . . . this is the essential meaning and concept of my two books, one of which, the *Sonnets to Orpheus*, is already in your kind hands.

I had friends visiting here for Easter and have read aloud (for the third time now) these poems; in doing so I experienced, every time, how much one can aid comprehension by small explanations given on the side. But for this a personal reading aloud is necessary. . . . During the reading the other evening, I thought of you, dear Most Gracious Countess, and wished so very much to look through this book with you, page by page, in order to present each single poem to you in all its power. I know now that there is none which is not clear and productive, even if some are so close to the inexpressible mystery that they cannot be explained but only endured. But I experienced how much my voice, involuntarily, contributes to the interpretation, if only because the whole mystery of the creation of these verses still vibrates in it [in the voice] and transmits itself with indescribable vibrations to the listener.

If I am not mistaken, I have already told you of this too: that these strange *Sonnets to Orpheus* were no intended or expected work; they appeared, often many in one day (the first part of the book emerged in about three days), completely unexpected in February of last year, when I was, moreover, about to collect myself to continue those other poems—the great *Duino Elegies*. I could do nothing but take in my stride the dictation of this inner impulse, clearly and obediently; I, too, understood only gradually the relation of these lines to the image of Vera Knoop, who died at eighteen or nineteen, whom I knew little and saw only a few times in her life, when she was still a child, admittedly with strange attention and emotion. Without my arranging it this way (with the exception of a few poems at the beginning of the second part, all the sonnets kept the chronological order of their emergence) it so happened that only at one given time do the second-to-last poems of both parts make reference to Vera explicitly, address her or call forth her image.

This beautiful child, who first began to dance and caused a sensation among all who saw her then by the art of movement and walk which was inborn in her body and soul,—unexpectedly declared to her mother that she no longer could or would dance . . . (this was just at the end of childhood); her body changed strangely, became, without losing its beautiful Slavic conformation, strangely heavy and massive . . . (which was already the beginning of the mysterious glandular illness that later was to bring death so rapidly). . . . During the time remaining to her, Vera

354

played music, finally she only drew—, as if the denied
dance came forth from her constantly more quietly,
constantly more discreetly. . . . I knew her father,
Gerhard Ouckama Knoop, who had spent the greatest
part of his life as an engineer at the big Knoop spinning
mills in Moscow. A heart condition, whose strange nature was a puzzle to the physicians, later compelled
him to withdraw from this activity; he came with his
wife and two daughters (of whom Vera was the
younger) to Germany and still had time to write a few
books that did not remain unknown, but the great
uniqueness of experience that concerned and imbued
this humble man can perhaps not be sufficiently recognized through these [books]. His last years must have
been full of magnificent insights and clarity—and his
death, favored perhaps by the particular condition of
his heart, was a complete release of the things of this
world in an indescribable transfiguration of the spirit.
. . . He died knowingly, flooded, so to speak, by insights into the eternal, and his last breath was blown
to him by the wings of the angels, excited by him.
. . . I did not know him well, because living in Paris,
where he only visited me once, I lacked the possibility
of a closer relationship with him . . . but there existed
between us, from the beginning, that instinct of confidence, that joy in one another, which needed no further proof—which perhaps stemmed from the same
source as the exorbitant inspiration that now endowed
me so inconceivably to erect this monument to the
young Vera!—

It would lead too far would I now try to comment
on single sonnets, also I would very much like to let
this be a reason for a future meeting. Nevertheless, so
that you may read the book correctly, I thought I might
be permitted to write you the explanations above,—

they will now yield so many things that will act as light accompaniment during your reading hours.

Perhaps it is also good to know that the XVIth sonnet (of the first part), page 22, is addressed to a dog: I deliberately did not wish to make a footnote about it, because that would have almost had the effect of an exclusion (or at least a setting apart) of the creature, whom I wanted especially to take completely into our event. (Does one perhaps, would one guess, that a dog is being addressed?)

I will close, Esteemed Countess. The anemones! I wonder what you said to them (in case they arrived still slightly recognizable). Last year I was told that this dark-violet-furred species of the Pulsatilla is at home only in the Valais; inexperienced as I unfortunately am in botany, I was pleased to believe it, but this year someone passed through who called the little flower with disgraceful familiarity "cow-" or even "kitchen-bell" and assured me *que c'était tout ce qu'il a de plus commun*. . . . Well, that would not, after all, detract from its beauty, but it surprised me, because as it first comes up here among the rocks, in the protection of its silver fur equipped for all disaster, it looks really rare and noble.—Did you know it? Do you have the same in Hungary?—

I had music here at Easter, I have to tell you, splendid music—an occasion for me, who so seldom gets around to taking in music (and perhaps not at all wishing or daring to be receptive to it more often). With my Swiss friends a very young violinist also came to me, who they assure me already counts among the best and most extraordinary artists of her instrument. She played Bach for me for three days, almost exclusively Bach—and how, how! With what maturity and certainty of the violin, with what determination. (Fates should be like this, and lives; but only in the things without destiny is there this austere strength—which contains in itself and protects the tender—and this exactness.) The young artist, Alma Moodie (Scotch on her father's side, Irish on her mother's, born in Australia, studying at the moment in Berlin with Flesch) is going soon, as far as I know, on a tour to Rumania. . . . If she comes via Hungary and plays in Budapest and it fits in, please hear her. . . .

I gave her (for Rumania) the charming book of Princess Marthe Bibesco, *Isvor, le pays des Saules*, two volumes. . . . A book full of deep experiences of life and feeling, stemming from the oldest tradition of the people there—pages of purest feeling and poetry: shall I send it to you? (For I believe it is difficult to receive French books abroad.)

In lasting devotion gratefully saluting you

Your

Rilke

/ *This letter is important for its account of the background of the* Sonnets to Orpheus; *the "friends visiting for Easter" were Werner Reinhart (1884–1951), Rilke's landlord at the Château Muzot, and Alma Moodie (1900–1943), the violinist; Vera (Wera) Ouckama Knoop (1900–1919) was the girl whose death, as recounted by her mother, was the basis for the* Sonnets to Orpheus; *Karl Flesch (born in 1871) was a professor at the Berlin Music School.*

TO COUNTESS MARGOT
SIZZO-NORIS-CROUY

from Château de Muzot sur Sierre, Valais,
1 June 1923

My Esteemed and Most Dear Gracious Countess,
it was a time of visiting at Muzot, ever since that Easter
(glorified by the great music of Alma Moodie); a coming, staying, and going, as really never before—and I
not only had to do the honors at my tower, which are
quickly done, but had to show off the Valais in general,
which (so little known) in its magnificence had something special and meaningful to offer each of my
guests. Only since Monday have I been alone again,
and really had ahead of me no greater joy than to
write you quietly and in detail: Your good letter
brought such very attractive opportunity to do so! Then
yesterday, unforeseen, I suddenly found it necessary to
travel to Zurich (and probably to Bern) on urgent business, I am leaving this noon—, and so there remains for
me just enough time to mail off the *Isvor* of Princess
Bibesco, my own copy. You have to forgive graciously
the many marks that I, in reading, have drawn on it,
some will please you, others merely accentuate the way
in which I momentarily (and often so delightedly and
appreciatively) received it.

As much as I notice and suffer from my increasing,
almost disgraceful immobility, especially at this moment when, unexpectedly, a short trip is demanded
of me, as much as I notice and suffer on this occasion
from my sluggishness, which began after the war (this

was different before!), and therefore have hardly the right to imagine that I shall soon and easily achieve bigger undertakings beyond the Swiss border—as much as all this is the case: nevertheless I would very much like to ask you to keep both my volumes of *Isvor* until such time that I may be permitted to collect them again at Adamocz in person.—The "wide-open portals" gave me much joy and made a deep impression!

Now I am not keen on writing you so many "explanations" of the *Sonnets* (apart from the fact that I constantly have to look at my watch today), so that something may still remain to be done, when I, sometime, beside you, while reading aloud, leaf through the book. Moreover, you were already in quite complete empathy: the sentence you wrote me, your insight that that "higher sphere" of the poems proves itself actually the one that is nearest, closest to the essence, thus a most familiar thing forgotten . . . is the most positive and most beautiful that, since their arrival, has been said to me about the Orpheus *Sonnets*. Compared with this feeling, of what significance are the small uncertainties here and there! It [the work] actually often concerns the most delicate, that which lies on the borderline of what can barely be expressed; sometimes I myself wrestle for the meaning that used me as an instrument, in order to burst through in human form, and the light of some parts I myself own only in unique blessed moments.

In the poem to the dog, by "my master's hand" is meant the hand of the god, namely Orpheus. The poet wants to lead this hand, so that it may also, because of the dog's infinite sympathy and dedication, bless him, who, almost like Esau, has put his hide on only because he knows in his heart of the heritage that does not belong to him: to take part in all things human with need and happiness.—

You see, therefore, you think too far, over and beyond the poem, when you think you need the help of the concept of soul-migration, which is alien to me in this sense. I believe that no poem in the *Sonnets to Orpheus* has any meaning that is not completely written out in it, often, it is true, with its most secret names. In my conviction anything that might be "allusion" contradicts the indescribable temporalness of the poem. In this way, too, no Christ-parallel is meant by the unicorn; but all love of the non-proven, the non-palpable, all belief in the worth and reality of whatever our soul has created and lifted up out of itself through the centuries may be extolled in it. This orientation of mine conditions also the great admiration I have for the book of Princess Bibesco. . . . Actually, the more tradition is externally limited and choked off for us, the more decisive it is for us that we retain our ability to remain receptive and conductive to mankind's widest and most secret traditions. The *Sonnets to Orpheus* are, this is how I more and more understand them, an effort, made in absolute obedience, in this profound direction . . .

The unicorn has all the meanings of virginity constantly celebrated in the Middle Ages: thus it is asserted that the unicorn, nonexistent for the profane, is reflected, as soon as it appeared, in the silver mirror the virgin holds before it (see: tapestries of the XVth century), and is reflected again "in her" as in a second, equally pure, equally secret mirror.

They are coming for the luggage—I have to close, esteemed Countess—may you forgive the haste of these lines.

Greet park and garden of Adamocz. I remain with

my whole heart inclined and recommended toward your kindness and friendship.

Your
Rilke

TO RUTH SIEBER-RILKE

from Château de Muzot s/Sierre (Valais),
on 8 December 1923

My dear, dear Ruth, has the time really come again to hold our birthdays up to ourselves, reproachful of the fact that we are not nearer, and forced (by the distance) to shout our wishes back and forth, like the cabbies? Well, you have shouted very heartily, with a very clear voice, and I have recognized it well by sound and intonation.—Now I shall try to do likewise. Attention!!! I shout:

A good, happy birthday, my dear Ruth! Health and joy and confidence in a new year of life!

But actually, it seems to me, this year we cannot show off much with our respective birthdays, surpassed as we are by the newest, brand-newest birthday of little Christine, which you, my dear Ruth, have achieved. All wishes one has and expresses or thinks draw themselves involuntarily toward the small, well-known little basket, which has not been inhabited for twenty years, and in which there is now movement again (and which in turn moves us, more than can be said). The dear small little basket (the swallows have returned, they come again and again to the same nest and signify happiness and joy!)—I have to imagine that living in the rooms of Altjocketa is at many moments just as festive and pleasant as our home in Westerwede suddenly became around that Christmastime when you lay in the small little basket and gave us to understand more and more that you thought you could enter into and accept this world, which we devotedly offered you. According to what you tell me, little Christine also might show some signs that she accepts the world of Altjocketa as the one that is in every way interesting and appealing to her. Too bad only that your little servant spirit herself has not grown up very far in this world—, at that time we had the stately "Eka Hayen" (and it was the time when she had not yet grown over our heads . . .). But to make up for it, many things were quite inconvenient and primitive in the Westerwede house, while it is probably comfortable and pleasant at the "lodge." Nevertheless, don't tire yourself too much, dear little Mama, permit yourself much good and joyful rest, think that it will all profit little Christine directly.

Greet Carl cordially from me. (And, if Helmuth is still with you, him too!)

I have succeeded with difficulty in obtaining for you a copy of the big edition of the *Elegies*, which right after publication was already sold out; however, it is in a rustic dress, a simple one, one might say a summery one,—which nevertheless might fit well into your rusticity. It was to be sent at the same time,—but I had forgotten that today there is a great feast of Mary, the post office is closed, and also tomorrow, Sunday; therefore the books can go off only Monday: and therefore this letter cannot be registered. But the letter I will not let wait and be delayed, and I hope it arrives nevertheless and has the power to assure you in time, that I, by most beautiful wishing, celebrate your feast day with you.

Thanks for throwing, on my feast day, into little

Christine's heart, which she mirrored infinitely clearly, a part of your wishes for your

Papa
(your grand-daddy)
Rainer-Maria

/ The birthday of Ruth Sieber-Rilke, the poet's daughter, was on 12 December; Christine was her daughter, and Carl was her husband, Carl Sieber; Helmuth was Clara Rilke's brother, Helmuth Westhoff.

TO COUNTESS MARGOT SIZZO-NORIS-CROUY

from Château de Muzot sur
Sierre (Valais), Switzerland,
the second-last Sunday before Xmas
[16 December] 1923

. . . Your letter, dear Most Gracious Countess, indicated to me that, after the journeys of the summer, you were pleased to return home, and so I may be allowed to imagine that you again welcome the quiet months at Adamocz, with all their domestic and inner tasks; once you wrote so beautifully about this compliance to the will of the season; these are the days of turning toward the inner self, of increasingly taking possession of oneself, which, under apparent repose, goes on in the most intimate workings of the heart. Exactly as in the "sleeping tree." With this you have written the title for all the winter tales of life, the wise and comforting title, which time and again translates the story, where it might be sorrowful, into something great and valid, especially when one remembers therewith the steadfast and magnificent oak tree, under which you have written this sage sentence, so divining of all trust in life. That all emptiness, all absence, all apparent abandonment cannot be anything else in the natural unadulterated existence but a turning inward of that which appears lost or past, a recollection and gathering together, and quiet, deep-down working, which is about to renew the momentarily invisible and almost unprovable, in order to recreate it inexhaustibly, like new, as if for the first time with the next rising wave of the year.

. . . In this connection [of a visit at Bothmar Castle near Malans] I thought of—it just occurs to me at the right time—availing myself of some information from you: among the most stately female portraits of the seventeenth and eighteenth centuries, several drew our attention to themselves by the fact that the portrayed held in her calmly displayed hands, unobtrusively and yet with a certain emphasis that may be attributed to the symbol, the same object time and again: a lemon. Salis was of the opinion that by this stereotyped attribute (mostly quite strongly and expressively painted, by the way) was expressed the fact that the bearer, at the time when she was thus reproduced with the appearance of her prime or advanced years, had already passed away; however, he was not quite certain of this interpretation, the question remained open. I looked forward to passing it on to you on some occasion; perhaps you have in your own home similar representations, or remember having seen or heard of similar ones. If that is actually the meaning of the lemon provided, then it nevertheless still remains unexplained how this fruit came to have this symbolic usage. As far as I know, it has not played a rôle in any death cults; is it this combination of last bitterness and maturity that could make it a sign of having passed away—that would seem to me almost too derived and too subtly reasoned. (Its fragrance, by the way, the fragrance of this fruit, has for me an indescribable power of penetration; during the winter, when the senses are deprived of so many outside influences, I always have a glass dish with lemons in my workroom. Their bitterness, as astringent as it may prove itself in taste, breathed in as fragrance gives me a sensation of pure vastness and openness—; how often have I regretted that in the face of all such experiences we definitely remain so silent, so speechless. How I experience it, this lemon smell, God knows what I owe to it at times . . . and when I actually, literally, have to repeat what it dictates into my senses: Fiasco!)

How constantly limited is the field of our eloquence: recently in Bern (I went there from Malans via Zurich) I thought it over again. Each time the "Historical Museum" is the great event for me there, because of its fabulously magnificent tapestries, which the Swiss of the fifteenth century had captured for themselves from the Burgundy treasury of Charles the Bold. These splendid collections have recently become enriched in other ways, through the legacy of a collector of oriental objects: miniatures, arms, tiles, bronzes of incomparable value; this time, however, I happened on one special discovery, shawls—Persian and Turkestani cashmere shawls, such as were set off in a touching manner by the softly sloping shoulders of our great-grandmothers; shawls whose centers are inserted circles, squares or stars, with black, green or ivory-white backgrounds, each a world in itself, yes, truly, each a complete happiness, complete bliss and perhaps complete renunciation—each all this, full of human touch, each a garden in which the whole heaven of this garden was also told about and contained, as in the fragrance of the lemon probably the whole room, the whole world around communicates itself, which the lucky fruit included day and night in its growth. As with the laces years ago in Paris, this I suddenly understood, standing before these spread-out and variegated fabrics, the essence of the shawl! But to say it? Another fiasco. Only thus, perhaps, only from the variations that a tangible slow handwork permits, do there result complete secret equivalents of life, which the language reaches always only in paraphrase, except when it might succeed off and on to manage with magic appeal that some more secret countenance of existence remains turned toward us in the dimension of a poem. . . .

. . . The occupation with these two large volumes of letters [Dehmel's] has in many ways touched and also shamed me; I understood how much closer one could have been to another, without the caution, without the diversion and distraction of life; oh, that one might never lose anything! Oh, that one may never have to reproach oneself, when looking back on any human countenance that was ever turned toward one seriously and openly, for having betrayed or missed it. But here one lives in the confines of one's own body, which alone in a purely physical way (because one can start only with this, likewise physical, ego) forces upon one a special standard: one lives, I mean to say, within the limits of this body and the surrounding world in which one moves, bringing other ties and limitations with it . . . and thus one is not always so free, so loving and unsuspicious as one might be allowed to be according to one's own resources and convictions. Often it is also the uncertainty and, indeed, distractedness that limit one: what an amount of magnanimous self-possession would be necessary to have ready, for each voice that reaches us, the truest ear and most unperturbed answer. I have admired this presence of mind in Victor Hugo before the droll and absurd, when last year the protocols came into my hands, in which appears the account of the progress of those remarkable séances which were undertaken at the home of Victor Hugo with the *tables tournantes*. Strange, and in part very beautiful results. But it is amusing how the great, serene poet cannot be confused by any of these "spirit" voices, how he takes each in his stride and in his reply often goes so far as to suggest to the unknown power (where it manifests itself in his own field) the change of an odd-sounding verse!

But enough! The Sunday has almost completely passed during this communion with you, forgive the too-much; a long pause had to be made up for.

The poor little dogs! So much calamity. But it has frightened me that you thought you had to pay with this for some beautiful joy: *avec cette arrière-pensée, on prépare soi-même la pente à quelque revers futur* . . . But if it has to be anyway (I know, alas!, how difficult it is to rid oneself of the habits of [certain] feelings), why not rather imagine, every time, that fate had come to owe one, on the basis of such affliction, another new joy? That is, is it not?, the same account, only at any given time moved up by one entry!

I remain, Most Gracious Countess, gratefully and always devoted to your kind friendship,

as your

Rilke

TO ALFRED SCHAER

from Château de Muzot s/Sierre/Valais,
26 February 1924

. . . In my *earliest* period, twenty-five or thirty
years ago, one might indeed speak of "influences" that
can be easily and specifically cited. The name of Jacobsen alone signifies here a quite definite epoch in my
life: he was really the "year's regent" of my planetary-
terrestrial year. And when I think of Bang (of the *Gray*
and the *White House*), a star of the first magnitude
might be indicated there, by whose appearance and
position I found my way for a long while in the darkness of my youth (which was differently dark and differently twilit from periods of youth today). Liliencron's name was very wonderful to me in those years,
Dehmel's hard and significant; Hofmannsthal's existence somehow proved to one that the most absolute
poet was possible as a contemporary—, and in Stefan
George's relentless creating one sensed the rediscov-
ered law which henceforth no one, if he is concerned
with the magic of the word, would be able to ignore.
Into these experienced relationships worked the Russians, Turgeniev first, and the man who had directed
me to this master, Jacob Wassermann, through his personality as well as through his first, already singularly
controlled works. To recognize the Michael Kramer of
Gerhart Hauptmann, with whom I also had personal
relations, was a pride of those years. With my first trip
to Russia (1899) and my learning of the Russian language in which I then experienced quickly and almost
without hindrance any more, the spell of Pushkin and

Lermontov, Nekrassov and Fet and the influence of so many others . . . with these decisive inclusions the situation then changes so basically that a tracking down of influences seems absurd and impossible: they are countless! How many things had effect! One by its perfection, another because one at once understood that it should be better or differently done. This, because one immediately recognized it as akin and exemplary, that, because it obtruded itself antagonistically without being comprehensible, indeed, almost without being bearable. And life! The presence of the suddenly exhaustlessly disclosed life which in Russia opened up to me still like a picture book, but in which, since my moving to Paris (1902), I knew myself included, everywhere com-municating, co-imperiled, co-endowed! And art . . . the arts! That I was Rodin's secretary is not much more than an obstinate legend that grew up out of the circumstance of my once, temporarily, for five months (!), assisting him in his correspondence. . . . But his *disciple* I was in a much better and much longer sense: for at the bottom of all the arts there operated the one, same challenge which I have never received so purely as through conversations with the powerful master who at that time, although of a great age, was still full of living experience; in my own *métier* I possessed a very great and praiseworthy friend, Emile Verhaeren, the poet so human in his hard glory,—and as the most forceful model, from 1906 on, there stood before me the work of a painter, Paul Cézanne, every trace of which I pursued after the death of the master.

But I often ask myself whether that which was in itself unaccented did not exercise the most essential influence on my development and production: the companionship with a dog; the hours I could pass in Rome watching a ropemaker who in his craft repeated one of the oldest gestures in the world . . . exactly like that potter in a little Nile village, to stand beside whose wheel was, in a most mysterious sense, indescribably fruitful for me. Or my being granted to walk with a shepherd through the countryside of "Les Baux," or in Toledo, with a few Spanish friends and their women companions, to hear sung in an impoverished little parish church an ancient novena that once, in the seventeenth century, when the carrying on of this custom had been suppressed, was sung in the same church by angels . . . Or that so incommensurable an entity as Venice is familiar to me, in such degree that strangers could ask me successfully among the manifold turnings of the "calli" about any destination they sought . . . all this was "influence," wasn't it?—, and the greatest perhaps still remains to be mentioned: my being permitted to be *alone* in so many lands, cities and landscapes, undisturbed, exposed, with all the diversity, with all the hearkening and heeding of my nature, to something new, willing to belong to it and yet again compelled to detach myself from it.

No, into these simple transactions that life performs with us, books, at least later, cannot extend entirely decisive influence; much from them that lays itself in us with its weight may simply be outweighed by meeting with a woman, by a shift in the season, yes by a mere change of atmospheric pressure . . . through, for example, a "different" afternoon unexpectedly following upon such and such a morning—, or something else of the sort that is continually happening to us.

The question about "influences" is naturally possible and admissible, and there may be cases where the answer carries with it the most surprising disclosures; however, no matter how that answer reads, it must promptly be rendered again to the life from which it stems and in a sense be newly dissolved in it. Pursuant to this feeling, I have tried here, in order to answer at all, to prepare something like a "solution." May it appear not too diluted in your test-tube, my dear Doctor, and may it manifest a few more properties which will repay the investigation and observation you wish to expend upon it.

/ *Alfred Schaer (born in 1874) was a lecturer at the University of Zurich; [Herman] Bang (1857–1912) was a Danish writer; Rilke had known Jacob Wassermann (1873–1934) when they were young men in Munich.*

TO HERMANN PONGS

from Château de Muzot
s/Sierre (Valais), Switzerland,
21 October 1924

An imminent journey, matters to be wound up and preparations in connection with it, compel me to be briefer and to use more trite phrases than I otherwise would in dealing with the ideas suggested to me by your letter and the "questionnaire."

I must restrict myself to the most factual and then, after filling out the answer-side, will start tying in some supplementary material with the answers that refer to individual passages in your letter or its enclosures.

First the questionnaire:

Prague period. Final
school examination 1894   (or 1895)
  As student in Prague
until middle of 1896?   Yes

Memories of professors? Painting? (Klimt?)

—: none at all. Painting played no rôle, except that (very incompetently) I myself tried my hand at it. Klimt? thinnest gilt paper, even at that time.

Perhaps Ernst Mach's Philosophy?

Have never read philosophers except perhaps in those years a few pages of Schopenhauer (aversion to that sort of systematization).

What impressions were behind the strong social inclinations that came to expression in *Wild Chicory*?

The inclination to give away *Wild Chicory* may have been not so much "social," as rather brotherly and human; arising from my having myself been cut off from books and intellectual connections.

Wouldn't it be worth while to collect and republish the prose pieces of the whole early period?
"Hoar Frost" 1897
Without Present (Drama) '98
Along Life's Way (Short Stories) '98
Two Prague Tales '99
Everyday Life 1902
The Last 1902
About God 1900
or any others?

For reasons I have already indicated recently, this early production is without lasting value; besides which I, like most of those who were first carried away by the poem, was incapable of writing even a tolerable prose. The proof, that I could let myself go in the *Cornet* to intermingle these two widely separated forms, a tastelessness which for

372

years made that little improvization of a single autumn night unendurable to me, until finally I again gave it credit for the naïveté of its youthful manner.

Munich Period. How long? Memories of modern painting?

Munich 1896 till fall 1897 with interruptions. Painting, yes, but wrongly seen, from the point of view of subject. Uhde, with whom I had the opportunity of becoming personally acquainted.

Stay in Italy 1897

First stay in Italy 1897 (after having already at the age of eight visited our Italian Littoral [Görz and surroundings]. Since then have spoken and occasionally read the language).

When is the Worpswede period?
When the first Russian journey? 1899?
When the second? When with Tolstoy?

First Russian journey 1899; longer stay in Russia the following year. Called on Tolstoy both times. (1899 in Moscow, 1900 at Yasnaia Poliana.) Learning of Russian between the two journeys, without a teacher; reading Tolstoy (the great novels).
Westerwede near Worp-

When and through what did *The White Princess* come into being?

When for the first time Paris?

How long with Rodin?

What French painters preferred?

(Van Gogh?) (Cézanne?)

When in Sweden?

What came between parts I and II of the *Book of Hours*? (1899 and 1901?)

What between parts II and III? (1902 to 1903) (in the way of works and travels) (study of mysticism?)

Is the dense rhymeless style of the "Requiem" determined by a particular model?

What gave the first incentive to translations? Even before 1908? (E. Browning?)

swede: residence from 1901 to 1902 (from my marriage, which provided the reason for settling there).

Removal to Paris: fall 1902; residence there until 1914; with many journeys, for example, winter 1904 to 1905 (almost a year) Rome. Appended to that the months in Copenhagen and Sweden (Skåne).

Between *Book of Hours* I and II therefore came Russia; the second part came into being in Westerwede, the third (coming from Paris) at Viareggio in Italy, where, in the glorious *pinete* I did a great deal of work. Mysticism I read as little as philosophy.

The *Sonnets* of Elizabeth Browning were translated in honor of a friend who was of English descent on her mother's side and loved these

When first acquainted or acquainted at all with Simmel's works? And with which?

How (after a four-year interval) did *The Life of Mary* come about? (1913?) through what impressions? Perhaps through plastic art?

What impressions produced the occult incidents in *Malte?*

Besides Jacobsen is an-

poems above everything. Sole attempt in English, the most remote and alien language to me.

With Georg Simmel I came in contact only socially (1908–1900) [1899–1900]; at that time I was living in Schmargendorf near Berlin.

The Life of Mary (see letter)

The "occult occurrences" in *Malte:* in part accurately recounted experiences of childhood in Prague, in part things experienced and heard in Sweden. Here moreover one of the reasons why the fictitious figure of M. L. Brigge was made a Dane: because only in the atmosphere of the Scandinavian countries does the ghost appear ranged among the possible experiences and admitted (which conforms with my own attitude).

From the time I read

other prose now also contributive? (Maeterlinck?)

Danish, besides Jacobsen, Bang; Maeterlinck probably too for a time, but not as an element contributing to the development of my prose.

What personal impression of the late pictures of Paula Modersohn?

Paula Modersohn I last saw in Paris in 1906 and knew little of her works of that time or her latest, with which even now I am not yet acquainted.

Your inner relation to things? Relation to Van Gogh?

Only in passing, the great event to me in painting was Cézanne, whom however I began to study only after his death. Previously the great French impressionists had had an effect, and, in passing, Cottet, Lucien Simon, Zuloaga.

Tolstoy: it would be wrong to attribute to those visits to him an influence on my works of that time; ultimately he confirmed for me only the discovery of Russia, which was decisive for me. His figure was to me the embodiment of a fatality, a misunderstanding, and it struck me so by reason of the fact that, for all the obstinate injustice this tremendously restless man inflicted upon himself and was constantly ready to inflict upon others, that (I say) it still affected one as so touchingly protected and valid in his desertion of the tasks that were his greatest and at which he was most skilled. Only thus could a young person, who had already resolved to pursue art all his life long, comprehend that contradictory old man, who in himself was working at the constant repression of what had in the most divine sense been imposed upon him; who disavowed himself with infinite effort right into his own blood and never mastered the tremendous forces that were inexhaustibly renewing themselves in his repressed and denied artistic genius. How high (and pure!) he stood above those, the majority in Europe, who, on the contrary, worried all their lives about these forces and were determined, by practice and falsification (by "literature"), to conceal the occasional slackening or defection of their fruitfulness. The meeting with Tolstoy (whose moral and religious naïvetés exercised no attraction whatsoever upon me,—shortly before my second trip the disgraceful and silly pamphlet *What Is Art* had in all superfluity come into my hands—) so thus strengthened in me precisely the opposite of the impression he may have wanted to leave with his visitors; infinitely far from bearing out his conscious renunciation, I had seen, even into his most unconscious behavior, the artist secretly retaining the upper hand, and particularly in view of his life filled with refusals, the conception grew within me of the positiveness of artistic inspiration and achievement; of its power and legitimacy; of the hard glory of being called to something like that.

Only the meeting with Rodin, vouchsafed me two years later, and the years of close association with him, could still further strengthen this so grandly conceived idea, could bear it out more thoroughly. Here an error that has become more and more ingrained might incidentally be corrected. I was, strictly speaking, never (as your question sheet expresses it) "with Rodin," if by that a kind of position is meant. When I moved to

Paris in 1902, Richard Muther had suggested that I write about Rodin; for his work (though even then of plastic art little, according to its true value, had as yet become significant to me), I seemed prepared, inasmuch as my wife has the right to consider herself a pupil of Rodin's; through her, who as a young girl had been allowed to bring him her weekly work for many months (and later again and again), a turning had been prepared in me: I had become more capable of comprehending works of art from the standpoint of *form* and seemed a trace more safeguarded against chance overpowerings by mere relations of content, which act upon the unprepared person, even through the most inadequate handling of form, if they in any way touch him.—At the time I came to Paris, one could get to know Rodin's work, with exception of the few pieces that even then belonged to the Luxembourg Museum, almost only at his own place; so it was natural for me to go out often that fall, finally every day to Meudon. Out of our from the very beginning quite lively conversations, a real relationship rapidly developed, the funds for which on the one side my gradually increasing admiration sufficiently provided, while to meet this self-probing feeling a response grew up on the Master's side which, without presumption, even at the end of the first year, I might call one of friendship. If journeys kept me away then, how often it was an unexpected, sympathetic word from Rodin that came to strengthen me in my own work. In 1905 [1904], during my stay at a little Swedish castle in the neighborhood of Lund, there reached me from several German and Austrian cities invitations to lecture on Rodin; I did not see myself capable of completely satisfying these demands without previously coming into new contact with his continually growing work, and decided, in agreement with Rodin, to return to Paris earlier than had actually been my intention. To my inquiry whether I should find him in Meudon, Rodin had replied in the affirmative, moreover with the invitation to lodge this time with him. Scarcely had I declined this, when, I remember, a telegram arrived from Rodin's secretary which repeated the invitation so pressingly that I had no further scruples about accepting. This telegram read: *Monsieur Rodin y tient, pour pouvoir causer.* And so with that began those five months when I really was "with Rodin"; first as a guest in his house, later, as I did not want to stretch this hospitality further without also (my own work, part two of the Rodin book, had meanwhile been concluded) being somehow useful to him, when I devoted my free time to assisting him with his extensive correspondence, which was continually far in arrears, I cannot boast of the letters I wrote for him at that time. This occupation for which my pen, which knows no haste, was not the most apt, soon grew up over my head and—what was worse—it threatened to force our association out of its natural course in that it compelled me often to substitute for our otherwise fluent discussions the most irksome reminders of letter-debts and other obligations of correspondence, leading of necessity to a distortion of our relationship, which it was infinitely crucial for me to keep sound and fruitful. So by May of the following year I moved back to Paris, completely my own master, and my relations with Rodin, which had passed into a curious region, fell back into their earlier channel which they were then, through the years, to fill in a stronger or weaker stream. Here once again (gathering from your questionnaire how much you are further looking about for "influences") I will linger and emphasize how far this direct and manifold influence of the great sculptor outweighed anything that stemmed from literature and in a sense made it superfluous. I had the good fortune to meet Rodin in those years when I was ripe for my inner decision and when on the other hand the time had arrived for him to apply with singular freedom the experiences of his art upon everything that can be lived. The opposite of what I had observed in Tolstoy took place here: A man who had assented fully and actively to the inner mission of his creative genius, the infinite divine play, was taking possession, by means of the insight there acquired, of more than just his art; it looked for a while as if everything for which, his hands bound in the work, he had been unable to reach, were of its own volition giving itself to him as well. . . . And so it may be too, not only for the artist of highest intent, but for the simple craftsman, if only he has once bitten open the kernel of his *métier*: the intensity arrived at within his characteristic achievement appropriates to him (automatically, one might say) everything that is and has been which corresponds to the same degree of intensity. From thence stems the wonderful wisdom of craftsmen (which is being lost), thence the spiritual spaciousness in shepherds' souls. . . .

And now (we are not so far from it) the difficult attempt to do justice to your striking reflections on "rich" and "poor." The turns your letter takes are not entirely intelligible to me, which may well be due to my not finding your point of departure, and so having to join your thought along the way, without knowing from whence it may have started. If it comes from the conception of the "social"—as it appears to—then I must at once assert that one would be wrong in classifying any one of my efforts under this rubric. Something of a human likemindedness, something brotherly is indeed spontaneous in me and must have been laid down in

my nature, otherwise the liberating of this characteristic under the influence of the Russian example would
not have moved me so deeply and familiarly. But what
absolutely differentiates so joyous and natural a tendency from the social, as we understand it today, is the
utter disinclination, even aversion, to changing anyone's situation or, as they say, to bettering it. The situation of no one in the world is such that it could not be
of peculiar use to his soul. . . . And I must confess that,
where I have been required to participate in the destiny of others, this above all has always been important
and urgent to me: to help the person oppressed to recognize the peculiar and special conditions of his plight,
which each time is not so much a consolation as an (at
first unapparent) enrichment. It seems to me to create
nothing but disorder if the general effort (for that matter an illusion!) should presume schematically to allevi-
ate or remove oppressions, a thing which injures the
freedom of the other person much more drastically
than does the plight itself, which with indescribable
adaptations and almost tenderly confers upon him who
entrusts himself to it, indications of how—if not outwardly, then inwardly—it could be escaped—. To want
to better the situation of a human being presupposes
an insight into his circumstances such as not even the
poet possesses concerning a figure of his own invention.
How much less still the so infinitely excluded helper,
whose scatteredness becomes complete with his gift.
Wanting to change, to improve, a person's situation
means offering him, for difficulties in which he is practiced and experienced, other difficulties that will find
him perhaps even more bewildered. If at any time I
was able to pour out into the mold of my heart the
imaginary voice of the dwarf or the beggar, the metal
of this cast was not won from the wish that the dwarf

or the beggar might have a less difficult time; on the contrary, only through an extolling of their incomparable destiny could the poet, suddenly bent upon them, be true and fundamental, and he would have to fear and avoid nothing so much as a corrected world in which the dwarfs are stretched and the beggars enriched. The God of completeness sees to it that these varieties do not cease, and it would be most superficial to regard the joy of the poet in this suffering multiplicity as an esthetic pretext. So I too have a conscience clear of any reproach of having prevaricated if, faced with the concepts "rich" and "poor," I unquestioningly claim for my poem the justified impartiality of artistic expression. It can never have been my intention to play off the poor against the rich or to espouse the one with more conviction than the other. But the task may well have been set me of measuring poverty and wealth for a while with their purest measures.—For, even here again, how should one not come to praise both when one discerns them rightly.

In a world which tries to resolve the divine into a kind of anonymity, that humanitarian overestimation must come into effect which expects of human aid what it cannot give. And divine goodness is so indescribably linked with divine hardness that a time which undertakes, in advance of Providence, to dole out the former, at the same time also drags forth the oldest stores of cruelty among men. (We have experienced it.)

I have finished; or rather I must decide to do so. Glancing over your pages once more, I notice I have still left two points unconsidered, or three, or more. . . .

Quickly still to these. (Concerning the letter:) No, it would have little sense for you to lay a *Book of Pictures* before me for the dating of the individual poems and poem-groups; my own memory is too unreliable and inadequate here. Most to be recommended would be a comparison of the first edition with the later ones, which would show you what works of later origin were little by little taken into the whole. (I am never provided with my own books and possess none of these editions to assist you in this survey.)

The origin of *The Life of Mary*, with which (in the winter of 1912) I resumed an older tone I had long since got beyond, was quite externally conditioned: I learned at that time that Heinrich Vogeler, in whose guest-book I had occasionally written Mary poems in those Westerwede years, was intending to publish those (early) verses with his drawings. To prevent this and at least to furnish him, in case he were to stick to his intention (which did not happen), with better and more connected texts, I wrote in a few days, consciously feeling back, these (except for one or two) unimportant poems, for which the painters' book of Mount Athos with its picture-legends served as objective support.

How difficult it often is to make credible the causes out of which a poem arises! You ask about *The White Princess*. At Viareggio, I lived in a villa facing the sea with a stately garden. In this there appeared, while I was standing at the window one afternoon, a friar collecting for his brotherhood, the white hood drawn before his face; he evidently did not dare enter the house but, in expectation of making his presence felt, kept at some distance on the garden path. Now whether he noticed me at one of the tall windows or not, the fear seized me that the uncanny stranger with the veiled face might take my slightest movement for a sign and enter. And from this fear I fell into a strange, paralyzing numbness. Moreover on the same evening (something which makes the day unforgettable to me) a dachshund belonging to the house died; that morning I had been surprised to find the animal, which was friendly with me and otherwise disposed to be playful and interested, sitting close up to the house, motionless, his long face turned as if in boundless meditation to the wall. . . .

Mustn't we be (you say it yourself) strangely constituted if from these two occasions, lifting itself up by them as it were, a year later, the poem could come into being that is called *The White Princess?*

And now, as a real close, a greeting to your little four-year-old son who has accorded my name the most beautiful and most direct recognition. This "poem" has the virtue of being short; should he ever want to memorize it, I would prefer for this effort the expression they have for it in French: *qu'il le saurait "par coeur."*

See whether his spontaneous "conjuration" has brought you in something serviceable and elucidating, and continue to regard me as

Yours sincerely,
R. M. Rilke

Postscript, the following day:

I am making use, dear Dr. Pongs, of this remaining fourteenth page to append one more contribution to the theme of "rich and poor." The little incident here reported (the greatness of which for the rest one may judge for oneself) expresses what my personal attitude would be, if I were to give thought to it, so completely and so validly that I should have nothing to add to it.

Does the name *Jammersminde* (Danish, translated by the expression "memory of suffering") remind you of anything? These are the journals, very widely circulated in Denmark, even taken up in schools, of Countess Leonora Christina Ulfeldt, a daughter of King

Christian IV, drawn up for her children and grandchildren during her twenty-six-year imprisonment in
the blue tower of Copenhagen. Her husband, Imperial
Steward Korfitz Ulfeldt, charged with high treason,
had managed to save himself in time by his flight to the
Tirol; the Danish government deemed it in order to assure itself at least of the Countess, who remained loyal
to Ulfeldt. She was at the English court seeking help
for her husband. There they knew how to reach her
and on some pretext or other to invite her onto a Danish ship where she believed herself to be a guest while
in reality she was already the prisoner of her custodian.
Into this moment is to be set the little scene which is
reported in the introduction to *Jammersminde* (in the
Danish edition at least). One of the younger officers of
the ship, in his youthful zeal, thought he would advance himself when he prematurely approached the
still unsuspecting Countess and respectfully but definitely demanded the jewelry she was wearing on her
person. One can imagine the astonishment of the person thus addressed. It cannot have been quite easy for
the young lieutenant to sustain with grace the look his
covetousness brought him. But then the beautiful and
stately lady who, in accordance with the mode of the
time, was richly adorned with jewels and chains,
stepped up to the mirror of her cabin and slowly, without haste, one after the other, removed the rings, the
pendants, the brooches, the bracelets and earrings that
piled up, warm and heavy, in the frightenedly out-
spread hands of the officer. When, already quite uncertain, he went with this royal booty before his comman-
dant, the latter's surprise and finally his rage knew no
bounds. He did not doubt that his secret intentions
were now discovered and the whole bold undertaking
had miscarried. Flaring up at his lieutenant with the

hardest words, he refused all responsibility and left it
to the unfortunate man to make good his arbitrary and
disastrous rashness—, he could find out for himself how!
Pale, trembling, the fabulous abundance even yet on
his overladen hands, the annihilated officer again appeared before the tall lady. Stood, stammering. . . .
She left him, regally, for a suitable moment in his state
of despair, but only (though she must really have understood all that would follow) to step again to her
mirror and, slowly, as if from the hands of a servant,
to take and put on the manifold trinkets with precisely
the same serenity she had previously shown in giving
them away, and already absorbed in her reflection as
it festively completed itself again in the glass.

P.S. Reading over my pages, though it is superfluous
(for you already, I think, understand me correctly) I
would nevertheless like to have noted down one thing
more: I am never giving *judgments* here of the manifestations and things you questioned me about, but am
showing them, most one-sidedly in the perspective of
the digressions from them that I may at times have
made. As "judgment" most of it (for instance the Tolstoy item) would be awry and laughable. But it was a
question here of the explanation of a specific situation
interesting you at the moment (which for that matter
makes me ashamed of taking it so seriously). I have
tried my utmost to satisfy your wishes and am once
more, as already yesterday, your:

R.M.R.

/ *Professor Hermann Pongs (born in 1889) was a literary
historian, and lecturer at Wunsch; he later lived in Göttingen. He was to write a number of articles about Rilke
and his work.*

TO WITOLD VON HULEWICZ

[postmarked Sierre, 13 November 1925]

. . . And am I the one to give the *Elegies* their proper explanation? They reach out infinitely beyond me. I regard them as a further elaboration of those essential premises that were already given in the *Book of Hours,* that in the two parts of the *New Poems* tentatively played with the image of the world and that then in the *Malte,* contracted in conflict, strike back into life and there almost lead to the proof that this life so suspended in the bottomless is impossible. In the *Elegies,* starting from the same postulates, life becomes possible again, indeed, it experiences here that ultimate *affirmation* to which young Malte, though on the difficult right path *des longues études,* was as yet unable to conduct it. *Affirmation of life-AND-death appears as one in the Elegies.* To grant one without the other is, so it is here learned and celebrated, a limitation which in the end shuts out all that is infinite. *Death* is the *side of life* averted from us, unshone upon by us: we must try to achieve the greatest consciousness of our existence which is at home in *both unbounded realms, inexhaustibly nourished from both.* . . . The true figure of life extends through *both* spheres, the blood of the mightiest circulation flows through *both: there is neither a here nor a beyond, but the great unity* in which the beings that surpass us, the "angels," are at home. And now the place of the love problem, in this world extended by its greater half, in this world only now *whole,* only now *sound.* I am amazed that the *Sonnets to Orpheus,* which are at least as *"difficult,"* filled with the same essence, are not more helpful to you in the understanding of the *Elegies*. These latter were begun in 1912 (at Duino), continued in Spain and Paris—fragmentarily—until 1914; the War interrupted this my greatest work altogether; when in 1922 I ventured to take them up again (here), the new elegies and their conclusion were preceded, in a few days, by the *Sonnets to Orpheus*, which imposed themselves tempestuously (and which had *not* been in my plan). They are, as could not have been otherwise, of the same "birth" as the *Elegies*, and their springing up, without my willing it, in connection with a girl who had died young, moves them even closer to the source of their origin: this connection being one more relation toward the center of *that* realm whose depth and influence we share, everywhere unboundaried, with the dead and those to come. We of the here and now are not for a moment hedged in the time-world, nor confined within it; we are incessantly flowing over and over to those who preceded us, to our origins and to those who seemingly come after us. In that greatest "*open*" world all *are*, one cannot say "simultaneous," for the very falling away of time determines that they all *are*. Transiency everywhere plunges into a deep being. And so all the configurations of the here and now are to be used not in a time-bound way only, but, as far as we are able, to be placed in those superior significances in which we have a share. But *not in the Christian sense* (from which I am more and more passionately moving away), but, in a purely earthly, blissfully earthly consciousness, we must introduce what is *here* seen and touched into the wider, into the widest orbit. Not into a beyond whose shadow darkens the earth, but into a whole, into *the whole*. Nature, the things of our intercourse and use, are provisional and perishable; but

they are, as long as we are here, *our* property and our
friendship, co-knowers of our distress and gladness, as
they have already been the familiars of our forebears.
So it is important not only not to run down and degrade
all that is here, but just because of its provisionalness,
which it shares with us, these phenomena and things
should be understood and transformed by us in a most
fervent sense. Transformed? Yes, for it is our task to
imprint this provisional, perishable earth so deeply, so
patiently and passionately in ourselves that its reality
shall arise in us again "invisibly." *We are the bees of the
invisible. Nous butinons éperdument le miel du visible,
pour l'accumuler dans la grande ruche d'or de l'Invisible.* The *Elegies* show us at this work, at the work of
these continual conversions of the beloved visible and
tangible into the invisible vibrations and excitation of
our own nature, which introduces new vibration-fre-
quencies into the vibration-spheres of the universe.
(Since different elements in the cosmos are only different vibration-exponents, we prepare for ourselves in
this way not only intensities of a spiritual nature but
also, who knows, new bodies, metals, nebulae and constellations.) And this activity is curiously supported
and urged on by the ever more rapid fading away of so
much of the visible that will no longer be replaced.
Even for our grandparents a "house," a "well," a familiar tower, their very clothes, their coat: were infinitely
more, infinitely more intimate; almost everything a vessel in which they found the human and added to the
store of the human. Now, from America, empty indifferent things are pouring across, sham things, *dummy
life* . . . A house, in the American sense, an American
apple or a grapevine over there, has *nothing* in common
with the house, the fruit, the grape into which went the
hopes and reflections of our forefathers. . . . Live

things, things lived and conscient of us, are running out and can no longer be replaced. *We are perhaps the last still to have known such things.* On us rests the responsibility not alone of preserving *their* memory (that would be little and unreliable), but their human and laral value. ("Laral" in the sense of the household gods.) The earth has no way out other than to become invisible: *in* us who with a part of our natures partake of the invisible, have (at least) stock in it, and can increase our holdings in the invisible during our sojourn here,—*in* us alone can be consummated this intimate and lasting conversion of the visible into an invisible no longer dependent upon being visible and tangible, as our own destiny continually *grows at the same time* MORE PRESENT AND INVISIBLE in us. The *Elegies* set up this norm of existence: they assure, they celebrate this consciousness. They cautiously fit it into its traditions, in that they claim for this supposition ancient traditions and rumors of traditions and even in the Egyptian cult of the dead evoke a foreknowledge of such relationships. (Although the "Land of Lamentation" through which the older "lamentation" leads the young dead is *not to be identified with* Egypt, but is only, in a sense, a mirroring of the Nile country in the desert clarity of the consciousness of the dead.) When one makes the mistake of holding up to the *Elegies* or *Sonnets* Catholic conceptions of death, of the beyond and of eternity, one is getting entirely away from their point of departure and preparing for oneself a more and more basic misunderstanding. The "angel" of the *Elegies* has nothing to do with the angel of the Christian heaven (rather with the angel figures of Islam).
. . . The angel of the *Elegies* is that creature in whom the transformation of the visible into the invisible, which we are accomplishing, appears already consum-

mated. For the angel of the *Elegies* all past towers and palaces are existent, *because* long invisible, and the still standing towers and bridges of our existence *already* invisible, although (for us) still persisting physically. The angel of the *Elegies* is that being who vouches for the recognition in the invisible of a higher order of reality.—Hence "terrible" to us, because we, its lovers and transformers, do still cling to the visible. —All the worlds of the universe are plunging into the invisible as into their next deepest reality; *a few stars immediately intensify and pass away in the infinite consciousness of the angels—, others are dependent upon beings who slowly and laboriously transform them, in whose terrors and ecstasies they attain their next invisible realization. We are, let it be emphasized once more, in the sense of the* Elegies, *we are these transformers of the earth; our entire existence, the flights and plunges of our love, everything qualifies us for this task* (beside which there exists, essentially, no other). (The *Sonnets* show details from this activity which here appears placed under the name and protection of a dead girl whose incompletion and innocence holds open the gate of the grave so that, gone from us, she belongs to those powers that keep the one half of life fresh and open toward the other wound-open half.) *Elegies* and *Sonnets* support each other constantly—, and I see an infinite grace in the fact that, with the same breath, I was permitted to fill both these sails: the little rust-colored sail of the *Sonnets* and the *Elegies'* gigantic white canvas.

May you, dear friend, perceive here some advice and elucidation and, for the rest, help yourself along. For: I do not know whether I ever could say more. . . .

/ *Witold von Hulewicz was Rilke's Polish translator.*

TO ARTHUR FISCHER-COLBRIE

from Château de Muzot sur Sierre
(Valais), Switzerland,
18 December 1925

So I thank you for a sympathy that, straight and strong as it is, is the outcome of such long experience with my books: your letter was full of evidences of true interest, how should I not want to answer it with equally true thanks.

I never read what my works call forth among the critics in the way of opinions, either in newspapers or periodicals: these voices do not seem to me to belong among those reactions that I would have to take into consideration again: also they are indeed destined altogether for the reader and must, as you yourself mention, reckon with his resources. However (as I was laying it with the rest of its kind) my glance fell on the first lines of your article. Let me, in confidence, clear up what you were impelled to point out there.

To President Masaryk I offered my respects, not this time indeed, but on an earlier occasion, through his Bern representative of that time: this feeling existed long before the revolutions of 1918 raised him to that more conspicuous position; how could I help feeling called upon to give approval when a man of universal intellectual significance assumed the topmost place in my native country, from which I am sufficiently detached to be loyal, independently, to its particular destinies.

As to the other point: I have lived since 1921 in an old tower of this French canton; Switzerland in gen-

eral, its soil, the relationships that have supported me
here, and not least the event of the grandiose landscape
of the Wallis to which I have become more deeply attached with every year: all these facts together consti-
tute that which, after the evil interruptedness and all
the confusion of the war years, has become a salvation
of my life and of my work. I cannot enumerate the individual circumstances that make my being taken in
here seem the most marvelous dispensation, but it is
easier to prove that it has been the most productive.
One has only to consider that the *Elegies* (begun at the
war-destroyed castle of Duino in 1912, continued fragmentarily until August 1914 in Spain and in Paris . . .)
had been left interrupted by the external circumstances into which the fortunes of wartime had
plunged me and even more through my inner torpor;
nowhere but here, in the Wallis, a country then completely unknown to me, could such a store of unfore-
seeable supports have been assembled: for here took
place, and everything was conducive to it, in the rigor-
ous solitude of the winter of 1921–22, the reuniting I
scarcely hoped for any more with the breaks in my
work of 1914, and it was so clean and so passionate,
and at the same time of such mildness in the healing
together, that out of a few weeks of indescribable devotion the whole of the *Elegies* arose as if it had never
been broken off, even gone rigid in its separate pieces.
That a person who through the wretched harassings of
those years had felt himself split to the roots, into an
Aforetime and a dying Now not to be united with it:
that such a person should experience the grace of per-
ceiving how in yet more mysterious depths, beneath
this gaping rift, the continuity of his work and his soul
re-established itself . . . seems to me more than just a
private event; for with it a gauge is given of the inex-

haustible stratification of our nature, and how many, who for one reason or another believe themselves cleft apart, might draw from this example of possible continuation a singular comfort.

(The thought readily suggests itself that this comfort too may somehow have entered into the achievement of the great *Elegies*, so that they express themselves more completely than they could have done without endangerment and rescue.)

Enough: out of all this should be understood merely that I have remained bound in a special way to this landscape in which I have met with the fullness of grace. Although I had seldom before become resonant through incentives of environment—, but here my glad and lively joining, together with the complete seclusion of my life, brought with it my setting down verses in the language which surrounds me and which is not accidentally that of these hill vineyards, the series of those *Quatrains Valaisans* around which other French poems, in most irrefusable dictation, have gradually arranged themselves. I saw no reason to ward off this spontaneous resonance that imposed itself on me in all purity, nor yet to resist when later, in Paris, it was proposed that I fill a little book with these examples of a happy inspiration. I was glad to give back to the country this most native gift in return for its eager and rescuing hospitality: with this is told the story of that "writing in French" which, as I learned little by little from various rumors, had occasioned such curious interpretations on the part of the public. It is enacted, this most incidental story, on quite different stages of the spirit from those they wanted to assign to it.

I know (to come back to your article) that you took up that version of the "discord" only for the sake of "accord," because this was after all the easiest insight that could perhaps be made attainable to the reader. Yet at this price particularly, I would least like to be more considerately handled. I know nothing of any disapproval, any "disapproving attitude of German literary circles." My work was dependent upon such reactions to a certain unavoidable degree only when I first published. Even at twenty-three, at the time of the *Book of Hours,* I ceased bothering about applause or disapproval, and since then individual voices at most have reached me which, whether they applauded or rejected or were undecided, work back into life and (unlike mere criticism) are resolved in it. I permitted anything to appear out of disillusionment or *rancune,* and it is the strangest misunderstanding that this suspicion so foreign to my nature should happen to throw its sullen shadow on the producing of those French poems, which for me signifies the brightest happiest having-been-given!

Do you think that by such "helps" the reader will become more capable of dealing with my books? But that is not meant as a reproach to you. Only you yourself, in view of your relationship to me, you yourself, that is what matters to me, should be among those who know better, those who truly know with me. The suspicion has crossed my mind that you too believed a bit in the possibility of a (how shall I say) revenge: well, that would be taking this innocent and spontaneous product, which I have with astonishment and delight seen appear out of my being's mystery, far too seriously and besides (how much!) misjudging it and me in it!

Straighten this out (with yourself)

and my grateful greetings:

Rainer Maria Rilke

P.S.: In Linz of course no one could give "information" about me; the unhappy months spent there comprise a time when I was quite unrecognizable to myself: how very much then I must have been so to others!

/ Arthur Fischer-Colbrie (born in 1895, in Austria) was a land official and poet; Thomas G. Masaryk (1850–1937) had become President of Czechoslovakia in 1918; Rilke's time in Linz was the fall of 1891 to the spring of 1892.

TO LEONID PASTERNAK

from Val-Mont par Glion sur Territet (Vaud), Switzerland, 14 March 1926

No, I cannot write you in Russian, but I did read your letter . . . and even if I could no longer read Russian (I still can quite well, but unfortunately seldom get to it . . .) but, even if I no longer could, the joy and the great surprise of reading you, dear valued friend, would, for a moment, have given me back all my knowledge: *this* good letter I would have understood in all circumstances and in all languages. And now I want to assure you at once how *your language* and all that concerns the old Russia (the unforgettable secret Skaska), and how everything of which you remind me in your note has remained close, dear and sacred to me, forever embedded in the substructure of my life! Yes, we have had to let much change pass over us, your country above all: but, even if we are no more to experience it in its resurrection, the deep, the real, the ever surviving Russia has only fallen back into its secret root-layer, as once formerly under the Tartarshchina; who may doubt that it is *there* and, in its darkness, invisible to its own children, slowly, with its

sacred slowness, is gathering itself together for a perhaps still distant future? Your own exile, the exile of
so many most loyal to it, is nourishing this in a sense
subterranean preparation: for as the real Russia has
hidden itself away under the earth, in the earth, so all
of you have only gone away in order to remain true to
its momentary hiddenness; how strongly, with how
much emotion, dear Leonid Ossipovitch Pasternak, I
felt that last year in Paris; there I saw again old Russian friends and found new ones, and the young fame
of your son Boris touched me from more than one side.
Also, chronologically, the last thing I tried to read there
were poems of his, very *beautiful* ones (in a little
anthology of Ilya Ehrenburg's, which I then unfortunately gave to the Russian dancer Mila Sirul; unfortunately: because at times since I would have liked to
reread them). Now it moves me to know that not only
he, Boris, the already recognized poet of a new generation, has not ceased to know about me and to be
familiar with my work, but that with you and yours too
my existence has remained in your hearts and sym-
pathies, that you, dear friend, have let your memory
and affection for me prosper and grow in your family,
infinitely increasing in this way something good that
has remained dear to me.

To know you living and working in comparatively
normal circumstances, surrounded by a part of your
family, is a good happy knowledge to me! And prejudiced though I am against having my portrait made, if
proximity in space permits and we see each other
again, I shall be proud to occupy a modest place in the
ranks of your models. But it is much more likely that
you will see Clara Rilke, who still lives in Germany,
near Bremen, or with our daughter, who is married and
living on an estate in Saxony and already something

over two years ago made me a grandfather by the arrival of a granddaughter! . . .

/ *Professor Leonid Pasternak (1862–1945), the painter, father of the poet Boris Pasternak, had introduced Rilke to Tolstoy; "the Tartarshchina" was the rule of the Tartars.*

TO DIETER BASSERMANN

from Val-Mont par Glion,
Territet (Vaud), Switzerland,
19 April 1926

Unfortunately I was able after many hindrances only yesterday, Sunday, to look through the proposed texts: I would have no objection to their being printed in this form. At most this: it disturbs my ear for language a little to feel a letter passage, which is by nature of a different density, joined as a direct supplement to the older essay. I should prefer to have you indicate by a few dots the not quite definitive character of the prose pages taken from the *Insel-Schiff*, in order to append the passage from my letter to you with more visible differentiation, after a more emphatic break, to the preceding text. In this typographical setting it would round out the former even better, in that the interval would become apparent which separates a note going back years ago now from my attitude of this very day, which is still similarly oriented; thus the curious persistence with which this idea, in a sense, keeps overtaking me, becomes more striking.

Meanwhile not only have the numbers of your periodical I asked to have sent again reached me, but, via my permanent address, the copies previously sent have also found their way to me. I have looked through them attentively. What surprises me is to find the talking-machine praised almost exclusively as a reproducer of musical material, as if it had so far concerned itself little with the spoken *word*. And yet, through its exact repetition, it could render strict control services to those whose business it is to give a speech or recite a poem, just as it does, in his sphere, to the practical musician. The talking-machine could further contribute, in the service of the poetic word, to a new orderly sense of responsibility toward the *reading aloud* of a poem (by which alone its whole existence appears). How many readers still miss the real relationship to the poem because in running over it silently they only graze its individual qualities, instead of bringing them awake. I picture to myself (after some resistance) a reader who, reading along with a poetry book in his hand, listens to a talking-machine in order to be better informed of the existence of the poem in question; that would surely be no mere "artistic pleasure," but very penetrating instruction, somewhat as certain tabulations in the school-room present and charge the eye with something in its relative proportions that is otherwise invisible. The prerequisite for such an exercise would in any case be that the talking-machine had received the sound picture of the verse sequence from the poet's own lips and not indirectly by way, say, of the actor. On the contrary, this means of education would not be unsuited to making the actor innocuous as an interpreter of poems (he almost always errs and goes astray). Preserved in the disks, the poem would then persist, to be called up at any time in the form intended by the poet: an almost inconceivable advantage! But of course for *us* to whom certain revelations seem to get their most indescribable quality of greatness, melancholy and humanity from their fabulous uniqueness, such a mechanical survival of the most mysterious and rich form of expression would be almost unbearable. It is still (besides being a need) also a strength and a pride of our soul to consort with the unique and irretrievably transitory.

/ *Dieter Bassermann (born in 1887) is one of the foremost German interpreters of Rilke; "the proposed texts" are some passages from Rilke's letters published in* Schallkiste *for June 1926.*

TO BALTHUSZ KLOSSOWSKI

from Château de Muzot sur Sierre,
26 June 1926

My very dear B.,

Then it is true that you will soon travel again and revisit beautiful Italy, which I have within two steps of me without ever taking them, those two steps! I am awaited, at Milan, at Venice, at Florence . . . and I have the necessary visa in my passport, but I am no longer *l'homme qui voyage,* everything holds me back, and none of the trains, even the great beetle-colored express with all its destination signs, that from my Bellevue balcony I daily see passing, does not stir up toward me the least breeze of temptation. I will end by having little barbed roots, and it will be necessary to come to sprinkle me from time to time (but not too much, I remember my cold feet).

My friend, I want to tell you: do not leave without sending me your Poussin (mine: I say with pride). It would seem as if my very walls had changed their clothes in order to receive it in a worthy manner: it will probably be their only decoration; the room has become so very pretty this time, with those green panels of my own invention, that I should not wish to put back in their place the old etchings (even though missing them, considering that they have provided me with such charming company . . .).

I should like, B., to know your opinion concerning the church by J.-M. Sert, now being exhibited in Paris. Have you seen these decorations and do you agree with the article by Claudel, which I am enclosing? How magnificently he expresses himself at times; according to him there could be a painter in our time who was capable of achieving this miracle: to create a complete painting-lining for a cloak for God. Only a Spaniard or a Russian in our time could be attracted by a task so enormous, by this amount of painting, which ought to be a totality of life and of faith. Would you give me your opinion on that? If it does not disgust you too much to find suddenly between your fingers a poor pen instead of a brush, let me hear from you occasionally, also when you are in Italy. Where will you go first?

I have learned that the French version of *Malte* has appeared, but I have not yet seen a copy; I am going to telegraph to Betz about this. . . .

Cordial greetings from your friend to you three.

I embrace you warmly,

René

(*From the French*)

/ "*Your Poussin*" *refers to Balthusz Klossowski's copy of Poussin's* Narcissus; *J.-M. Sert is José Maria Sert y Badia, a Parisian painter born in 1876 in Barcelona; Claudel was the French poet Paul Claudel (1868–1955).*

TO RUDOLF KASSNER

15 December 1926

My dear Kassner, so this it was of which my nature has been urgently forewarning me for three years: I am ill in a miserable and infinitely painful way, a little-known cell alteration in the blood is becoming the point of departure for the most horrible occurrences scattered through my entire body. And I, who never wanted to look it squarely in the face, am learning to adjust myself to the incommensurable anonymous pain. Am learning it with difficulty, amid a hundred resistances, and so sadly amazed. I wanted you to know of this condition of mine which will not be of the most passing. Inform the dear Princess of it, as much as you consider well. I learn through Princess Gargarine that Princess Taxis will settle down in her beautiful apartment in the Palazzo Borghese for the winter. And you, dear Kassner? How was Paris for you? I was happy to find the *Eléments de la Grandeur Humaine* in the issue of *Commerce!*

All love, Kassner!
I think much, much of you.

Your
Rilke

/ *In October, when one of Rilke's fingers became badly infected from a wound made by a rose thorn, his illness was diagnosed as acute leukemia; "the dear Princess" refers to Princess Marie von Thurn und Taxis; Princess Gargarine was a Russian friend;* the Eléments *was the translation of Kassner's book,* Die Elemente der Menschlichen Grösse (*1911*).

TO JULES SUPERVIELLE

> from Clinique de Val-Mont sur
> Territet par Glion (Vaud)
> 21 December 1926

My dear, dear Supervielle, Gravely ill, painfully, miserably, humbly ill, I recover myself for an instant in the sweet consciousness of having been able to be reached, even here, on this indeterminable and so little human plane, by your message and by all the influences it brings me.

I think of you, poet, friend, and in so doing I think still of the world, poor broken fragments of a vase that remembers being of the earth. (But this abuse of our senses and of their "dictionary" by the pain that goes leafing through it!)

> Rilke

/ *Jules Supervielle (born in 1884, in Uruguay), the French poet, had met Rilke during his last visit to Paris, in 1925; Rilke, who was to die on 29 December 1926, would accept no drugs to deaden his pain—and his awareness—during this last illness; according to Frau Wunderly-Volkart, one of the last things he said was, "Life can give me nothing more—I have been on all the heights."*

[TO NIMET ELOUI BEY

from Valmont
(22 December 1926?)]

Madame, yes, miserably, horribly ill, and painfully so, to a degree which I had never dared imagine. It is this nameless suffering which is named by doctors, but which is, itself, satisfied, if it but teach us two or three cries, in which our voice is not to be recognized. That voice, which had been educated to nuances!

No flowers, Madame, I entreat you, their presence excites the demons which fill the room. But what came to me *with* the flowers will be added to the grace of the unseen. Oh thank you!

(Wednesday)

/ *Nimet Eloui Bey, a Circassian beauty, met Rilke in Switzerland not long before his death; the letter above was published as "written on the eve of his death," but this could hardly be right, since he died at five in the morning of Wednesday the 29th; rather, this letter, probably written a week before the poet's death, seems to be the one that prompted Mrs. Eloui Bey's answer on the 24th ("Do not interrupt your repose to write to me. Your silence does not make you less present, I assure you"); Mrs. Eloui Bey is an important part of the Rilke legend, for it has been said that the wound in his hand at the beginning of his fatal illness was caused when, during a visit she made to Muzot, the poet was picking a rose for her.*

ANCHOR BOOKS

DOLPHIN BOOKS AND DOLPHIN MASTERS

The bold face **M** indicates a Dolphin Master. Dolphin Masters are Dolphin Books in the editions of greatest importance to the teacher and student. In selecting the Dolphin Masters, the editors have taken particular pains to choose copies of the most significant edition (usually the first) by obtaining original books or their facsimiles or by having reproductions made of library copies of particularly rare editions. Facsimiles of original title pages and other appropriate material from the first edition are included in many Masters.

FICTION

POETRY AND DRAMA

HISTORY AND BIOGRAPHY

PHILOSOPHY AND RELIGION

Wilmington Public Library
Wilmington, N. C.

RULES

1. Books marked 7 days may be kept one week. Books marked 14 days, two weeks. The latter may be renewed, if more than 6 months old.

2. A fine of two cents a day will be charged on each book which is not returned according to the above rule. No book will be issued to any person having a fine of 25 cents or over.

3. A charge of ten cents will be made for mutilated plastic jackets. All injuries to books beyond reasonable wear and all losses shall be made good to the satisfaction of the Librarian.

4. Each borrower is held responsible for all books drawn on his card and for all fines accruing on the same.